When Time Management Fails

When Time Management Fails

How Efficient Managers Create More Value with Less Work

Hunkar Ozyasar

2006

When Time Management Fails

"When Time Management Fails shatters the assumptions of 'what it takes' by providing concrete advice on how to climb to the top and still have a life. Beware, if you read this book, all excuses for inefficiency may quickly vaporize only to be replaced by actionable strategies for doing more with less time."

Paul G. Stoltz
Author of *Adversity Quotient*
CEO of Peak Learning Inc.

"When Time Management Fails goes beyond traditional time management techniques and proposes a highly effective and sustainable solution for the overloaded manager. Rewarding to both managers and their employees alike!"

Bob Nelson
Author of *1001 Ways to Reward Employees*
President of Nelson Motivation Inc.

"Ozyasar presents a smart, savvy and insightful look at ways to build your career while making a meaningful contribution to your organization. If you want to have more success in what you do, then read *When Time Management Fails!"*

Raymond Smilor
Author of *Daring Visionaries*
President of Beyster Institute for Entrepreneurial Employee Ownership

"Packed full of useful career tips for managers who want to accomplish more with less effort."

Richard Koch
Author of *The 80/20 Principle*

"Tired of being tired? Then this is the book for you."

Bob Rosner
Author of *Working Wounded*, Co-author of *The Boss's Survival Guide* and *Gray Matters*

"When Time Management Fails is a unique book in that it instructs the reader on how to control *what* work needs to be done, and their chance of success, instead of just how to be more efficient. The book does a great job at debunking the myth that working longer hours necessarily leads to success, and that success necessarily requires working long hours. It is all about working *smarter* not harder!"

Karen Chinander
Co-author of *The Input Bias: The Misuse of Input Information in Judgments of Outcomes*
Ph.D., Operations Management Professor, Florida Atlantic University

"Many managers feel they have to make a choice between leading a normal life and creating a successful career. Hunkar Ozyasar gives us sound advice on how to manage our lives so we can have success in both those worlds. *When Time Management Fails* is a must-read."

Kevin Daley

Co-author of *Talk Your Way to the Top*, Author of *Socratic Selling*
Founder and Chairman of Communispond Consulting

"Hunkar Ozyasar knows his subject well, and provides valuable tips and insights into how the aspiring lower and middle manager can survive and prosper in today's corporate world."

Thomas F. Schopflocher

Author of *The Turnaround Experience*

"Wow! If you're like me, you're tired of working too many hours—and tired of being told to just 'work smarter.' At last, here's a book that offers practical, easy-to-follow advice on how to get our lives back and reinvigorate our careers in the process. If you're burnt out, read it today. Me? I'm done for the day—and going to the movies."

Allan Halcrow

Co-author of *The Boss's Survival Guide* and *Gray Matters*

"Hunkar Ozyasar is a worldly professional who impresses me with his unique perspective on managing one's workload. He is street-smart, honest, and down to earth. His scanning of the field for what works and what doesn't transcends traditional, tired old mistakes that only work in a perfect world. Seeing true organizational savvy in the form of his real-world pragmatics makes his approach 'not your father's time management program!' "

Rick Brandon

Author of *Survival of the Savvy*

"Everybody in the world of work today struggles with the demands of 'fitting twenty pounds of potatoes into a five pound sack'. This book explains how the solution is NOT to expand the sack-the answer is to reduce the amount of potatoes! And it shows HOW in explicit, pragmatic ways."

Michael Feiner,

Author of *The Feiner Points of Leadership*
Consultant and Professor, Columbia Graduate School of Business

Dűnya'da benden kendisine bir kitap ithaf etmemi talep edecek en son kişiye
Hayatta tanıdığım en mert, delikanlı ve yűrekli adama
Engin zekası, eşsiz esprileri ve hayat felsefesiyle bana ışık tutan canım babam
Erkan Őzyaşar' a...

To the last person in the world who would demand that I dedicate a book to him
To the most trustworthy, genuine, and courageous man I have met in my life
To the one whose enormous intelligence, peerless sense of humor, and philosophy have illuminated my way
To My Dear Father *Erkan Őzyaşar...*

CONTENTS

ACKNOWLEDGEMENTS

I strongly urge anyone who wishes to write a book that will truly satisfy him to not attempt such an absurd feat. For longer than I can or wish to remember, this project has occupied most of my life. Therefore, I would like to take this opportunity to express my gratitude not only to those who have directly contributed to this book, but also to a number of people who have made my life more bearable. So, special thanks to:

My Mother, for tirelessly supporting every crazy thing I have done since the day I started standing up on my feet, for her progressive and open mind always ready to accept the rational, and for her infinite love

My Sister, for allowing me to witness the growth of possibly the wittiest and sweetest child of all times, and for continuing to listen to and put up with me after all these years

My dear friend *Hakan Aras,* whom I proudly consider my brother and a member of my immediate family, for showing me the true meaning of friendship, courage, and resilience (Ailemin bir ferdi ve kardeşim saymaktan gurur duyduğum sevgili dostum Hakan Aras'a, bana gerçek dostluğun, cesaretin ve metanetin anlamını öğrettiği için)

The irreplaceable genius and giant philosopher *Aykut Şahin,* for bringing out the best in me with his stunning and daring insights, and for allowing my insanity to unfold in a logical pattern

Kerem Çelikoğlu, for opening up his vast and inventive mind as well as his beautiful soul to me, and for our friendship which has grown in direct proportion to the distances fate has tried to put between us

"Il Professore Dell'Amore" *Daniele Ghiotti,* for sharing the fruits of his immense and exceptional intelligence with me throughout the years, and for never ceasing to believe in the power of the forbidden

The world's best street racer *Egemen Karaduman,* for allowing me to ride as his co-pilot in the beautiful streets of Ankara

Ali Sofyalıoğlu and *Ömer Gönül,* for helping to make the aforementioned streets more dangerous

Bülent Esen, for all the inspiration he has provided in and out of the weight room, and for never forgetting the great moments we shared (Spor salonunda ve hayatta bana ilham veren ve beraber geçirdiğimiz o güzel anları asla unutmayan Bülent Esen'e)

My jiu-jitsu partners *Alastair Onglingswan, Eitan Zachodin,* and *Robert Thierer,* for all the kata gatames, armbars, and wonderful times on 36th Street

My European confidants *Emmanuel Hemmerle* and *Manel Carril,* for helping to warm the cold winters of Evanston with their Mediterranean flair

Sunao Goto for repeatedly kicking my butt in K-I Grand Prix on PlayStation, and for all his help in trying to get this book published in Japan (which I promise will happen one day)

Dan B. Levine, for making my life on Wall Street a bit more colorful

Mehmet Altınok, for all the help he has provided in packing and shipping me across the Atlantic

Howard Nesbeth, also known as The Great Gatsby, for introducing me to the sweetest ladies in New York, and for countless hours of fun at his legendary Friday Night DINAs

Sincerely

Hünkar Özyaşar

January 2006 - New York

FOREWORD BY DAVID ALLEN
Bestselling Author of *Getting Things Done* and *Ready for Anything*

A sure-fire formula for making more money is to simply make yourself more valuable. Then you can send bigger invoices for your time and attention. If you were to lose everything, you would still have your self, and that self has more or less marketable value, based upon what you know and can do. Value is a two-way street, however; someone has to recognize your worth for you to capitalize on it.

Hunkar Ozyasar has provided a manual for enhancing precisely that kind of value, targeted to a very specific population: organization managers.

When Time Management Fails is full of useful perspectives and great tips. To me, though, the real elegance is in its unique approach to defining a key part of organizational efficiency that has remained elusive at best; how things really get done in larger structures through the relationships at the more amorphous levels of the hierarchy of knowledge workers. How we perceive and interact with the people around us affects how things do and don't get done. He explains why, as I have personally experienced many times, when some people disappear and aren't replaced, output and morale may both go up. Active bodies are not always productive ones. As an old personal-growth axiom goes, you can't ever get enough of what you don't really need. What most people and organizations don't need is harder work and longer hours. Hunkar's premise that typical "time management" is adding only slightly incremental efficiency to a much faster growing volume of commitments than any such techniques can deal with is an accurate and important one. But rather than leave us with another platitude about "smarter not harder," he really tackles head-on the issue about reducing the volume of the work itself.

On a cursory read, some of Hunkar's advice (and truths about how the game really functions) might seem more Machiavellian than some people would feel comfortable acknowledging. But in my experience we are all calculating, political beings, attempting to control and manipulate our environments. Those who try to ignore or deny that fact are usually its most obvious victims. By accepting those realities, however, and understanding better how they operate, we become more effective. It's refreshing to have someone as intelligent, observant, and (I'll dare say) sensitive as Hunkar is, call it like it is—especially when it's framed with such clear how-to information for better navigating these often murky waters. For the most part, we're all good people doing our best to do good work. To assume, though, that we don't need to understand and operate within a lot of situations that don't fit this definition is naïve.

I have a small company, to some degree outside the pale of the typical larger corporate environment of which this books speaks. But if each of us on my team integrated only a portion of Hunkar's counsel here, all of our lives would be better off.

INTRODUCTION

As the clock on the wall hits 6:30 PM, you slowly and painfully reach for the menu pinned on your wall. The discomfort has nothing to do with the quality of the food you will be eating. In fact, you are about to order a luxurious dinner at the expense of your employer. However, the thought of having yet another dinner in the office is deeply depressing. After staying in the office until 8 PM for the last two days, you were hoping to leave relatively early today. Maybe it was a romantic dinner with your loved one, a few beers with friends, or you simply wanted to see a movie after work. Well, whatever it was, it isn't happening. After another day full of interruptions from coworkers, unfair demands by your boss, and being forced to correct other people's mistakes, there is now little chance of getting out on time.

As if the disappointment of having to cancel your plans is not bad enough, a sense of guilt begins to creep up. You know that your workplace is not perfect by any means and not all of this is *your* fault, but could you have been out by now if you had spent a little less time surfing the Internet? Could you be sipping a nice glass of wine, instead of stale coffee from the vending machine, if it wasn't for the long chat you had with your college buddy on the phone?

If this scenario sounds familiar, you are not alone. The vast majority of individuals working for large corporations are under the mistaken impression that things would be dramatically different if only they could schedule their activities with greater care, prioritize their work more intelligently, and minimize distractions; in other words, if they were better at time management. Unfortunately, time management alone will not solve the problem. It certainly cannot hurt to be better organized and more disciplined, but if you simply have too much work to realistically finish over the course of a normal business day, time management will inevitably fail.

That's where this book comes in. Here you will find practically no mention at all of classical time management tools such as planning, scheduling, and prioritizing. Instead, this book will attempt to show you something much more fundamental: how large corporations function. You will find out how that immense workload flows through the organizational hierarchy and is distributed unfairly across the desks of managers. You will better appreciate how giant companies dole out fame and blame. You will learn how some managers in these large corporations produce more valuable outcomes with smaller workloads; how they obtain the appreciation, compensation, and promotion they deserve without staying longer in the office than their peers. You will also see how these masters of efficiency do all of this in an ethical and sustainable manner. So please join me in an exciting journey where we will explore what is going on inside those intimidating organizations, and inside the minds of the master managers who have discovered how to easily succeed within them.

PART I

The Basics

CHAPTER 1

The Inspiration

Of all the things on earth, why obsess with managerial efficiency?

If desperation is the best inspiration, as they say, I must consider myself fortunate. I was blessed with an almost infinite supply of this resource during the early days of my career. Before graduating from college with a degree in business, I already had a year of, what I considered, real-life experience from an entrepreneurial venture and a part-time position in a brokerage firm. I felt confident that this background would give me a head start in my new job as an assistant brand manager, and couldn't wait to learn the insider secrets of marketing from one of the world's biggest consumer goods manufacturers.

Like many new employees of glamorous firms, however, I soon found out that reality had little to do with the propaganda. My dreams were shattered almost instantly. The happy faces in the interviews had all but disappeared. The sales figures we were shown on campus looked nowhere as impressive, once I found out that the firm was giving away a fifth of those products under the name of promotions. Almost half of the marketing department had left over the last year, and morale was anemically low as the firm was losing market share in practically every category.

Believing that, at least, there couldn't be any more bad news to receive and that the company had nowhere to go but up, I was able to keep my hopes alive for a while. Although I knew I couldn't change the big picture, I thought I could provide a fresh perspective and make a difference in my little world. But when I was finally introduced to my boss, I realized that they had saved the worst for last. We were a horrible match. While I could ignore the bottom line of the firm, it was impossible to ignore the pain and suffering my supervisor inflicted on me.

The first thing I noticed was that she had absolutely no clue where our critical documents were. The previous assistant had long gone, so I had no one around to answer my questions. Although we were trying to file our data electronically, e-mail was not as prevalent back then. Most documents were kept in physical folders of which I probably had over 50. Documents seemed to have been stuffed into those folders randomly, making it impossible to throw away anything. I was drowning in paper and would often search for hours just to locate the simplest files.

Virtually everyone in the firm disliked my boss, and consequently people were reluctant to help me no matter what I did. I was associated with an individual who people referred to as a "pain" and there was nothing I could do about it. The worst, however, was the lack of communication between my supervisor and me. She simply could not give clear directions. What instructions she did give were often not until the last possible moment.

She was so disorganized that both of us were always scrambling to meet tight deadlines. To make matters worse, she constantly changed her mind about what she wanted. The more important the project we were working on, the more nervous and unpredictable she became. I often had to calm her down instead of the other way round.

Since I keep a diary, I know that I was in the office every single day for the first nine weeks. During my first six weeks, I also ate every meal in the office on workdays. I would get up at 7:00, rush to the office, and grab some junk along the way for breakfast at my desk. At noon, I had a quick lunch, which would sit in my stomach like a brick because I was so stressed and ate in such a hurry. By the time I had my dinner delivered, I was totally drained and was often the only one left in a depressing office, still with a ton of work to do.

Imagine sixty-three straight days without a break. No wonder I was close to a nervous breakdown by the end of my second month. Still, I wouldn't have considered looking for another job had it not been for a heartbreaking event that came after four months. As ridiculous as it sounds now, I somehow saw it as a challenge: if I quit, my boss would win and I would lose. I guess I wanted to take revenge from the very system that hurt me so much by rising through the ranks and crushing those who made me suffer.

The straw that broke the camel's back was watching helplessly as a very valuable relationship was forever lost. In spite of all the help and understanding that I received from my girlfriend of many years, I couldn't even show up at her mother's funeral. I failed to give her a fraction of the support she had so generously provided for such a long time. I couldn't even listen to her after 14 brutal hours in the office, let alone make a comforting comment or two. I simply had nothing left to give to anyone.

Looking back, I can clearly see that my mind was completely numbed from work. I had become so detached from reality, that I convinced myself that she was being unfair when she finally left me. I thought, "What difference would it have made if I had traveled hundreds of miles to attend a funeral? Would it have brought back her mother?" and easily bought my own ridiculous argument. But after a few days, reality slowly and painfully sunk in.

At once, it all appeared so pointless. I started to feel like I was fighting an enemy I couldn't see, hear, or even define. What was I trying to prove anyway? And most importantly, to whom? Would my boss really see how wrong she was, if tomorrow I miraculously managed to drive all our competitors out of business by disobeying her orders? Or would she simply step forward and claim it was her idea? Even if I got her fired, would I feel truly satisfied? With the most important person in my life already gone and most friends slipping away from me, who would share the joy?

After the most depressing weekend of my life spent contemplating the facts, I made an appointment with a headhunter the following Monday and called up all of my old friends to let them know that I was looking for a new job. Although I couldn't quit without a new source of income, I knew I had to do something before my stomach cramps turned into an acute ulcer.

As if all this wasn't enough, another surprise awaited me. In the midst of this turbulence, my boss unexpectedly announced that she was pregnant and would take a maternity leave for six months. Typically, she told me at the last minute and left a week later. She had somehow gotten a much longer leave than was typically granted and simply disappeared. The manager of the department announced that since my boss would be gone for "only" six months, there was no need to replace her, and I would report to him directly during this period. He also added that he was "fully confident that I would rise to the challenge and not disappoint him."

At first, my panic was enormous. I thought that I was simply finished. While my boss had been the source of most of my pain, she was still doing a good deal of work—or so I thought. After all, she was there eight hours a day. No matter how much more efficient I could become without having her breathing down my neck, I figured that I couldn't squeeze much more into my days. Besides, I felt that I wasn't ready to handle a brand management position, even under ideal conditions. In fact, I was so certain that I would be fired soon, that a few hours after the announcement I called my landlord and asked how much he would charge if I canceled my lease sometime over the next two months.

But, to my amazement, things went almost perfectly during those six months. It appeared that my simple math was wrong. I was somehow able to squeeze into each day what the two of us used to do together. Although the first month was hard, I quickly developed a great relationship with the department head—a very supportive person who gave me almost unlimited freedom. With a little help from senior brand managers, I completed two projects that had previously been chronic pains. My new supervisor was so satisfied with my performance that he promoted me to brand manager of another major brand when my boss returned.

The most incredible thing was that I accomplished all of this by working fewer hours. During those six months, I came in only five times on weekends and never on both days in a weekend. Previously, I had clocked at least 70 hours a week, and my boss worked another 40 hours—a minimum total of 110 hours. (In fact, I spent 75 to 80 hours in the office, but I wasted so much time waiting for my boss that actual work hours were around 70.) Now, I was doing more in 50 hours a week. Plus, in spite of the two-fold productivity increase, the stress was much lower. I was leaving with a fresh mind and had a life outside the office. The change was so dramatic, that I did not even bother talking to the few firms that contacted me after I sent my resume.

But as my anger at my former boss slowly subsided over the following months, an equally frustrating sensation set in: I felt extremely vulnerable. Although I had a lot more time and energy outside the office, I just didn't feel secure enough to make long-term commitments or use that energy for anything meaningful. After all, it only took one lousy boss to turn my life upside down, and I had no way of knowing when the next such supervisor would show up. When I asked myself whether I could do much better if I was forced to work for a similar person again, unfortunately my answer was "no." To make things worse, bad supervisors were not the only danger. As I was going through my own troubles, I observed how the restructuring of the quality control department was sucking the life out of a young engineer I had befriended. There were rumors that the marketing department would be similarly reorganized. Therefore, I reasoned that before I could make long-term commitments, I had to learn how to protect myself in this new—and very strange—world. So, my search for the truth started.

First, I began by asking coworkers what they saw me do differently after my boss left and filled up page after page with notes. Next, I read every single time-management book I could lay my hands on and started studying organizational dynamics. I observed numerous companies to understand what made some managers work hard and long only to find themselves spinning their wheels, while others had lives outside the office and still succeeded in reaching their professional goals. I also began to interview colleagues who seemed to have particularly efficient work habits.

What started as an exercise in dealing with inefficient supervisors quickly turned into a comprehensive and obsessive study of managerial efficiency, covering all aspects of office life. When I took this a step further and asked my college classmates to put me in touch with the most efficient managers they knew, so I could interview them for my project, everybody thought I was crazy. To avoid revealing my personal story to every interviewee, I started to tell people that I was conducting a survey to publish my findings in a scientific journal or a business magazine. Although at first it was just an excuse, as time passed, I started to warm to this idea more and more. I kept accumulating tons of material that didn't seem to be covered anywhere else.

After two and a half years in marketing, the next step in my career was as a copywriter for an international advertising agency. I then pursued a business venture with a partner selling fresh fish to supermarkets and catering firms. This period in particular was highly enlightening, since it gave me the opportunity to observe a large number of organizations. I was absolutely amazed how different the workloads could be among similar positions in a given firm.

We often sold to numerous stores of the same supermarket chain. In countless situations, one store manager was always on site, while the manager in charge of a very similar store with no more support personnel was constantly out for personal reasons. Yet somehow, it was not at all unusual to see the second store purchasing larger quantities of our product and providing a cleaner and friendlier atmosphere to shoppers.

Feeling like a kid in a candy store, I interviewed as many of these people as I could. I soon realized that an article would be completely inadequate to capture the essence of the matter. I repeatedly got the impression that something big was missing from even the best time-management books and felt the urge to fill that gap. My desire to gain a better understanding of the relationship between managerial success and hard work, or the lack thereof, was the most important motivation to pursue an MBA at Northwestern University's Kellogg Graduate School of Management.

Kellogg was a wonderful experience. Not only did I have the opportunity to study the theoretical aspects, but I also benefited from the experiences of my classmates, who came from diverse backgrounds. In addition, I was given the exciting opportunity to complete part of my studies in Thailand, which further broadened my perspective and gave me a chance to interview managers who operated in an entirely different culture.

In graduate school, I realized that my classmates had amazingly similar experiences during their tenures in large organizations. Whether people came from a consulting company in London, a commercial bank in the Philippines, or the U.S. Navy, their complaints were almost identical. Interdepartmental fights, bosses who couldn't assess which of their employees added more value, rigid constraints imposed by senseless five-year plans, and a host of other issues came up over and over again when I asked people about their frustrations. But those working for smaller entities rarely encountered such problems. A clear picture started to emerge. The size of the organization seemed to matter a lot more than its mission. It appeared that when a company grew beyond a certain size, unique dynamics developed and major inefficiencies arose. While management literature was full of advice for making such giant and sluggish entities more profitable, I couldn't find a resource that addressed the kinds of problems that kept me and my classmates chained to our desks for 80 hours a week. To better understand these unique social structures, I started to study sociology with the help of my sister, who is a sociologist by training. In the meantime, I continued to interview as many managers as I could.

Following my graduate studies, I joined a major financial institution as a researcher. After spending several months in London, I settled in the New York office. Soon after that, I decided to collect my observations in a book. When compiling the past interviews, I noticed that although the data clearly pointed in the same direction, there were still some unanswered questions. To fill in the gaps, I accelerated the pace of the interviews.

Over the next three years, I interviewed nearly 100 more people, bringing the total number to more than 300*. I am very grateful to all the participants, as without their help this work would not have been possible. The following chapters consist of the findings of this in-depth study, spread out over eight long years. In Part I, I discuss the insights obtained from the interviews and attempt to bring everything together in a new framework. The remaining chapters focus on how you can apply these lessons to your own career to reduce your workload without sacrificing success.

As you will notice, the names of the interviewees have been left out. This is due to the fact that prior to every interview, I had assured each individual that no personal details would be published. I found this guarantee made people much more willing to talk. Some interviewees pointed out that they saw no problem with having their names published, but I have still refrained form this practice because, naturally, people have the liberty to change their minds during the years that have passed since I talked to them. The enormous task of tracking them down to reconfirm their willingness to disclose personal details would not have been feasible or realistic. Therefore, most of the great people who have kindly contributed to this work will simply be referred to as "interviewees".

Does the world really need another management book?

Most books catering to the overworked manager seem to be looking for the solutions in all the wrong places. Time management resources, for instance, will teach you how to finish routine tasks faster in order to squeeze your current duties into fewer hours. The next group is what I call the "it's all in your head" books. They claim that excessive stress and burnout are the result of our psychological response to what goes on in the office and advise us to change our outlook. A further category, work-life balance books, assert that by learning how to be happy with less money and a smaller title, we can build better lives outside the office.

These approaches treat the symptoms as opposed to the illness. The fundamental problem of most managers is not working too slowly, worrying excessively, or desiring the impossible. The problem is having too much work to do. The books mentioned above will show you how to complete your immense duties a little faster and with a better attitude, but they rarely help you figure out why the organization is expecting so much from you in the first place.

Please take a moment to think about the most efficient colleagues you have known: people who succeed with many fewer hours than their peers. Were they really leaving the office earlier because they managed their time better? Can their shorter work hours be explained by their calmer demeanors or more realistic goals? I doubt it. In all likelihood, these people have figured out a way to succeed with less work. I am not referring to proper scheduling or being better organized. I mean less work in that they have fewer phone calls to make or they are asked to give less frequent presentations. These individuals somehow end up with more manageable projects and get more help from others while performing their already easier tasks. And when they reach their goals, they get more credit than an average manager in their situation would. As a result, they achieve more appreciation, compensation, and promotion with less work.

In this book, you will find the secrets of these managers in an easy-to-understand, down-to-earth format. I explain what these people do differently and show how you can adopt their habits. I provide concrete solutions as opposed to abstract answers. If someone constantly takes your e-mails and forwards them as if they were his own work, I will tell exactly what actions you can take to solve this problem, as opposed to suggesting that you use a "Triangular Resolution Model" or the "Five Bs of Conflict Management."

Is this book for you?

As I mentioned, my studies led me to conclude that, whenever people work together in a midsize or large organization regardless of its industry, similar dynamics develop. So if you are (or will be) employed by a medium to large organization to perform a managerial task, you will find a lot of relevant information in this book to reduce your workload without sacrificing success.

If you are employed by a very small organization, however, you may find some of these lessons irrelevant. The number of employees is much more important than the financial transactions of the establishment. If you are working for a real-estate broker in Hollywood with only five employees, you could be facilitating enormous transactions, but you won't see the interdepartmental conflicts, year-end performance reviews, or useless marathon meetings that a larger organization lives by. Therefore, you will benefit less from this book. Around 100 employees divided into at least three to four departments seems to be the minimum required for those large-organization dynamics to develop.

In addition, you need to perform a managerial task. In other words, you should have some control over how to manage resources, even if the only resource you are in charge of is your own time. If you do nothing but enter the parking tickets written in New York City into a computer, you cannot change much about your job. There probably will be a clear procedure in place, the task will be highly formalized, and you will be working mostly as a one-person team. Thus, suggestions such as presenting your work in a certain way or securing the cooperation of others to minimize your workload will be irrelevant for you.

Keep in mind, though, that people almost always underestimate the amount of potential freedom in their jobs. As an assistant brand manager, for example, I felt that I simply had to do what I was told and that no one would ever take me seriously. But after the departure of my immediate supervisor, I found that under the right circumstances—which one can at least partially create—a lot more autonomy can be gained than we realize. Therefore, when assessing if you can benefit from this book, do not think about how much freedom you are currently given, but think about how much freedom you could possibly obtain.

For the sake of simplicity, most of the examples have been taken from corporate settings. But as I mentioned, what the organization does or whether it is trying to make a profit won't impact the common dynamics we see in large entities. What matters is size. As long as your employer meets the above criteria, you will be able to use the advice in this book.

Lastly, be assured that I won't ask you to become someone other than yourself. Since most self-help books are boot camps in disguise, you may wonder if this book, too, will attempt to turn you into a Navy SEAL or a model citizen. Every suggestion in this book comes from ordinary people who have successfully put the techniques to use. None of the interviewees had a privileged position or a unique talent that you cannot duplicate. I haven't made a conscious effort during my interviews to avoid people who were married to the company's founder or spoke seven languages. But I haven't quoted such managers because they almost never had anything substantial to say. This is hardly surprising; if you are not forced to become more efficient, you simply won't. In fact, most interviewees worked under much more difficult conditions than the average manager will ever face.

Most of the strategies were developed to deal with insane supervisors, lazy coworkers, never-ending corporate restructurings, and crushing workloads. If the lessons work even under such circumstances, think how much easier they will be to apply under more normal conditions, once you spend a little time to understand them. I know from firsthand experience that people like you do it every day. There is no reason why you cannot do the same.

Is this ethical?

As I explained above, I think that everyone working for a medium—to large-sized organization in a managerial role will benefit from this book. This, of course, translates to millions of readers all over the world, and brings up the question whether I can satisfy the ethical values of so many different people. In order to deal with this challenge, I did my best to adhere to two ethical standards.

First, I tried to ensure that if I owned a large company, I would have no problem in giving a copy of this book to every one of my employees. This meant excluding any suggestions that would compromise the productivity and competitiveness of the company. The end result, I believe, is a manual that will not only do no harm to the organization, but actually make it more productive. Although the mission of this book is to help the reader become more efficient, the fortunes of the individual and the employer are often tied. Therefore, helping him to accomplish more with less work also makes the organization more productive. As I point out in the introduction to Part 3, many suggestions that look self-centered, such as advertising your achievements, will actually add a great deal of value to your employer.

Second, I constantly asked myself who the most conservative reader could be and made sure that even such an individual would get his money's worth if he bought this book. My reference point was a bishop trying to rise within the hierarchy of the Roman Catholic Church with fewer work hours and less stress. I cannot claim that this imaginary reader would approve of every solution suggested here. However, I am convinced that even he would find enough suggestions that apply and get an excellent return on the time and money invested in this book.

CHAPTER 2

The Reality of Management

In Chapter 1, I said that this book is for individuals who perform a managerial task. However, due to the games organizations play with titles, it is difficult to tell if a person performs such a task by looking at his business card. So let us start by analyzing what a manager is and why he needs something beyond conventional time management tools to reduce his workload.

What is a manager anyway?

The typical, and incomplete, definition is that if you are in charge of one or more individuals, you are managing them and deserve the title of manager. A better definition of a manager is:

An individual who is given a set of objectives to reach, as opposed to specific tasks to complete in a predetermined amount of time, and manages various resources to do so.

Thus, if you are the assistant to the finance manager, helping him with tasks such as keeping files up to date, providing budget figures to marketing and working with IT to ensure that your boss's systems run smoothly, according to this definition, you are a manager. Although you may not be supervising anyone and may appear too "small" to be called a manager, you are responsible for results and are managing resources, such as data systems and brand managers, to achieve those results.

Let's take a closer look at the last resource—brand managers—to demonstrate the critical difference between a managerial and a clerical function. During budget season, your boss will probably go over strategic issues regarding next year's budget with the head of marketing. They will agree on a set of rough figures, but the details will be worked out later after many rounds of painful revisions, where junior people run the show. Your boss will probably tell you something like "Make sure that marketing sends the numbers by Wednesday." How to handle this task will be up to you. Chances are that Scott, the junior brand manager who is swamped in work, will moan and whine when you tell him the deadline, and you will have to somehow convince him.

You can give a boring lecture over the phone about the importance of this project for the company's financial health or try to help Scott by offering to "go over the numbers together to make his job easier." Other strategies include appealing to Scott's more humane side, telling him that your situation is much more miserable, or use bribery by promising that if he helps you this time, you will make him your number one priority whenever he needs your help. You can probably see now that as a financial assistant you are result driven and have at least some freedom in how you accomplish these results by managing resources, even if your job may look mundane and clerical from the outside.

Now, contrast this with the individual who enters receipts into a database and ensures that they add up at the end of the day. Although his title may not sound much different from our assistant, the nature of the task is entirely different. He will probably work alone in front of a computer with almost no freedom at all. Since the job is very straightforward, he won't need to make judgments on how to achieve the results. In other words, he won't need to manage resources; instead, he will do exactly as he is told.

Notice that the difficulty of the task is not the deciding factor. Entering hundreds of receipts into the computer by hand every day could be more tiring than being in charge of an entire department. Also note that a lot of jobs that are not considered "managerial" actually consist of managing resources as opposed to carrying out predetermined tasks. In fact, a lawyer, a chef, or a detective may perform just as many managerial duties as a brand manager does.

A perfect acid test to find out if your job is a managerial position is to consider your job description. If you could tell your grandmother what you do for a living in one or two sentences, you are probably not a manager. If, on the other hand, your job description is complex and vague, if what you do on a daily basis depends on the particular task at hand and is very difficult to describe to an outsider in general terms, there is a good chance that you are a manager.

Managers are responsible for results, as opposed to specific tasks, and must be willing to do whatever it takes to achieve them. Since the best way to achieve those results will change constantly based on circumstances, an exact description of what you do will be very hard to provide to an outsider. On the other hand, a specific task can be described in one or two sentences no matter how unique or bizarre it is ("I am the guy who checks the thickness of the silicone layer on the 900 Megahertz processors used for military applications.")

In short, managerial jobs are complex in nature, while task-based or clerical functions are much more clear-cut. Because of the inherent complexity and the need to make constant decisions, managers are usually much more stressed out than clerical workers are. Due to that same reason, managers are also paid more.

This complexity is further compounded in large organizations where the number of goals, the frequency with which they change, and the number of people that a manager must interact with are significantly higher. In the earlier example, the financial assistant must not only deal with the whims of numerous brand managers, but he also has to grapple with changes in the deadline due to the requests of the manufacturing department, and new constraints imposed by the distant headquarters. He wouldn't face all these challenges in a small company. Therefore:

Management = Complexity

Consequences of complexity

The most important implication of this complexity is in performance evaluations. When not only the outcomes we are asking for, but also the circumstances under which they must be achieved change constantly, it becomes extremely difficult to quantify an individual's performance. Thus, a manager can only be assessed subjectively by people who understand the intricacies of the job (i.e., his superiors.) On the other hand, the performance of the worker who enters the receipts can be measured very easily by the number of entries and their percentage of accuracy.

Let's consider another example to see how difficult it can be to measure a typical manager's success. Suppose that an executive in charge of the sports drinks division reports worse numbers in all major areas—sales, profits, quality, and order volume—compared to two years ago when he took over the job. Based on this data, can you conclude that he was a failure? Not necessarily.

He might have focused on the future by investing in R&D and could have several gangbuster products in the pipeline. Since a business is worth its discounted future cash flows, he might have actually added value during his tenure. But suppose that his bosses do not buy this argument. It would still not be so easy to conclude that he has failed. He could demonstrate that the decline was caused by the now-fired head of sales, the new tax code, and the increase in raw material prices, adding that he did a great job in limiting the damage.

Similarly, positive results do not necessarily prove managerial ability. They may have been the result of fortunate developments such as a competitor going bankrupt or the booming economy. To what extent these factors account for the numbers is very difficult to quantify. So, just as the jury cannot conclude that a man arrested at the murder scene is the killer without considering all relevant information, one cannot simply look at a handful of numbers to judge a manager, because managerial jobs are extremely complex in nature.

Once again, the problem is magnified in large organizations. Although the boss can see every move of his people if he is managing a business with five employees, this becomes impossible in a department of 30. In addition, the tasks are often so specialized in large companies that the boss cannot be an expert in every job, and rarely knows what the correct yardsticks are.

Management = Complexity

Complexity = Immense Difficulty in Performance Evaluations

Consequently, fairness becomes harder and harder to find as you go up the organizational ladder. While you will rarely see a welder getting promoted if his cars constantly break down, a divisional manager can leave his department in worse shape than when he started, and still advance to the next level. The higher you go in an organization, the more complex everything becomes and the harder it gets to measure results.

For the welder, the relationship between work and success is straightforward. Since his performance is easy to judge, hard work will always show and lead to appreciation. On the other hand, laziness cannot be hidden and will automatically result in disapproval.

Simple, non-managerial function (Ex: A welder)

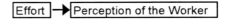

However the manager's effort has to pass through several stages in order to result in appreciation. First, hard work should create results, but due to the complex nature of the job, this may not always be the case. While the welder has little choice in how he does the job, a manager must work not just hard but, more importantly, smart. Otherwise his effort may be wasted.

Yet, even if he can successfully convert his effort into better results, his superiors may not understand the significance of the feat. Remember that one must be aware of the circumstances under which a manager operates before one can decide if the numbers are good or bad. And even if he can convince the world that the numbers paint a pretty picture, the manager is not yet done because it is still not clear that he deserves credit for the outcome. While a welder can never make better cars by chance, a manager can simply get lucky or achieve success at the expense of his colleagues. Therefore, he must also prove that the performance is the result of his managerial aptitude before he can reap the benefits.

The Managerial Value Chain

To define this multistage relationship between work and appreciation, I will borrow a term from production and call it *the managerial value chain*. Just as raw materials have to pass through several stages in a factory to become a finished product, a manager's effort has to pass through several stages to turn into the finished product he is looking for, namely appreciation.

Managerial function

The same way as a problem at any stage in a factory can diminish quality, any breakdown in this process can result in a lack of appreciation for the manager. To get the most success with least effort, a manager must produce strong results, ensure that the significance of the results are understood by colleagues and superiors, and finally communicate how those results would have been impossible without him.

I developed the first version of the managerial value chain soon after my boss took her maternity leave. Her fundamental mistake became crystal clear in the context of the value chain. Despite being a manager, she thought like a welder, assuming that if she worked hard on something it would always show. She never asked herself if the hard work would lead to results that others actually cared about, or if they would give her credit for those results. For example, she never realized how many people in the company assumed that the advertising spots magically materialized when you wrote a check to the ad agency. Consequently, she failed to understand why people refused to give us credit for those flashy campaigns.

On the other hand, I always attempted to look three steps ahead, investing my time into tasks that others valued and were convinced that only I could accomplish. If something needed to be done that no one would give me credit for, I tried to package it differently so people would see its significance. When that was not an option, I tried to postpone it until people realized its importance or else tried to delegate it. I didn't measure myself by the amount of effort that I put into my job and never expected others to do so. My boss, however, used the number of hours she worked as a yardstick to measure her worth, and assumed that others would do the same.

Since I use the terms "result" and "perception" frequently, it is worth explaining them. Every noticeable outcome of your actions is a result. Therefore, the term encompasses a whole lot more than the typical criteria such as sales or profitability. Whether the accounting department gets the monthly figures from you on time is an important result. Similarly, a "thank you" e-mail or a phone call to the head of sales by the regional manager can be a critical result with far-reaching consequences.

Perception refers to what people think of the results that you produce. People's perception of you refers to what they think of you as a manager, and this perception holds the key to many rewards. Envision your job as a game of Monopoly, where you win an amount of play money based on how successful, capable, and valuable you are perceived to be. At the end of every round, you can exchange this money for such things as a bigger salary, a promotion, or a corner office. This book will show you how to maximize the play money in your account for every hour you spend in the office.

Two myths you must erase from your mind

Now that we have analyzed the relationship between effort and success in a managerial role, let us dispel two common myths that arise from failing to grasp this relationship.

i) Myth number one: A manager's workload is dictated by the job

Because of the structure we analyzed above, the amount of work a manager has to do is not a fixed constant. It is a variable factor that the manager can actually influence. Right here and now, erase from your mind the misconception that your job requires you to work X hours a week. For some jobs, you may need to stay in the office longer than for others, but as a manager you have at least some control over the number of hours that are needed to accomplish your objective.

Never forget that you are ultimately trying to create a favorable impression in the minds of those whose opinion makes a difference, as opposed to performing a set of rigid tasks that require the investment of a certain amount of effort and time. By using maximum leverage at every step of the value chain, you can create this favorable impression with less work. Failing to see this fact, most managers believe that there is a direct and unchangeable relationship between the first and fourth boxes in the value chain.

This misconception is part of a cultural heritage inherited from earlier generations, when we all worked like the welder. More effort always translated into a better perception of the individual because tasks were simple and straightforward. Each job required a certain amount of work and there was little you could do to change that. If you worked less, you would simply be fired or go out of business. For today's highly complex managerial jobs, however, this is no longer the case. If all of this sounds too abstract and theoretical, consider the following examples:

Assume that, on average, you work 50 hours a week and take a two-week vacation once a year. During your absence, 100 working hours will be lost. While you will probably work longer the week before you leave and put in some overtime when you return, chances are you won't put in 100 hours of overtime during those weeks. Even considering that colleagues will lend a helping hand while you are away, some work simply evaporates and is never replaced. Where does it go?

Next, consider a situation where an individual is absent for a longer period, such as for a maternity leave like I described earlier. Another person fills in for several months. My example was certainly an extreme and the person filling in often has to work longer hours. But very rarely will he end up working the same number of hours as he and the previous manager did together.

In fact, during reorganizations certain positions will be completely eliminated, yet each department will carry out the exact same tasks as before. While workloads of the remaining managers do go up, this increase is rarely proportional to the reduction in personnel. What if 20% of the workforce is cut from a department? Senior managers, people who are so unhappy with their jobs that they lost all sense of fear, and folks with only a few years to retirement surely won't step in to fill the gap. If total workload remained the same, the other half would have to work 40% longer. This rarely happens. If it did, someone working 50 hours a week would have to step it up to a brutal 70 hours. Think of the reorganizations that you have witnessed. Did you really see such a dramatic jump in work hours? If not, what happened to some of the workload?

Finally, and most importantly, consider this: if the requirements of a job determined the workload, then equally successful managers doing the same type of job should be working the same number of hours. In reality, this is very rare. Sales managers in charge of similar regions or brand managers managing similar products often have significantly different workloads. An even better experiment would be to compare the number of hours of a predecessor and his successor for a given position. Throughout my career, I have observed countless situations where an individual who worked like crazy would leave, only to be replaced by someone who worked many fewer hours but got the same job done just as effectively, if not better. I am certain that you, too, will recall similar situations.

These examples clearly demonstrate that, under the right circumstances, a managerial job can be handled with much less work without sacrificing success. As we will later see, a manager can always contribute to those favorable circumstances. But first, he must erase from his mind the notion that the job needs him there X hours a day and there is nothing he can do about it.

ii) Myth number two: Managers who work less succeed less

The second misconception is that there is a strong correlation between hard work and success. Once again, this impression is inherited from an earlier era when there often was only one correct way to do a job and the results were easy to evaluate. Successful carpenters were those who worked hard, because it was practically impossible to find a clever way to make a chair in half the time. Furthermore, there wasn't a lot you could do to promote a chair. Regardless of what you say, or don't say, such a simple product can be evaluated by anyone. To be successful you simply had to put in the hours.

While this may still be true for today's carpenters, welders, and mailroom clerks, it is not the case for managers. There are a large number of ways to accomplish a managerial task, and even more options to sell the results. So simply putting in the hours is no guarantee for success. The hours may not yield useful results, and those results may go completely unnoticed. Likewise, fewer hours do not automatically lead to less success.

This, too, may sound like an academic theory at first, because we are hard-wired to think that more work equals more achievement. Please take a moment and visualize the people who rose to the top in your present or past organizations. What were the top three things that differentiated these individuals? It is highly unlikely that hard work will be among your answers. An ability to motivate others, developing alliances with power groups, inspiring a sense of confidence in shareholders, or being able to hire the right people are common answers, but hard work is not.

Still not convinced? Pick up a copy of Forbes or Fortune magazine and read an article about a star manager. How do the authors explain the person's rapid rise to the top? Strategic genius? Possibly. His insights into future consumer trends? Probably. His persuasiveness? Maybe. But hard work? Very unlikely.

So erasing the "my job needs this much work" and "hard work equals success" mantras from your mind is a prerequisite to reducing your workload. However, spending too much time in the office is not the only price you will pay for this erroneous mindset. In the long term, this approach can easily ruin your career.

CHAPTER 3

How Hard Work Can Ruin Your Career

Our worst mistakes can often be traced to very simple and seemingly innocent assumptions. An event I witnessed a long time ago at a health food store beautifully demonstrates this. While I was looking for some healthy late-night snacks, three young men walked in. From the conversations, I gathered that one of them refused to eat the hot dogs that his buddies were happily munching on and dragged them in to get a protein bar.

Over the next ten minutes, I watched in disbelief as he read the label of every single nutrition bar in the store while his buddies were literally trying to pull him out. His questions to the clerk revealed that this bodybuilder was obsessed with nutrition and was searching for the highest protein content. In the end, he bought just one bar and walked away with two very angry friends.

Unfortunately, this young man is the norm rather than the exception among amateur athletes. Due to our obsession with protein, hundreds of millions of dollars are flushed down the toilet every year without adding any muscle onto the buyers' already over-nourished physiques. The typical Western diet includes ample amounts of protein. Hence, protein deficiency is almost never the cause for unsatisfactory muscle or strength gains. If this obsession only led to a waste of money and time, it wouldn't be a big deal. Sadly, excessive protein ends up as fat around your midsection and, at extreme doses, it can even become toxic.

Similarly, the average manager is already working hard enough. Lack of effort is rarely the cause for dissatisfactory salaries or overdue promotions. And, just like an obsession with protein, excessive work does not only lead to waste and absurd behavioral patterns, but can be highly toxic for your career at extreme doses. Here is why.

A hard work mentality will debilitate your career development
In your job, like with most other things in life, you can compensate for shortcomings by working harder than you need to. This, however, is an inefficient method of reaching your objectives, and more importantly, it prevents you from becoming aware of your weaknesses. As I will attempt to demonstrate throughout this book, the higher you move in an organization the less critical hard work becomes. An assistant brand manager, who doesn't understand the

principles of effective advertising, can survive by working unnecessarily hard. But this will no longer be possible once he becomes a brand manager and must defend his brand against new competitors.

Even more importantly, junior managers can often make up for a lack of human management skills when they have no direct subordinates. But this flaw will certainly be exposed once they are expected to supervise others. Let us return to the assistant finance manager in our earlier example. Most financial officers will have no problem with an assistant, who spends his weekends in the office updating the marketing spreadsheets, because he couldn't convince the brand managers to send their contributions on time. As long as the correct numbers arrive in a timely manner, the boss will probably not care how the assistant is getting them.

The problem is that someone, who is making up for a lack of managerial skills in this fashion, will fail to duplicate his moderate success after a promotion. If five people are directly under your command, it is impossible to compensate for all the inefficiency you are creating for yourself plus five subordinates by staying longer. You simply won't have enough hours in a day.

Always compare your work hours to those of other reasonably successful colleagues in similar positions and strive to be on the lower end of the spectrum. If you must consistently outwork them to obtain similar results, something is wrong. You'd better identify the problem before it becomes a pattern. In the following chapters, I will outline the skills you need to thrive in a modern organization and help you to recognize where your shortcomings might be.

A strategy revolving around hard work is unsustainable over the long-term

Trying to differentiate yourself by working harder is like trying to sell a product with a deep price cut; both strategies are extremely difficult to sustain. Such an approach puts you in a very vulnerable position and makes it relatively easy for a newcomer to beat you at your own game. For example, no matter how efficiently you can manufacture, a competitor may suddenly appear out of nowhere and offer a price that you cannot match. This new player could enjoy advantages such as lower taxes in its country, access to cheaper raw materials, or favorable exchange rates.

Similarly, if you rely solely on hard work to differentiate yourself in the office, someone may suddenly show up and work harder than you ever thought possible. He may have just moved into town and know absolutely no one there; he may be trying to forget a broken marriage and using work as an anesthetic; or he may simply be able to live on only five hours of sleep. To put it in consulting terms, hard work does not provide a sustainable competitive advantage, because it can be copied with relative ease.

If, on the other hand, a manufacturer has a unique asset such as a strong brand image or patent, it is virtually impossible for an outsider to come out of nowhere and match those advantages. Likewise, what you need to develop is a strong brand image and a set of unique capabilities that make you a rare gem. How likely is it for someone to appear out of the blue and know your customers as well as you do? Or match the excellent relationships you have developed with other departments over the years? But a newcomer can always produce more presentations, return more calls within five minutes, and put in a lot more face time than you do.

Another problem with excessive work hours or rock bottom prices is that you will always live on the edge and have very little wiggle room. Manufacturers that rely solely on price have a wafer-thin profit margin, which can evaporate in an instant. If the product costs 98 cents to make and you are charging $1, you'd better pray that your workers don't ask for a raise or that the utility company doesn't increase the price of electricity.

In the same way, if you have built your entire life around your work and the only other things you can squeeze in are laundry and an occasional haircut, even a minor disruption will dramatically impact your performance. Under these circumstances, you simply cannot handle life's natural challenges such as illness, a death in the family, or a new baby. Two investment bankers I interviewed mentioned how they thought that they could continue to work 80 hours a week indefinitely, until life put other priorities in front of them. One had to resign after getting married, while the other "…went through hell" after his father passed away and he had to commit a large chunk of his time to his family for six months. Someone who has a life outside the office, however, can usually handle such challenges by temporarily suspending his social activities or physical training and get away with much less damage to his career.

Also consider the fact that you, too, will age and will probably need or want to slow down as the years go by. So if your strategy for getting noticed and being promoted is plain hard work, ask yourself for how long you can continue to do that.

CHAPTER 4

Four Pillars of Managerial Efficiency

Before we go on, let us review what we saw thus far, and try to visualize the big picture. We saw that a manager is someone who manages various resources in a complex environment to achieve a set of objectives. As we discussed, the complexities, which arise from having to do whatever it takes to achieve volatile objectives in a large organization make it extremely hard to judge a manager. A single number, such as sales or profitability, will never tell the entire story; managerial performance can only be judged subjectively by other, more senior individuals.

As a result of the difficulty and subjectivity in performance evaluation, hard work does not necessarily equal success for a manager, because hard work does not always show. To succeed, a manager must produce strong results, make people aware of the significance of those results, and ensure that his colleagues and superiors attribute the outcome to him as opposed to the circumstances or to others who have little to do with the outcome. This relationship holds true in any large organization regardless of the entity's mission or culture. It is complexity that gives rise to this relationship, and complexity is inevitable when performing a managerial role within a large system. The managerial value chain sums up the steps that lead to the appreciation of a manager.

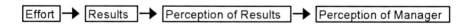

But, despite its clarity and precision, the value chain alone does not tell you what to do. To better understand the day-to-day application of the ideas behind the managerial value chain, let us look at what the efficient managers do differently. Their behaviors fall into four broad categories and form the main pillars of managerial efficiency.

1—Efficient managers have a proactive and strategic mindset
Since managers usually produce intangible—and often invisible—outcomes, those accomplishments are difficult to perceive unless people are made

aware of them. Therefore, efficient managers think and act like good salespeople and constantly promote their goals, ongoing efforts, and past achievements. In a large organization, the "clients" that a manager must deal with range from bosses and subordinates to external customers. By viewing the world from the perspective of those whose opinions matter and emphasizing different aspects depending on whom they are interacting with, efficient managers build a wide base of support. This enhances their productivity and makes it easier to get more credit for the results they produce.

In addition, efficient managers proactively redefine their jobs. Most successful workers in this day and age have learned to evolve in response to changing circumstances. However, very few people actively shape their environment to improve their efficiency. By constantly modifying their assignments, efficient managers find more advantageous ways of reaching their objectives and new ways to market the results. An example would be turning your job into a hybrid and unique role to relieve the pressures of direct peer comparisons, as we will see in the next chapter.

Efficient managers also prioritize strategically and ruthlessly. They consider the contribution of each task to their perceived value and never try to divide their time democratically between tasks. Finally, efficient managers never judge themselves by the number of hours they spend in the office and, therefore, live without guilt.

2—Efficient managers know how to handle people to maximize efficiency

Since our education and early experiences do not adequately prepare us for the challenges presented by giant entities, most managers fail to understand the intricacies of human interactions in a large organization. When they need the cooperation of others, they use the same approach regardless of whom they are dealing with. Yet, due to the distinct layers in large companies, a one-size-fits-all approach such as "being nice," "playing tough" or "empowering people" will not solve the problem.

People who are above, below, and at the same level as you present at least three different sets of challenges and require different approaches. Efficient managers know how to build coalitions with people at their level, how to minimize the intrusions of the individuals above them while still making these officials happy, and how to improve the efficiency of those under them. They are able to distinguish between the real goals of people and propaganda and they help others to achieve their true aspirations. Efficient managers also know how to handle troublemakers, who can wreak havoc on your efficiency.

The ability to handle people correctly helps at every step of the value chain. By getting more help from others, efficient managers can create better results with less work. In addition, the people who are involved in a project can appreciate its significance much more easily. Finally, by working closely with others as opposed to operating in isolation, efficient managers create more opportunities to demonstrate how they have contributed to the bottom line.

3—Efficient managers work to build a positive image over time

We all project an "image." Those who radiate a sense of success and competence are supported much more vigorously, while also enjoying a much higher tolerance for their mistakes. Unfortunately, this aura is the cumulative result of many small things that we rarely pay attention to. Therefore, our careers are often full of missed opportunities.

Efficient managers are aware of those little details that contribute to their image and make the most out of every occasion. Among other things, they know how to inspire a sense of confidence in their colleagues, put in more face time without staying longer in the office, impress people in meetings, and communicate the importance of their jobs with subtle but strong messages.

This strong image has tremendous implications at every stage along the value chain. Since people are much more likely to contribute to missions that they believe will eventually succeed, efficient managers can enlist the help of others much more easily. Every project of efficient managers, no matter how small, is like an entrepreneurial venture headed by a star CEO. Just as Wall Street rushes to invest in such ventures, colleagues readily help efficient managers, because they expect a successful outcome from these winners and want to be associated with it.

When it is time to sell the results, everybody is much more likely to appreciate the value of the outcome because what we believe in is largely determined by what we expect. The same is true at the last step of the value chain. If managers A and B contribute equally to a successful project, but A radiates success while B pales in comparison, who do you think will get more credit?

4—Efficient managers accumulate political power and use it wisely

Political power is the ability to change the course of events or, in other words, to have it your way. By giving you the ability to shape your work as well as the work of others, this valuable resource enables you to reorganize tasks around the principles of the managerial value chain. Choosing the easiest and most visible tasks in a group project or ensuring that you end up with the richest clients are among the many uses of political power. Just like image, power is the accumulation of many little actions that often appear insignificant to the untrained eye.

Efficient managers are aware of the constant struggle for power and masterfully spot the opportunities. By identifying the true objectives of coworkers, efficient managers can provide compelling reasons for colleagues to join forces with them. In other words, they know whether to dangle a piece of meat or a carrot from the stick to get others to follow their lead. Efficient managers also know how to use common tools in large organizations, such as official plans or formal studies, to gain more power. As a result, they obtain results with much less work. Since they appear powerful enough to make big things happen, they also have a much easier time convincing coworkers that they are the ones who deserve the credit for the miracles. As we will see later on, people won't give you credit for anything that you look incapable of doing.

These topics, which will make up the following chapters, maybe aren't what you were expecting when you picked up this book. Perhaps, subjects such as how to organize your desk for maximum productivity or managing your schedule would have sounded like more natural solutions for getting out of the office faster. The problem is that such strategies treat the symptoms instead of the underlying disease. If you have too much work to fit into a day, scheduling will, at best, provide a slight relief. The question that must be answered is "Why do you end up with so much work in the first place?"

Maybe, you are consistently saying the wrong things in front of superiors, and they are not aware of how much work you are already doing. In this case, you must pay more attention to your image and promote your work. Or could it be that you always end up with the hardest projects in your department because you lack the political power? The objective of this book is to isolate these fundamental problems that are responsible for your over-cluttered inbox and solve them.

Point number one, the right mindset, will be analyzed in the next chapter and will conclude this part. The remaining three points, however, are more elaborate and, therefore, each one will be analyzed in a dedicated part with several chapters. Since these chapters contain a great deal of material and the typical reader of this book may not have a lot of time, here is a road map of what is to come, so you can navigate the book a little more easily.

Part 2, which focuses on building rewarding relationships, will be especially helpful when:

i) You must depend heavily on negligent individuals to do your job

Typical examples are accountants who cannot get their work done because the expense sheets aren't filled out properly or lawyers who are not provided with the full terms of an agreement that they must draft in a timely fashion.

ii) You are sabotaged by others who compete for the same resources

Especially during budget cuts, other departments or even managers from within your group may sabotage your efforts in order to divert resources to their own projects. Also, some organizational cultures overemphasize internal competition, judging managers solely on how they fare in comparison to others. Especially common in sales, this may lead others to harm you to look better themselves.

iii) You lack the resources to do the job

Superiors may simply not have given you the training, personnel, or budget that you need to accomplish your objectives.

The common element in all of these cases is a lack of cooperation by the people around you. As a result, the managerial value chain will break down in the first stage and your efforts will fail to produce the results that the organization needs. Part 2 (Chapters 6-11) will remedy this problem by showing you how to build mutually beneficial relationships.

You may be particularly interested in Part 3, where we will talk about image, if:

i) You have a very technical or highly specialized job

If very few people understand what your job actually involves, colleagues and superiors may not appreciate the results even if they are clearly visible. Although technical jobs, such as IT or engineering positions, are the first to come to mind, this problem can also plague managers who perform simple duties. If you are the only salesperson covering Hispanic customers, nobody in the firm may grasp the difficulties that arise from cultural differences (Note, however, that this problem is solvable, and the advantages of having a unique job actually outweigh the drawbacks.)

ii) You are responsible for control, backup, compliance, or security related functions

There are certain people in every organization that you'd rather not see. If, for example, the compliance department in a brokerage firm is working properly, all procedures mandated by the Securities and Exchange Commission will be followed. No one will hear either from the SEC or the compliance guys. After a while, however, people may start to think that the compliance department is doing nothing, since they are never heard from. It can also be very hard to gauge if compliance is doing an excellent job or just the bare minimum to keep the SEC away.

iii) Your job is centered around long-term projects

If you are rewriting the 1,200-page internal audit manual in nine months, you may have little to show until the final product is ready. Consequently, superiors may underestimate how much progress you have made.

In these cases, the value chain is prone to breaking down at the second stage, meaning that the organization may fail to understand the significance of the results that you produce. Part 3, Polishing Up Your Image to Cut Your Workload (Chapters 12-17), should be particularly useful for any manager faced with this problem. It will show you how to communicate the importance of your job and the implications of your achievements.

You will especially like Part 4, which discusses power, if any of the following is true:

i) Your job involves a lot of joint projects

Especially if the individual responsibilities of team members are unclear and top managers are unaware of the internal structure of the team, it may be very difficult to dole out credit in a just manner when the final results materialize. Another precarious situation arises when the team is dominated by one or two departments that can overpower other participants. If you are the only financial representative in a product development team of six engineers, it won't be too hard for the R&D department to frame the effort as their own initiative and give you zero credit.

ii) Your organization enjoys a clear advantage over its competition

As we will see later, the strengths of your employer can easily turn into your weaknesses. If the company makes a clearly superior product, for example, the success may always be attributed to the product as opposed to you, the salesperson, no matter how much you sell. Similarly, if you are given an unusually large budget or a lot of manpower due to the importance of the initiative, you may have a hard time getting credit for the results unless they are truly spectacular.

iii) You are working for a very politicized and fragmented organization

Clashes inside the organization can impact both your chances to achieve meaningful results and your ability to claim the credit you deserve. Colleagues will usually provide very little help and may even sabotage your efforts in such places. However, once you make it to the finish line despite the lack of support, others will rush to claim a portion of the results.

In these cases, the value chain will short-circuit at the last stage and you won't get the credit you deserve even if people appreciate the significance of the outcome. Part 4, "Gaining the Power to Do Less" (Chapters 18-22), is especially useful for a manager stuck in this situation. Here you will learn how to claim the credit that you deserve for your work.

Let us now kick off our journey by diving right into the brain of an efficient manager...

CHAPTER 5

The Mindset of the Efficient Manager

During the twentieth century, corporations have grown so quickly and evolved so rapidly that even those educational institutions specifically designed to prepare us for such corporations were left far behind. Even today's finest business schools fail to instill in their students the kind of attitude and mindset that is necessary to make the most out of a career as a manager in a giant entity. Despite all the wonderful science that is taught, the general setting in these academic institutions is far too stable, sane, and simple to prepare people for the challenges of the real world. Telling the students, often half a year in advance, what exactly they will have to learn, when they will be tested, and how well they must do on the exams will hardly give them a taste for what they can expect upon graduation. As a manager in a large organization, you will be assessed without even knowing it. You are lucky if the CEO gives you five minutes' notice before asking the most critical question in a board meeting. To make things worse, you cannot check your test scores online, and the professors as well as the passing grades will constantly change.

Consequently, most of us start our careers with the wrong expectations as well as the wrong mindset. And once we join the rat race, there is rarely a chance to stop and evaluate our mistakes. Most managers never lose the student mindset. They behave as if they were in an orderly, stable, simple atmosphere. Amazingly, they expect to come to work each morning, simply do what they are told, and—only by virtue of working hard—to succeed. Although they evaluate countless alternatives to reduce the cost of producing a particular brand of margarine without affecting its taste, these individuals go through their entire careers without asking themselves what they can do to reduce their own work hours without affecting their career prospects.

Efficient managers, on the other hand, know that they will have to survive in a turbulent environment and that no one will give them a roadmap. They approach their own careers with the same proactive, strategic attitude that they use to improve the productivity of their companies. As a result, they achieve better results with less work. In this chapter, I will attempt to condense the mental mode of operation of efficient managers into easily digestible pieces.

The efficient manager always thinks like a salesperson

No matter how impressive your title, in a large organization you will always be a small part of a giant puzzle. Hence, you can do very little without the cooperation of others. You need the help of other departments, coworkers within your division, your superiors, and your subordinates to achieve meaningful results and to convert those results into appreciation, promotion, and compensation. Luckily, all of these people will need your input, too. There is a constant bartering process going on. Regardless of whether you realize it or not, you are constantly selling your ideas, achievements, and plans to those who can give you a bigger salary, the corner office on the top floor, or the respect you deserve. To get a good deal out of this trade, you need to think like a salesperson.

The single most important quality of a great salesperson is his ability to see the world from the perspective of the buyer. He knows that his ultimate success depends on how satisfied the client is with the product or service he delivers, as opposed how much he himself likes what he delivers to the client. A good car salesman, for instance, will gather as much information about you as possible before saying a single word about the car, so he can emphasize the qualities of the vehicle that are important to you. If you arrive at the dealership with a baby, he will talk about the safety features of the car, whereas he will likely emphasize dependability and the low cost of maintenance if you check the sticker prices closely and appear cost-conscious. Bad salespeople, on the other hand, get emotional about the product and talk about the features they like the most. Such a seller will likely explain how the sweet V6 engine glued him to the driver's seat on the highway or how easily the spacious cabin accommodates his 6'3", 230-pound frame even if you will use the vehicle mostly in the city and weigh only 160 pounds. No matter how sincere or passionate the salesperson, such a sales pitch is unlikely to succeed.

Similarly, efficient managers are guided by the desires and priorities of those whose opinions matter. If all of the folders have to be meticulously searched for a lost file, the subordinate matters the most and he must be convinced of the necessity of this task. When trying to get a bigger promotional budget, the board of directors is the client. So, for the next two hours the efficient manager will look at the world from the perspective of a board member and assess how an increase in trade promotions will sound when the board addresses the shareholders at the end of the year.

A lack of this "managerial empathy" is the single biggest problem of inefficient managers. These men and women often have an inflexible mental picture of the "ideal" budget file, promotional campaign, advertising slogan, or whatever, and strive to achieve this ideal regardless of what other people value. Consequently, they are forced to do more than their fair share. Since their goals are not in line with those of their coworkers, people are rarely motivated to help them.

More importantly, even if they achieve what they consider to be the ideal outcome, they are not compensated sufficiently, because their ideal is almost always a compromise solution from the perspective of others.

Like practically every other virtue I will emphasize in this book, managerial empathy is much more important in a large entity than in a small organization. If the company has only five employees, the priorities and goals of these individuals will probably be well aligned. What you consider ideal will not be too different from what your coworkers are after. Furthermore, there won't be as broad an array of personalities around you. Since there is less departmentalization and specialization in small firms, these companies often attract generalists as opposed to clusters of specialists. But in a large company, you will be selling an idea to the ultra-precise engineers in the morning and bargaining with the image-driven marketing department at noon.

Keep this principle in mind while reading the following chapters, and the material will make a lot more sense. Whether we are analyzing the importance of building an argument on people's existing beliefs, obtaining more help from coworkers by making them look good, or saving time for top managers by providing them printouts they can read in a cramped cab, the essence of almost every principle involves empathy. Like a good salesperson, look at the world from the eyes of those whose opinions matter and you will go further with fewer steps.

The efficient manager takes the initiative and redefines his job

Another trait of efficient managers is their willingness to constantly redefine their jobs. Due to the ever-changing conditions in a large organization, the standard procedures adopted by a predecessor or dictated by top management are rarely the most efficient mode of operation. Since the goals as well as the resources are evolving, the job must too. Knowing that others won't provide a roadmap for this evolution (or will do so only after the manager fails) efficient managers take charge and continuously reshape their jobs.

i) He looks for new ways to perform his duties

This message cannot be overemphasized: The workload of a particular managerial job is not a constant that you must obediently accept; instead, it is a dynamic factor that you can influence. The reason is that a managerial job isn't a collection of clear-cut tasks. It is a dynamic assignment that you can modify as long as you reach the desired objectives. Although it may look easier to work within the existing framework established by your predecessor, you cannot improve your efficiency much beyond that of your forerunner with such a passive approach.

When I started to work in purchasing, we never knew how many tons of each raw material to purchase until sales forecasts came in for the next year. So, we had to squeeze all contract negotiations into the second half of December. This was both stressful and inefficient. After my first year, I realized that volume wasn't as important in our business as shipment size, lead times, and specifications. I went to sales in November and asked for rough volume forecasts that I could use to negotiate for a quarter of the raw materials. We agreed to renegotiate if there was a big change in the forecasts, but there wasn't. Although my boss was skeptical at first, he loved it because we were done before Christmas. The following year, we negotiated all purchases in this way and completed everything in half the time. You must take a step before someone tells you to. Only then can you experiment without your boss bugging you and find more intelligent ways to do things.

The manager in this interview solved a problem at the first stage of the value chain and found a way to achieve one of the results with less effort. He also reduced the workload of his supervisor, which will have a further positive impact on his image. As the interviewee correctly identified, the key is to be proactive and act before your back is against the wall. This way, you can experiment without your boss breathing down your neck and pleasantly surprise your superiors, as opposed to looking like you are just putting out fires.

ii) He looks to add or subtract new duties to differentiate his job

Always watch out for opportunities to differentiate your job, because a unique and highly specialized job will dramatically improve your freedom. Stated differently, the less people understand what you do for a living, the less they can interfere. You have probably worked with people who had fancy titles like "LAN Systems Support Manager" and wondered what in the world they did. Whatever you ask them for turns out to be "impossible with our current infrastructure," and whenever you go see them they are playing with their handheld computers. Unfortunately, you cannot object, since you have no idea what these people are supposed to do.

I used to work with a manager whose main duty was to obtain regulatory approval for new products. Due to the legal intricacies and the boring nature of the task, nobody knew or wanted to learn about what he was doing. With all due respect, I doubt that he was doing much at all. A law firm handled the paperwork, leaving our "expert" with nothing more to do than follow up on the status of approvals and translate the correspondence for brand managers. Yet nobody could question him, because we had no defense whatsoever to the technical terms and legalese he would throw at us in response. Although this person's behavior was extreme and is not desirable, it nevertheless shows how advantageous it can be to have a unique and specialized job.

Another advantage of a unique position is that it practically eliminates the possibility of direct peer comparisons. For most managers, especially those in sales, the pressure to outperform peers can be tremendous. In such a competitive atmosphere, people are also less willing to help each other. Performance standards are usually very high, as members push themselves to the limit. Most importantly, such environments severely restrict your ability to promote your results. While you can always make a case for why it wasn't possible to attain a higher volume when you are selling a unique product, your argument will fail if the next guy works 15 hour days and sells more of the exact same product using the same promotional budget.

Seek unique positions where direct performance comparisons are impossible and you are the only expert in what you are doing. If your existing job does not provide this luxury, try to add or subtract a few duties to make it significantly different from the jobs of your peers.

Suppose that you are one of the many relationship managers with a portfolio of ten key customers, and the firm decides to build a new "prospective client database" for a new market it wants to enter. The task is too much for a manager to take up on top of his existing job, yet not so time-consuming that it justifies a dedicated person. This could be a great opportunity to propose transferring five of your clients to other managers and taking on this additional role. Not only will you turn your job into a hybrid position, thus making direct peer comparisons much harder, but you will also be the only expert in an area.

As long as you keep an open mind, you will realize that such opportunities abound. Do not be afraid to take up totally new and unfamiliar tasks. Remember that the more complex and incomprehensible the subject appears to outsiders, the better. The time invested in learning these new topics may be well worth the comfort later on.

You don't need to revolutionize your job with the addition of one such giant task. You can slowly evolve over time, making small changes along the way. When there are a bunch of new clients to choose from, go for the different ones. If you can advertise in a variety of newspapers, always pick the one that is not used by others around you. Every step you take to differentiate your job and to become the only expert in a particular field is a step in the right direction.

Please do not view the task of redefining your job as a huge challenge. Today's large organizations are changing at such dizzying speeds that your job will evolve anyway. All you need to do is to slightly alter the course of this change. As a salesperson, for example, you will inevitably lose some customers and add new ones or deal with different departments as time goes by. What is required is that you make a little bit of effort to influence the ones you end up with.

iii) He outsources as much as possible to become the client rather than the seller

You should constantly look for ways to shift your support functions to outsiders, as opposed to obtaining such services from other departments or divisions in your own organization, because he who pays the bills has an enormous power advantage. To illustrate this point, let us look at two different relationships: brand manager and R&D manager within the same firm vs. brand manager(BM) and the account executive(AE) working for an independent advertising agency.

Although the BM enjoys, at best, a slight edge in power and prestige when dealing with the R&D manager, he is absolutely dominant in his relationship with the AE, because his company is paying the bill. If the BM does not like the AE, he can call the AE's boss and complain, while the other side can never do the same. If things don't improve, the BM can request that the AE be replaced and, with a little support from his marketing director or VP, he will probably succeed. I have witnessed the above scenario firsthand and I am sure that most experienced BMs have, too. On the other hand, I seriously doubt that an AE ever got a BM in serious trouble. The sole reason is that one side is writing the check. In comparison, the number of BMs who have such a huge influence on their colleagues in the R&D department is extremely limited.

As a manager, you will immediately notice the difference between the attitudes of those you pay and those you don't. The first thing I noticed as an assistant BM was that no internal party such as R&D or finance would return my calls, while the AE, who was much older and more experienced than I, would call me right back and apologize that she had missed my call. The amount of time you can save with such cooperation is amazing. If everyone I dealt with had operated that way, I probably could have gone home at noon every day. However, nothing comes for free and my gain was the AE's loss, as she had to schedule her entire day around BMs.

To enjoy these benefits, purchase your services from external parties whenever you can, as opposed to sourcing them from another department within your organization. In Chapter 21, we will return to this subject and analyze how you can maximize your leverage when dealing with suppliers, to minimize your workload.

The efficient manager prioritizes ruthlessly

One important obstacle to redefining your job is the guilt produced by prioritizing your responsibilities. Since we are constantly told that we can do everything perfectly if we work hard enough, we cannot accept the fact that, at times, less important tasks have to be sacrificed in favor of more critical matters. One of the first things I noticed about efficient managers was their willingness to prioritize brutally. Thus, they could focus on what mattered more and used the leverage from the favorable outcomes to defer, or even completely eliminate, the minor tasks.

In my first week on the job, I was shocked to see a colleague hang up on the regional manager when he received a call from a client. He did not even put the client on hold for a moment. When I probed, he said, "There are a few guys whose calls I must take and this was one of them. In my caller ID, I have three zeros before their names. Those zeros are like a bomb alert to me, and I stop whatever I am doing when I see them. I'll call the RM right now to tell him that it was my biggest client. If he doesn't understand, he is in the wrong business. Even then, I would rather apologize to him than to my best client." I later realized that he was able to hang up on RMs, because his clients liked him so much. They insisted on talking to him and nobody else. This gave him amazing power with the RMs. It's kind of a paradox: In order to hang up on a RM or sacrifice other less important things, you need power. But you can never accumulate that power until you show the courage to hang up on RMs and really focus on critical tasks.

After you think about your priorities, you will probably come up with a different set of critical tasks, and maybe RMs and not clients will be at the top. The important thing to understand, however, is that certain factors will play a much more important role in how you are perceived. Hence, your priorities must be in the right order for maximum efficiency.

Once you start to deliver critical results, not only will your superiors bug you a lot less about details, they will also be more tolerant of an occasional mistake or negligence in a non-critical area. This is why most efficient managers never return certain phone calls or simply don't reply to some e-mails and get away with it. People wonder how someone so unresponsive got to where he did. What they don't realize is that to get there, you have to do the important things really well, which sometimes requires being unresponsive somewhere else.

The efficient manager doesn't judge himself by how much he works
We are so conditioned to measure our worth by how much we work that most of us are actually afraid to become more efficient and leave the office early. No matter how independently you think, you too will probably feel a bit guilty as you improve your efficiency and leave when others are still working. Fear also arises when you realize that superiors may use the lack of face time against you.

In Chapter 15, I will talk about face time in great detail and explain how you can defend yourself against hour counters—those incompetent supervisors who use the number of hours you spend in the office as the sole measure of your dedication and contribution. I also think that getting out of the office as early as possible will greatly boost your contribution to society. I don't think that anyone ever made the world a better place by staying at work longer than necessary. In fact, the exact opposite is true; society would be much better off without those wasted marriages, early heart attacks, and frustrated children, which are inevitable if one spends a disproportionate amount of time on the job.

Judge yourself with the results you are producing, not with the number of hours you spend in the office. Never miss the forest for the trees. The forest is your achievements. Less important details, including how much you work, are merely trees without which the forest can survive.

And a word of caution...
Do not try to swallow this book in whole

Now that we have covered the theory and the ideal mindset with which to apply it, we are ready to go into the details of application. Please note that the next 17 chapters contain an enormous amount of practical knowledge. Unlike most books, this one is not simply the opinions of a single wise person. It represents the experiences of hundreds of managers. Therefore, you cannot expect to retain everything you are about to read.

Think of this as an open buffet dinner, where you would start with your favorite dishes and would go back for a second round if you still have room after that. Similarly, start by applying the most relevant lessons in this book and wait until you digest them before you attack new topics. If you bite off more than you can chew at once, you will only frustrate yourself and delay the learning process. Remember that you can always come back for more.

Do not worry about what percentage of the ideas you are able to retain or put to use. Even if you only pick three to four tactics from the whole book and save a mere 15 minutes a day as a result, this makes over 60 hours in a year. That is way more than you will need to read the book. Needless to say, I am confident that you will achieve a much higher improvement in efficiency.

PART 2

Managing People for Maximum Efficiency

Not every organization values its employees to the same extent. Some rely primarily on patents, brand names, or legal protection and treat their people as a secondary tool. However, your relationship with these people is always the key to success for you as a manager. In the end, it is always the people, not patents or best-selling products, who will have the final say on whether you will get that raise or promotion. Just as importantly, it is those people who will eventually determine how much work you must perform in order to succeed at your job.

How you handle top managers, or more precisely the people above you, plays a huge role in perceptions. This impacts the transition from the second to the third and from the third to the fourth box in the managerial value chain. It is the job of top management to apportion blame and fame. Hence, a success that top management does not attribute to you is not a success at all. The R&D department may develop the best formulation on earth for a lipstick. But if top managers attribute the market share gains to the flashy marketing campaign featuring supermodels, marketing will get most of the credit. Due to this reason, people who know how connect with top management can achieve an impressive degree of success with very little effort.

Peers and subordinates, on the other hand, play a tremendous role during the first stage of the value chain. By learning how to get the most out of these individuals, you can get a lot more done with the same amount of effort. Over the next six chapters, we will analyze each of these relationships in great detail. But first, let's start with some basics that apply to all interactions in the office.

CHAPTER 6

Building Rewarding Relationships

In Chapter 2, I explained why the amount of work that a manager must perform to succeed is not fixed. If you accept this principle, it should be easy to also accept that the total managerial workload in an organization is not fixed. After all, the sum of variable parameters cannot be constant. In other words, this is not a zero-sum game. But let's leave the academic jargon aside and look at an example that we can all relate to.

Assume that, at the end of a meeting, the leader calls for a follow-up session. Instead of asking the participants to agree on a date right there, your boss waits and then asks you to arrange it. Although it would have taken at most five minutes to find a mutually agreeable time when everyone was in the same room, it will now take you at least half an hour to send e-mails and make phone calls. So your boss has produced twenty-five minutes of additional work for you. If this was a zero-sum game, someone should have gained twenty-five minutes, but there is no winner here.

Just as it is possible to increase the aggregate managerial workload in an organization, one can also reduce it. Spending thirty seconds to double-check a file or promptly informing the factory of a change in shipment dates can save hours for your colleagues. In this chapter, we will explore fundamental human management skills that will help you reduce the total workload in your organization and retain your fair share of those savings.

Recall the Golden Rule: The more people trust you, the less you will work

If I had to pick the most critical asset of efficient managers, I would not choose experience, education, or charisma. Instead, I would say that it is the trust of their coworkers. The more people trust you, the more liberty they will give you to pick the most efficient mode of operation. Very few jobs, if any, have been designed with the managerial value chain in mind. Therefore, standard assignments must be modified according to the requirements of the value chain. If people don't trust you, this becomes impossible, as they will impose inefficient methods on you.

When working with my boss, I feel like I am preparing Christmas dinner with my mom. We constantly look over each other's shoulders and drive each other mad. We're so unproductive that only one of us working alone could do the same job faster. For example, when we have to organize big seminars, I prefer e-mail. I can keep track of things and express myself better in writing. But my boss insists that I use the phone, because he doesn't believe that I can get things done effectively via e-mail. He constantly asks me if I have called so-and-so, and when I tell him I sent an e-mail, he makes the call and conferences me in. I am completely inefficient in those calls because I can't think with five people yelling in my ear. I usually end up both writing the long e-mails and suffering through the calls. If he would let me work my way, I could probably do it all in half the time.

Here, the value chain breaks down at the first stage, due to the lack of trust and freedom. As a result, the work requires more effort than it needs to. But problems can arise at any stage. Another interviewee complained that his boss doesn't trust him enough to talk in important meetings, which makes it impossible to promote his achievements.

Perhaps the most common manifestation of insufficient trust is when colleagues double-check your work. This has terrible consequences on efficiency. For example, when you are asked for a market share graph, ideally you want coworkers to consult with you as to what competitors to include and whether to use number of units or dollar sales. Then, again ideally, they would request that you send them only the graph that you suggest. If, however, they do not trust you, and think that you will simply encourage them to accept whatever you have handy, they will ask for all possible variations, probably five or six graphs, and choose one on their own.

Other consequences of mistrust include long interrogations over the phone to verify the accuracy of critical data, or being asked the same question several times in slightly different formats to check for consistency. These things will significantly prolong your work hours, and there is very little you can do to prevent them if coworkers don't trust you. So how do you gain this trust?

i) Either accept assignments enthusiastically or reject them

When you are given a boring or painful task, the worst thing you can do is complain about it. The more apathy you display toward an assignment, the less people will trust that you will do a good job, and the more they will look over your shoulder. The restrictions they will impose and the additional information they will request to check your results will only prolong the task.

Either accept an assignment enthusiastically or fight to reject it. If you will end up doing the work no matter how much you complain, embrace it even if you feel like ripping the head off the person who dumped it on you. When you cannot raise objections because of the seniority of the other party, don't think you must whine and make faces to get your point across. This is a primitive mode of communication. In addition to leading to more scrutiny and more work, it will also damage your relationships. As I explain in Chapter 11, you have better options when dealing with unreasonable requests.

ii) Do not leave issues up in the air; help people cross items off their lists

Any issue that isn't 100% completed or delegated continues to occupy valuable space in our minds and reduces our mental performance. Best-selling author David Allen calls these "open loops." The e-mail that your colleague promised to send to the client but never gave you a confirmation about, or the expense forms that should be okay but have never been officially approved are examples of open loops.

Every open loop you leave in people's minds will erode their trust in you. They will think that you never fully complete anything unless constantly checked up on. One easy way to gain trust and sympathy is to help them close these loops by definitively concluding matters one way or another. An e-mail that just says "the expense sheets have been approved" or a phone call that lasts only a few seconds does the job.

Although you may assume that these follow-ups will lead to more questions or demands, in fact it is quite the opposite. If the other party has to call you to inquire about the status of an unfinished job, you will look bad for not having gotten back to him. This will give justification to make additional demands. Furthermore, you will look like you are hiding to get away with as little work as possible, which will erode people's trust and lead to closer scrutiny. To avoid this, get back to people to confirm the successful completion of all tasks, no matter how small. Always finish by telling them to call you in the future if they need something else. This will rarely result in more calls—if they need to call you, they will do so anyway—but will greatly help to build trust.

If you have bad news that will inevitably surface, communicate it aggressively before people find out. If you won't be able to send the promised file by the deadline, contact the recipient right away and explain the situation. Similarly, do not wait too long to tell people about bad market share numbers. On the contrary, send a message with those results even earlier than you would have if you had good news. Under no circumstances should people assume that you tend to remain silent whenever you have something unpleasant to tell. If they reach this conclusion, they will flood you with e-mails and phone calls every time you are a day or two late. This will devastate your efficiency.

iii) Clearly communicate and accept full responsibility for what you will deliver

We rarely work alone in a large organization and therefore depend heavily on others to help us keep our promises. Simply "doing our jobs" is usually inadequate for satisfying the demands of coworkers. It is often necessary to hunt down information and specific individuals and occasionally do other people's jobs to satisfy what is expected of us. Managers who do not understand this requirement and define their responsibilities too narrowly cause tremendous trouble in large organizations and quickly lose the trust of their coworkers.

> My new employees in relationship management usually make a big mistake by drawing thick lines between their responsibilities and those of other departments. When a customer asks for a budget, obviously the relationship manager must depend on accounting. But this does not justify missing the deadline because the accountant was late. I go insane when an employee tells me it isn't his fault. If the customer gets annoyed, it is your fault. When you must work with an unreliable accountant, ask your client for more time. Then call the accountant every hour to check up. If you're still nervous, ask me to step in. You will drive me crazy if you come to me fifteen minutes before the deadline and say that you did your best, but the accountant messed up. If you do that, you will be the one who messed up.

The problem is caused by a mismatch between our definition of responsibilities and people's expectations. Unfortunately, in a large organization colleagues will seldom understand exactly what you do and will always ask you for things that are not your responsibility. Smaller entities, where both processes and the roles of managers are much simpler, rarely present such problems. Having to work with individuals whose titles you can barely pronounce let alone understand what they do for a living is a constraint unique to giant companies.

The only way around this is to balance what is expected and what you can deliver. This is not to say that you should do everything that people ask for. You must, however, clearly communicate what you can do *before* you start to work on the requested task. In case of a discrepancy, you must either broaden the scope of your responsibilities or scale back the expectations.

Assume that you are asked for a budget that you need to get from the accounting department. You should either accept the responsibility and hunt down the accountant, or refer the other person to the accountant and step back. What you should not do is to promise to get the information, fail to do so, and then make an excuse by claiming that it was the fault of the accountant. It is better to be a tough negotiator who rarely agrees to deliver everything he is asked for, but always does what he says. Pumping up the expectations and then disappointing people quickly leads to erosion of trust and workload inflation for all the parties involved.

If you think that people are expecting an unfair amount, you should reduce their expectations by communicating how much you are already delivering, as I will explain in Part 3, especially in Chapter 13. Avoiding the topic and hiding behind job descriptions in the case of conflicts will only erode people's confidence and eventually increase your workload.

Improve your communication skills

Communication in the workplace is like the obesity epidemic in America—the more it is analyzed, the worse it gets. There are many reasons managers cannot connect with colleagues. First, large establishments require such specialization that coworkers only have a vague idea about what we do. Furthermore, the world is so fast-paced that it is hard to keep up with what is going on in our own areas, let alone following the evolution of someone else's job. Managers also have less time than ever before and must limit direct contact. The days when people would chat for an hour after lunch are long gone. Finally, large organizations are so politicized today that few people can speak their minds. As a result, we drive each other crazy. We request things at the worst moment, send wrong files, or say things in meetings that make others look like idiots. This leads to chronic workload inflation: a lose-lose situation where everyone ends up with more work to achieve the same results.

i) Efficient Communication 101: Ensure continuous information flow

Proper communication can only be achieved if information flows continuously instead of being sent in unmanageably large chunks. Since our minds can process only a limited amount of data at once, we don't absorb a lot of what people tell us in four-hour meetings or day-long seminars.

When I worked in advertising, a client was trying to establish a presence in the small pickup truck market. Over the weeks preceding the official debriefing, they had constantly mentioned the fuel economy of the vehicle. During the big meeting, however, they suddenly revealed that the advertising campaign had to focus on durability. The latest research showed that consumers were misled by the flimsy look of the truck and didn't think that it could handle tough tasks such as carrying construction equipment. Clearly, most consumers wouldn't buy the truck even if they knew how little fuel it consumed. After the meeting, a seasoned advertising executive beautifully explained the problems with such a sudden information overload.

> Now we need a miracle to come up with a creative idea on time, because the copywriters have been conditioned for so long to focus on fuel economy. You cannot put a brief in front of them and expect an idea overnight. I know one person assigned to this project had been spending time in gas stations, talking to people about their trucks and listening to the jokes they made about fuel prices. He probably wrote

many scenarios that are in the garbage bin and was waiting for the "eureka" sensation. This is how the mind of a copywriter works. Just as you can't make good wine overnight, you can't make good advertising in a week. You have to feed the information gently over time so it really sinks in.

Guess what happened in the end. The agency couldn't deliver on time and the schedule had to be revised. This delayed the entire launch and created tons of extra work—especially for the client.

Although most jobs are not as creative as copywriting, the same principle applies. If you don't supply digestible bits of information to the supermarket manager about the products he will sell next year and cram it all into the three-hour "annual planning meeting," you will overwhelm him. Then you will wonder why he failed to order enough refrigerators for the new brands of ice cream. Just like the copywriter, he needs time for the information to sink in, maybe spending a day in the ice cream aisle or talking to shoppers at the checkout. He needs time to think, plan, and digest. If you don't give him this time, he will order either too few or too many refrigerators and the resulting chaos will multiply both his and your workload.

To ensure that information flows continuously and in digestible bits, do not wait for the final decision, because by then it may be too late. The possibilities are endless. You could ask a secretary for another department's meeting notes, send prototypes to the logistics department, or invite suppliers to the crash test of next year's two-door coupe. The best way to ensure information flow, however, is to chat. This doesn't have to be nearly as time-consuming as you may think. Quickly stop by to ask coworkers what they think about making a purple toothpaste or offering a six-year warranty while these ideas are still in the development stage, and encourage them to do the same. Keep these conversations short, simple, and fun. Remember that frequent exchange of information leads to better communication and a smoother, less stressful operation.

ii) Efficient Communication 102: Allow others to express themselves

The second rule is to help others to open up by encouraging them to speak their minds without fear. Since managers are often ignorant about each other's jobs, we live under the constant threat of appearing stupid. The desire to preserve our images by keeping our mouths shut is one of the biggest obstacles to proper communication.

Ideas that are still in the development stage are particularly vulnerable, because most incomplete theories will sound foolish. Even the best organizations don't implement more than 10% of their ideas, so at least 90% of what is discussed will be infeasible. To encourage coworkers to communicate early and regularly, show them that you don't mind looking dumb once in a while. If you can laugh at yourself when you blow it, you make it much easier for others to open up.

It is also critical that you don't overpower others with your knowledge or experience. If coworkers sense that you know everything about a matter and have nothing more to learn, they simply will not talk. Be particularly careful with young and inexperienced subordinates. To gain the respect of their employees, many supervisors appear like gurus and intimidate their people.

> My boss's whole life revolves around banking. His office is filled with books and finance magazines. He actually taught finance in college prior to coming to the bank and still has the same attitude. He makes me feel so ignorant. I get sick when he asks me why I never go to him with suggestions. How can I?

Demonstrate enthusiasm for what you do, but keep some of your knowledge to yourself. If you don't know the answer, just say so. Welcome suggestions and, even if they sound ignorant, show appreciation for the effort. When someone comes to you with a bad idea, do not immediately correct his mistake. Get back to him after a day or two and offer the correct answer as an alternative inspired by his comments, rather than punishing him on the spot. That will only create the impression that you didn't even think about what he said. Even if you are a guru, let people discover the depth of your knowledge slowly. Remember that it is your character, more than your expertise, that earns you respect.

iii) Efficient Communication 103: First, ask yourself what they think

Work within the boundaries set by the other side's beliefs. Just like habits, convictions can only be changed slowly. What we can believe is largely dictated by what we currently accept as true.

Long ago, I met a personal trainer who was fiercely opposed to doing a lot of sit-ups to flatten the stomach. His theory, which is universally accepted today, was that only a few minutes of specific work was needed to strengthen the abdominal muscles. Further crunches would not result in greater fat loss around the belly. That, he said, could only be accomplished with diet and aerobic exercise. Naturally, I was shocked when I later saw him put a client through twenty minutes of abdominal work. When I confronted him, he said,

> Like most people, this woman thought she had to do hundreds of sit-ups and wanted to spend half of the workout training her abs. I only have ninety minutes for the warm-up, actual workout, stretching, and discussion about the diet. So I can't afford to talk about sit-ups for more than five minutes. There is no way I can change her views in five minutes. If I simply tell her to do three dozen sit-ups, she'll hate

me and go find another trainer who will give her forty-five minutes of stomach exercises. Having convinced her to do only twenty minutes is actually a victory. If she works with me, in a month or so, I can teach her how to flatten her belly. But I can't do it in one session—she is too prejudiced to accept it so quickly.

This brilliant analysis demonstrates an understanding of human nature that few managers posses. Before you communicate a viewpoint to someone, ask yourself what his current beliefs are and how much you can change them at one time. Then round off the sharp edges of your argument accordingly. Here is another great example.

When the new division manager revealed his plans to boost the customer base by 50%, I immediately knew he had no idea. In fact, we didn't have enough resources. If anything, we had to get rid of smaller accounts. So I focused on these problems in my presentation and explained why we couldn't handle more clients. In return I was accused of demoralizing the department. The funny thing is, after a month, the division manager postponed the expansion plan and hired more sales reps, as I had suggested, but I never got any credit. I now realize that it would have been better to give just a few hints about the problems in my first presentation, instead of throwing it all at him at once. After a few weeks he would have come to his senses anyway but he wasn't ready to accept it then. A simple pro vs. con analysis with a slight emphasis on the cons would have given him enough for starters and would have made me look much better.

Keep this example in mind and never give people more than they can accept. Instill just a small doubt in people's minds by using their beliefs as stepping-stones, and have them come back to you for more. The new division manager above should realize that he needs more data before he can act and return with questions. Then he will be ready to absorb information like a sponge.

iv) Efficient Communication 104: Understand people's true objectives

The discrepancy between official goals and real objectives can be a tremendous obstacle to efficient communication. You cannot connect with someone unless you know what he is trying to do. Unfortunately, real objectives are often politically incorrect, and therefore most managers hide them. Instead of asking people to be candid, which will only scare them, observe what they spend their time on, and gauge their responses to different stimuli. If a manager states that he really wants to build a strong sales force with new hires, but never takes the time to interview applicants, you can certainly question his motivation. Similarly, the marketing VP who constantly talks about improving synergies with sales but never picks up phone calls from the sales department presents an inconsistency.

> My company decided to integrate all of its Web sites, which required lots of work by product managers. One manager in particular always supported the project when the head of technology was around, but he rarely returned our calls and was absolutely reluctant to help. It all fell into place when I distributed a study stating that some products, including his, could lose visibility after the integration. He loved it and immediately appeared at my desk to talk. He was obviously worried about his total hits, but was afraid to bring that up. Going forward, I made sure to provide him occasional data that gently pointed to the negatives of the integration. After I realized what he was after, we went along great.

The clues are everywhere. Sometimes they slip out inadvertently, while at other times they are intentional. So keep your eyes open.

Do not commit the two deadly sins

There are two deadly sins that do irreparable damage to relationships. The first is making people suffer unnecessarily. Imagine this: Your boss harasses you for a report, you kill yourself to make the Monday morning deadline, and then you find it on his desk on Wednesday, still untouched. Another variation of this same abuse is asking for precise data when a rough figure is enough. Suppose that you are scheduled to talk about a new product idea at a business dinner and want to quote a ballpark profit figure. Common courtesy dictates that you ask accounting for an approximate number. Instead, most managers ask for super-precise figures to hedge against all risks. This forces the accountants to do a full-fledged analysis, instead of saving such a detailed study for the final phase. As a result, not only will accounting hate you for torturing them, but they will never believe you when you say, "This time we really are launching the product, so the numbers have to be exact."

Such lies are much easier to uncover than we realize. My boss once asked me to prepare a report before a meeting on Friday. When he got the printouts, he said that the meeting was postponed and went home, making me highly suspicious. After he left, I called the people he was going to meet and asked them if anything else was needed for the postponed meeting. As expected, the meeting wasn't postponed. It had originally been scheduled for Monday. I was outraged. I had suffered only because that _____ wanted to read the report in the comfort of his home. Worst of all, he treated me like an idiot and lied to me, thinking that I would never find out. How can you believe such a person again?

Second-guessing people behind their backs is the other cardinal sin. Many managers ask two people for the same thing because they have so little confidence that the job will be done right the first time. But if the individuals find out, and they often do, their anger will wipe out any trust that might have existed. A variation of this tactic is to withhold existing information, asking people to do the work from scratch to see if they come up with the same result as before.

> When my boss told me to build a financial model, I explicitly asked him if we had an old one at hand. He said that the old model was incomplete and he couldn't find it anyway, so I started to build a new one. After two days of work, he gave me some numbers to test my spreadsheet, but we couldn't agree on the result. Then he opened a near-perfect model that produced different numbers. I was furious. He had lied twice: the old model wasn't incomplete and he knew where it was. He was using it to check my work because he obviously had no confidence in me. Yet there really was no need for this pretense. Had he told me to build a new model without looking at the old one so he could double-check the results, I would have understood, because this was a critical project.

The scenario is similar to my experience with the "postponed" meeting, with similar results: How can you expect someone to trust you after all this?

While I will not assume the role of an ethicist here and tell you when to be honest, I want to leave you with a few thoughts on the impact of such lies on efficiency. First, remember that when you ask someone to do something for you, but lie about an aspect of the task that needs to be accomplished, such as a deadline, you are taking a tremendous risk. As we will see in greater detail in Chapter 10, the person who does the work will be so immersed in the project that he probably will uncover your fraud. He may run into a colleague and casually mention it, he may have to call the client when you are not around to answer a question, he may find an old model in the network or do some detective work like I did. And once he finds out, your credibility will drop to zero. Needless to say, this lack of trust will severely hamper your efficiency. Always keep in mind that the individuals who work for you are the hardest people to deceive in the company.

Furthermore, most of those lies are unnecessary anyway, because people's tolerances can be exceptionally high when you open up. An honest attempt to communicate the truth and an effort to reduce the burden on the other side is not only a safer solution, but will also save a tremendous amount of work for both sides. In the above scenario, for instance, the supervisor could simply have told his assistant that an old model was available, but had never been checked rigorously and therefore should not be used as a foundation for the new spreadsheet. To help the assistant, the boss could then give some hints about what the finished model ought to look like or maybe even reveal some portions of the old spreadsheet that he had confidence in. The bottom line is that there is often an alternative to lying, and these alternatives work much better in the long run.

Gently change those you can, and gracefully accept those you cannot

Inevitably, some coworkers will get on your nerves. The reasons could be job related or just personal. A colleague who sends messy files that take hours to figure out presents a job-related problem. On the other hand a boss who goes through your drawers to "borrow" the stapler is an example of the second type of provocation. (Here I am talking about good people with a few bad habits. Pathological cases are discussed in Chapter II, Dealing With Troublemakers.)

The most important rule when dealing with these annoyances is to assess what you can change and calmly accept what you cannot. Whether or not you can alter a behavior depends on how deeply rooted the habit is and how much authority you have over the individual. Personality traits are nearly impossible to change. If an employee is an introvert by nature and eats lunch on his own, do not try to open him up with your formal authority. Not only will the effort most likely fail, but it will severely hurt the individual.

If you must interfere, keep your criticism as focused as possible. Communicate that you are not trying to turn him into a different person, but are only concerned about the job. Do not ask him to "relax a bit and open up." Instead, tell him that you respect his right to spend time alone, while explaining that business matters may be discussed during informal gatherings. Telling someone that he doesn't have the right attitude will almost certainly backfire. You will achieve temporary results at best, but really alienate the person.

Since seniority is so important in how much you can change people, always start with the more junior person, even if his manners are perfectly legitimate. For example, if your boss gives you the numbers late and delays the report that you must send to accounting, talk to the assistant accountant first. Even if the deadlines have been set in stone, you have a better chance to get a concession from someone at your level than from your boss. In explaining, focus on issues beyond your control. Tell the assistant that you cannot meet the deadline because of your boss's critical business commitments.

Only if this fails should you go to your boss. Again, blame external circumstances and explain that you already tried to talk to accounting. Send the message that he is doing the right thing, but you must still ask for a concession. If you side with the accounting department in front of your boss, you will seriously undermine your chances. Telling him directly or indirectly that his behavior is putting you in a difficult situation will challenge his authority. You essentially will be asking him to suffer to relieve you pain, and will surely lose that tug of war.

Of course, even the best diplomat can change only so much and must put up with a lot of annoying behavior at work. In order not to destroy your relationships, maturely accept what you must. Most managers think that when they are mistreated, they should make the other person's life more difficult to show they can hit back. When a disorganized colleague forwards a messy file, they grumble, send annoying messages, and delay giving him what he needs. Even if this conduct does less damage to him than what he put you through, appearing fair on that basis, do not resort to such tactics. You will damage the relationship further and make it harder to change the person's behavior later, if an opportunity arises.

In addition, the other side will have no incentive to help you elsewhere, because you already took revenge. If, instead, you act maturely, expressing discontent occasionally instead of getting even, it is more likely that you will get a useful concession in a future negotiation.

Gain everyone's respect, no matter how unimportant they may seem

Although I have repeatedly stressed the importance of treating people according to their power and position, I don't want to imply that you can show disrespect to certain individuals. In today's dynamic organizations, your power is not purely a function of rank. At times, a secretary can be more powerful than a VP and an IT support person can seriously hinder a senior officer.

When I was working in advertising, the art director I was partnered with on a critical project had a huge system crash. It was around midnight, and the chance of finding a tech person was very slim. But since the project was due the following morning, we set out to look for help. I miraculously found someone, but was quickly disappointed because she said she was too busy to help. However, to my amazement, her attitude changed by 180 degrees when the art director and I walked down together to give it another shot. She came upstairs and solved our problem relatively quickly.

The next morning, I went to her to apologize for being so pushy. Given how quickly she had agreed to come up when I went there with the art director, I felt that I must have done something wrong the first time. Her response was completely unexpected. She said that she changed her mind only because she owed a favor to the art director and he was always so nice to her.

This experience helped me see a lot of things from a different perspective. Although the art director was a relatively senior person, both his and my destinies were in the hands of an IT person that night. If she did not want to help, there was nothing we could have done. Even if I had been the CEO, she could have taken a look at the PC and said, "Sorry, nothing I can do right now" and I wouldn't have been able to challenge her. Since then I observed many similar events.

I have particularly witnessed the power of secretaries. If you must catch the VP before he leaves in an hour, his secretary is the only person on earth who can help you. Only the secretary can tell you the right time to walk in and can put a few calls on hold to give you that five-minute window. Just like the IT person in the prior example, if a gatekeeper does not want to help, there is nothing you can do. The same is true when you lose your badge and ask the security guard to let you in at two AM.

You cannot be friends with everyone. And you shouldn't try, because it will look fake. But you can treat people with respect and try to make their lives easier. If you need to change your airline ticket, tell the secretary right away, instead of waiting until the last minute. If you have a technical problem, ask the IT service if they can give you directions over the phone so they won't have to come over. Remember that you tend to need the help of these "unimportant" people when you are in big trouble. So don't make enemies unless you need to.

5 Key Points You Should Remember

- Never complain about something you will be forced to do anyway
- Upon finishing a task, get back to people and help them cross it off from their to-do lists
- Give your coworkers constant feedback about your ideas during the development phase
- Do not secretly check the accuracy and quality of someone's work
- Gracefully accept the nature and work habits of the people you cannot realistically change

CHAPTER 7

The Easiest Ways to Satisfy Top Management

Although it has been over a decade, I still remember a scene from my favorite comic strip, "Conan the Barbarian." Conan was bringing a young prince to safety after rescuing him from the bad guys. While riding on his lap, the child started to brag that he would become the king one day and asked, "It's great to be the king, isn't it?" In response Conan said, "I don't know, I've never been one. But I've never seen a happy king, either."

While I don't hang out with kings, I have had the chance to observe numerous top managers in large organizations. I cannot say that all of them were unhappy, but they certainly appeared to be under tremendous stress. Since the challenges of top managers are unique, we will start by taking a closer look at the heartaches that go with managing a large operation, whether it is a department, company, or kingdom. Our goal is to understand how one can satisfy the unique demands of these people with the least effort while minimizing their intrusions.

In addition, the following discussion will provide valuable insights into the fundamental dynamics of large organizations. If you sometimes fail to make sense of what is going on around you, read on. Once you understand the mindset of the men and women who run large entities, the events in these institutions will make a lot more sense.

The hard life at the top

I always compared top managers to ducks—despite their calm demeanor on the surface, they are actually paddling like crazy underneath. They are so effective in concealing their true emotions, however, that very few people realize what top managers are going through.

i) The bigger your title, the bigger your troubles

The first source of heartache for a top manager is the scale of the problems he must deal with. Just as the fire in a skyscraper intensifies as it rises, trapping people in the top floors, problems in an organization move from the bottom towards the top. They often grow in the process until they trap top managers, who have no one to bump these problems up to.

Picture this situation that I witnessed through an interviewee working for a cement manufacturer. The customer rep is informed that his product has started to crack on a construction site, causing serious damage. Panicked, he calls the factory and finds out that they have received similar complaints from others. The customer rep is overjoyed to learn that this is related to manufacturing and has nothing to do with him. He can now push the matter up to his boss—the head of sales—and fade away. The head of sales calls the VP of manufacturing. The VP panics when he hears the news, because he realizes that his quality control system must have failed. Soon he finds out that a raw material is to blame, and the problem may surface in other plants, too. Since they may now have to close all their factories, the VP must call the CEO.

As this example demonstrates, by the time the problem reaches top management it is often a full-blown crisis. Otherwise, it wouldn't have gotten there in the first place. As a result, top managers spend a substantial amount of their time dealing with the most unpleasant issues. Strike threats, product recalls, lawsuits, and all kinds of disasters find their way onto the desks of top managers when they become too big to be handled at a lower level.

Because they constantly have to put out fires, top managers are almost always stressed. In addition, they find it very hard to focus on anything or to plan their lives. They are pulled in all directions by internal and external troubles. The results are mental fatigue and time-famine. Top managers may not necessarily spend more time at work than other employees. Walk into any office building at 10 PM, and more than likely, you will see the junior managers as opposed to VPs. However, these unexpected crises make it very difficult for top managers to stick to a schedule. The cliché of the CEO calling his wife to say that he won't be home for their wedding anniversary is very real.

This kind of life makes most top managers rather absentminded. They have to keep track of so many issues, most of which they don't have direct experience with, that there is little room in their heads for anything else. Their brains are constantly busy, and they cannot leave it behind when they go home. The mental burden of top managers can reach such proportions that they are often willing to pay enormous amounts of money to avoid having to think hard outside the office. They have decorators decide on the color of the curtains and dieticians plan their meals.

ii) The mightier you are, the less control you have over your destiny

As if the mental burden wasn't enough, the top manager also faces a loss of control as he climbs higher. The main problem for anyone in charge of a large operation is that he has to manage a mechanism whose parts he does not perfectly understand. Large organizations have become so complex that nobody can grasp everything going on in such places. In the past, candidates for a top spot were rotated through each department for a few years at a time before taking on a leadership position. Today, this career path is much less likely to achieve the desired effect. A year or two is hardly enough to learn about areas like finance or marketing where people now spend a lifetime to become experts.

More importantly, the pace of change has become so dizzying that, after a few years of absence from any field, people lose touch with latest trends. In addition, organizations have grown tremendously over the last two decades, and have many more departments and divisions. Yet we still put one person in charge of a department, factory, or even an entire company, and hold him responsible for everything. Since he cannot fully understand every one of its pieces, a top manager must run such a complex entity through other people, who know what he does not. This leads to tremendous stress.

When running a small operation, such as the accounting for three breakfast cereals, you will be the ultimate expert. You will know more than your subordinates do in every area. Since you won't have as many subordinates, you can closely monitor their actions and fully control the process you are responsible for. You can tell your people exactly what to do and catch most mistakes before they turn into crises. When lying in bed at night, you can be confident that everything has been taken care of in the office. In short, you can be in charge of your destiny.

As a CEO of a large organization, however, you can never have such control. You have no choice but to trust people whose jobs you don't perfectly understand and whose actions you cannot monitor. The accounting manager could perform the jobs of his subordinates if he had to, and therefore can tell his people exactly what to do. But a CEO never has that luxury. Nobody can know as much about each function in a large company as the VP in charge of each area does. Even if the CEO knew the job of every VP perfectly, he doesn't have time to closely supervise and direct those VPs. So he must trust them. As a result, the more senior you are, the less control you can exercise over the people you are responsible for and the less control you have over your destiny.

The public thinks of top managers as all-mighty figures. In reality, however, the lower your rank, the firmer your grip on the situation. In the early part of the twenty-first century, corporate America has been shaken by numerous scandals; top managers were accused of crimes ranging from cooking the books to price-fixing schemes. Rather understandably, many CEOs or VPs in these firms were unaware of what was going on under their noses for years. A careful accountant is in a much better position to catch a mistake or deception by his people than the mighty CEO or a powerful VP.

Top managers try to compensate for that lack of control by selecting people who are like them. When you are choosing an assistant accountant who will be the only person under your supervision, his ability to learn the job and his dedication matter more than his personal style. Since you know his job perfectly and will see almost everything he does, you can provide very specific directions. He can then execute these commands under your watchful eye. The CEO, however, does not have this luxury. He must select people who think like he does and who, even in his absence, will do what he would have done. This is the only way to retain at least some degree of control. As a result, the characters of big organizations closely reflect those of their founders or long-time CEOs. In this chapter, we will see how to become one of those people that top managers trust, delegate to, and leave alone. Remember, the less people poke their noses into your business, the less work you will have to do.

iii) The more they respect you, the less sincere you can be

An important duty of top managers is to preserve their images in front of the people who trust them. Consider a public company where shareholders such as mutual funds and wealthy families, who lack the expertise to judge the candidates, select the CEO. While the track record of nominees—things like the profitability of their respective divisions—provides a starting point, the way each candidate presents himself will make a tremendous impact on the final choice.

When we know too little to evaluate someone's skills, we often judge character and transfer this judgment to other fields (i.e. "image transfer".) We say an auto mechanic who impresses us with his confidence and jargon "knows what he's talking about," even if we have no clue what he just said. Due to the complexity of large organizations, the outsiders selecting top managers almost never know enough to judge managers purely on merit. Consequently, they rely mostly on how the person carries himself.

Most importantly, stakeholders want to see someone who looks like he is in charge of the operation and gives them the confidence to sleep well at night. They seldom realize that no one can be truly in charge of today's giant entities. Their need for reassurance forces top managers to put on a false face. Most top managers come across as cynical with their everything-under-control attitude. They often sound like seasoned politicians with vague answers and insincere manners, yet the world imposes these expectations, further compounding their stress.

Notice that "top manager" is a relative term. Think of an entity as a continuum, instead of dividing it into discrete groups of top, middle, and lower management. The higher up the manager, the bigger his problems, the less he has control over his people, and the greater the pressure to appear in charge of the situation. Even if you are not working with CEOs or VPs, you must consider these dynamics, because anyone above you will be more exposed to these sources of stress than you are. Now, let us see how these challenges should impact your attitude towards top managers.

The paradox of proximity

A phenomenon in large organizations puzzled me for years until my sister finally made sense of it by drawing upon her background in sociology. During my first years, like most overworked young managers, I stayed away from top officials. Whenever I talked to them, I either was asked difficult questions or was told to prepare a lengthy report. Yet to my amazement, I noticed that the people closest to top management had the easiest lives. Amazingly, the closer you were to senior people, the less they knew about the details of your job and the less they questioned you. And of course, this trust and freedom dramatically reduced your workload.

It became crystal-clear when my sister explained how the same was observed between teenagers and parents in practically every culture. Parents who have distant relationships with their kids feel the need to know where the child is going, whom he will hang out with, and when he will return before letting him go out. Parents who enjoy an intimate relationship and spend a lot of time with their children, on the other hand, have sufficient trust and do not ask as much. So, paradoxically, the closer the relationship, the less the parents know and the freer the child is.

Similarly, the closer you are to top managers, the less they inquire. They wish to empower you and leave you alone because they have too much to do and too little time. But first, they must see that you are like them and that you will do as they want even when they are not around. They cannot afford to lose control over the processes they are responsible for. In other words, you and top management must "click." You certainly cannot accomplish this by avoiding them; doing so will erode their trust and increase your workload. In contrast, getting closer to them will increase your freedom and reduce your workload. There are many ways to get close to them:

i) Appear calm under pressure and look in control

As we saw, senior officials need to look like they are in charge. Since they constantly operate under the pressure of keeping appearances, their worldview evolves over time and they start to impose the same expectation on their subordinates. When dealing with top managers, you must look in control of your destiny and give them the reassurance that they can comfortably turn their backs to you. If you are questioned about a project in the elevator, you must be able to provide a reassuring answer in ten seconds. If you look like a deer caught in the headlights and all you can utter is, "Um, well, actually it's fine. Let me e-mail you an update in five minutes," your image will be destroyed. An interviewee who was previously in the armed forces made a great analogy.

> A group of managers working together is like a SWAT team moving through enemy territory. I want the guy covering my back to exude a great deal of confidence. I want him to tell me with his eyes that nothing will escape his attention. If he appears lost when I look at him, I

can't trust him and will have to start watching my own back. That's when I'll lead my team into a trap.

Think of top managers as the SWAT team leader. Show them confidence when they look into your eyes. Only then can they focus forward as they should and leave you alone. Although we will talk extensively about appearing in charge of an operation in Chapter 12, let me briefly explain what to do when cornered by top managers.

First, stay calm. We often appear frightened to avoid punishment in the office. When we are confronted and have nothing to say, we often let our frustration show, hoping that the other side will see how much we are suffering and then stop pressuring us further. In a large organization, panic will only lead to more scrutiny by reducing coworkers' confidence in your ability to do the job on your own. Remember the golden rule: people leave those whom they trust alone. The exercise below helped a salesperson on Wall Street remain calm in front of clients and is equally useful when dealing with superiors.

> I used to panic and talk forever or just freeze when clients asked tough questions. To train me, my boss started asking questions that I had to answer in thirty seconds. "Where is the economy headed?" "How will stocks do today?" "Will consumer spending hold up?" He used to say that the key was to have three to five bullet points in mind about each subject, sorted in order of importance. The idea is to be able to go on automatic pilot so that you can respond to questions very swiftly without having to think or even when panicked. The right order is critical because if you are cut off, as often happens when talking to portfolio managers, you will have communicated the most important issues. I still warm up myself and my subordinates every morning with similar questions, trying to answer them in thirty seconds. In fact, we exchange bullet points every morning.

To be ready for a sneak attack by top managers, have a thirty-second summary about every big story that they might be interested in. If necessary, write down three to five bullet points about each issue and memorize them in the right order. It is well worth the effort.

Additionally, never appear overworked or frustrated to obtain more time or a bigger budget. This will only tell superiors that things are getting out of control and will provide them with a reason to restrict your freedom. Although suffering managers are occasionally told to take some time off, they are seriously pressured to do more work upon their return.

ii) Do what your superiors would do

Since top managers provide greater freedom to those who share their fundamental approach, you can significantly reduce your workload by adopting the strategies of your superiors. The message that you are giving by joining the ranks of the "supporters" is that you understand the importance of coherence and will help to implement the top-level strategy, even when you disagree with some of its details. This means that your bosses can turn their backs to you and use the time and energy saved by empowering people like you to closely supervise those who stubbornly insist on their way of doing things. These disbelievers who threaten to diverge from the strategy must be carefully monitored. They enjoy much less freedom, and therefore, must perform much more work than the supporters do.

If your boss prefers to talk to advertisers personally even for minor matters, because he believes that "Your vision can only be communicated by being there," you should also operate this way. This has nothing to do with flattery. You are just making a deal: "If you insist, I'll visit the agency in person. In return, get off my back and don't interrogate me after every meeting."

If, however, you fight him and try to prove that e-mail is just as efficient, you will lose. Since you cannot scientifically prove that one method is superior to the other, it will turn into a tug-of-war between your style and his. When you lose this battle, the boss will want you to obtain his approval for outgoing documents, ask tons of questions about every advertising-related project, and make you prepare notes for his review after every meeting. You can certainly imagine the additional workload that this will create. So by obeying his orders, you gain lots of trust and freedom, and in turn reduce your workload while enhancing your organization's productivity.

iii) Say what your superiors would say

It is equally critical to understand what top managers wish to communicate to the world and help them to get this message across, even if you think it is not the right message.

In the past, when a superior asked me to provide data, I'd give him what I would have wanted to know in that situation. Then, I wondered why I could never make them happy. Now, I first think about what they want to prove. They are mostly looking to make a point instead of showing the whole picture, and you must help them do that. For example, if the head of production asks for market share graphs and he's lobbying to close a plant, he'll want to make the products manufactured in that facility look bad. So I'll send him the charts that show the biggest decline for those products. In the past, I'd just provide a bunch of graphs without this sort of analysis, and he kept coming back until he found what he wanted. In the end, he'd still have his way, but I wasted a lot of time and looked clueless.

As this interviewee points out, engaging in unnecessary battles will not only inflate your workload but also lead top management to ignore many of your potentially useful suggestions.

This doesn't mean that you cannot state what you think. You definitely should, both for your own good and that of your organization. But first provide the information that supports the mainstream view at the top, before giving an alternative opinion. When asked to prepare ten slides about the disposable razor market, which top managers love, first show why the market can grow further. Only after providing this kind of data should you think about slides with a negative tone. If you only provide pessimistic ones, the boss will ask for ten upbeat charts and completely ignore your first set.

To anticipate their needs, you must know the true priorities of top managers. Since this point was covered in Chapter 6, I will only mention that grasping the real objectives of top managers is harder because their agendas are more complex and covert. So keep a close eye on them. Try not to miss meetings they will attend. Read their mass e-mails even if they bore you to tears. Find out where they are when they disappear for a whole week. If they ask you to rewrite a report, ask them, or at least the secretary, which comment bothered them. Only then can you understand what is going on in their minds.

iv) Accept full responsibility for the results and never make excuses

Since they are separated from daily operations, top managers will often be ignorant about what you can do and what you must depend on others for. Therefore, it is critical to bridge any gap between their expectations and what you can deliver. Communicate clearly what you can do and then either refer them to other people for the task or agree to do more than your fair share.

Although bridging this expectation gap will greatly enhance your relationships with top managers, sometimes you will still be blamed for things beyond your control. Due to their limited time and mental energy, some top managers won't get it when you explain what you cannot do. And a few of them simply won't care. If this happens and you are unjustly criticized for a failure, make no excuses. Once an action has been taken, it is too late to communicate responsibilities. Just step forward and accept the blame. You can explain the reasons for the failure and suggest preventive measures for the future, but never make excuses. Present your case and let top management decide whom to charge with the crime.

For example, assume that the sales director feverishly calls you from Russia. He is asking for next year's budget and won't call the finance department, despite your explanations that you have no access to those files. Left without a choice, you are forced to own the task. However, you cannot get him the figures and he misses the sale. In that case, do not say, "I told you I didn't have access to the files; it's not my fault," or blame the finance people who were too slow.

Due to their isolation from daily tasks and the many crises they must deal with, top managers often blame the wrong people for mistakes. There is nothing you can do about this. When it happens, get over it. Do not panic and start blaming others. Top managers know that they are often unfair (but they will rarely admit this, of course) and won't hold every failure against you. They just move on and want you to do the same by focusing on the future, instead of getting stuck in the past.

If you waste time trying to detach yourself from the failure, you send the message that you don't understand the game played at the top and have no place there. Such people are a top manager's worst nightmare. When times get tough, top officials have to baby-sit these oversensitive individuals. In the above case, suggest that the sales director sit down with you for five minutes before business trips to provide a list of data he might need while abroad. This will earn you high marks for your ability to think ahead. During this brief meeting you will also show that you depend on others for some tasks, without looking like a whiner.

Most importantly, never blame your subordinates in front of top officials. As we will see in Chapter 12, this shows that you don't understand your responsibilities. By accusing your employees, you admit your incompetence in selecting, motivating, and developing people. In other words, you simply admit that you are a bad manager.

Save them mental effort

Since their heads are overstuffed with a multitude of issues, top managers expect subordinates to save them mental work by thinking on their behalf. The first rule is not to expect them to remember anything. Recap what was discussed or exchanged whenever you can. If you are forwarding a thick research report to a superior, do not assume that he will remember why the research was originally commissioned. Include a summary of the original research brief and try to obtain an executive summary of the report. If your e-mail response is longer than one page, so that one must scroll down to see the original message, include a reminder at the top such as, "RE: In response to your request to summarize monthly production activity."

One interviewee often gets handwritten notes from a top manager asking for graphs and charts. He says that he always presents the printouts with the original handwritten note, because this reminds the boss what he had asked for and "the printouts look nicer next to the casual note." Finally, confirm all appointments with secretaries, as top managers may forget to do so.

Although these points sound trivial, they can make a big difference. In addition to saving mental work for top officials, these reminders create the impression of a faster response. When people forget what they said, they rarely admit to being absentminded. Instead, they assume it must have been a long time since they said it and reason that you were slow to respond. But if you attach a reminder of the original request to your answer, it will feel like you got back to them pretty quickly while things were still fresh in their minds. Second, if the data or report doesn't suit their needs, top managers can blame you for having given them the wrong thing. You can avoid unnecessary arguments by providing proof of the original demand. Over time, these things solidify your image as someone who operates smoothly and efficiently.

Executive summaries are another effective tool when dealing with top officials. If you can find an intern, secretary, or other support personnel to do them, by all means provide these valuable reports. But if you cannot, there are alternatives to the time-consuming process of preparing them. A couple of Post-Its on a report, together with a few highlighted sentences, can make a huge difference. Few people appreciate the shock of a senior manager upon receiving anything longer than five pages. Nor do people understand how much you can ease the pain with minor modifications. When used properly, these will convince the top manager that he doesn't need to read the whole thing. If, after skimming a few of your underlined sentences, he says, "This is exactly what I would have focused on," you are golden. Not only will you save him a lot of time, but you will also demonstrate that you are on the same wavelength and qualify as CEO material.

To enhance this effect, try to anticipate questions and either provide answers or show that you are seeking an explanation. If sales of a product that the manager is particularly interested in are down, do not just put an exclamation mark next to it. Explain the cause in two sentences or write in the margin that you have scheduled a meeting to investigate. (Being able to anticipate questions/concerns is yet another benefit of knowing the priorities of top management.)

The same principle applies to electronic documents or e-mails. When forwarding a message, give an insightful explanation for why the manager should or, more importantly, shouldn't read the material. By explaining in two sentences that, except for the highlighted areas, the forwarded e-mail contains nothing other than what has been discussed in the last meeting, you could save an executive many valuable minutes. Always remember that the vast majority of top managers hate reading long reports, and do whatever you can to spare them the effort.

Use these guidelines in verbal communication as well by talking only about what top managers can and want to understand. Do not say that the new server can back up 75 gigabytes in two minutes. Instead, say that it will save each sales rep half an hour per week. Remember that their heads are cluttered, and never dump too much information on top managers.

Save them time

As time-famine is among the greatest problems of top officials, they love people who can save them time. Most of what was mentioned above about reducing their mental burden will also save them time by speeding things up. But two points can be added to the list.

When organizing meetings, schedule the top executive as the first speaker. This way, he can address the crowd without having to wait for the prior person to finish. In addition, when the top manager knows that he will talk first, he is more likely to show up on time. Even if he doesn't, you can kick off the meeting with another topic. But if he is the last speaker and still arrives late, you may have to keep everybody on hold until he shows up, as all topics will have been covered.

You must also have a good relationship with the secretaries of top managers to use their time—and your own—more efficiently. Know in advance when the manager will be out of the office and when he will be traveling. Since most of them fly frequently, they are forced to get a lot of work done in cabs and airplanes. Consequently, they appreciate a well-timed report handed to them on their way to the airport. Furthermore, it pays to know when they will be in the office if you have anything that needs to be approved.

Impress top managers with quality, not with speed

Due to their reliance on other people for anything that does not require their direct attention, top managers can become totally detached from daily processes. Anyone who is more than one level above you will probably know very little about what you do on a daily basis. Therefore, a top manager can't really judge how long a particular assignment will take you.

Unfortunately, most people don't realize this and attempt to impress top managers by responding as quickly as possible to their requests. When asked for half a dozen charts, the tendency is to rush to the computer and try to make an impression by setting a new speed record. But the top manager will rarely know how fast is fast. He may not be impressed at all, even if you reply extremely quickly. Even worse, he will often assume that you simply hit the print button if you respond too fast and will undervalue your work. On top of it all, he will likely expect the same speed the next time around, which of course may be impossible.

The good news is that you can turn this problem into an opportunity. To do so, buy as much time as you can and deliver an absolutely perfect piece. Even if he cannot know how fast is fast, the person will always be impressed by quality. Logical organization, clarity, and precision are much easier to judge than speed. Also, do not assume that the reader will remember anything and remind him of what he needs to know with references to prior e-mails, meetings, and conversations.

Ensure that your work pleases the eye, and make things easy to read and understand. Whenever possible, use bullet points as you would in a presentation instead of full sentences. Top managers love this format because it saves a lot of time. They are used to presentations and can easily follow such files. Additionally, top managers can present these in meetings or forward them to their peers without having to ask a secretary to reformat the information. Always believe in your work and assume that the recipient will like it enough to forward it or use in meetings.

One final tip: Suppose a high-level official came to you directly and asked for some material. Since this happens only a few times a year, you are determined to impress him and start working right away. Halfway through, however, you realize that you forgot to ask a key question. But you don't want to look bad by going to him with such a simple issue. Simply print out what you've done thus far and request that he take a quick look to ensure that the two of you are on the same page. Then, just before you leave his office, casually ask your question. Make it sound like you want to double-check. Chances are he won't notice that you forgot to ask something last time.

Use the power of printouts

The attention span of top managers is usually so short that you need every bit of help to get on their list of priorities. Printouts can give you that little edge over your competition. First of all, hard copies are the only things one can read during a cab ride or while waiting in line to board the plane. Top managers often end up in such situations and, due to their obsession to work under every imaginable condition, they pick up the first available printout and start reading.

Therefore, a few hard copies provided on the way out to the airport have a much higher probability of being read than an e-mail. Furthermore, unprocessed printouts demand more attention than electronic messages. An e-mail can sit in the inbox of a busy executive for months without bothering him. A few pages scattered on someone's desk, however, are a bit harder to ignore and must somehow be attended to.

If you must e-mail the information, try to provide printouts of at least the most important pages. Customize the printouts slightly with a few lines of handwritten notes or one or two Post-Its. This will make them sufficiently distinctive and deter the top manager from throwing them away. Otherwise, he may ask if your e-mail contains the same data and, if the answer is yes, simply toss the printouts.

Do not become too friendly with top managers or your direct boss

Since conventional wisdom states that becoming friends with top managers helps you rise in the organization, it may be tempting to spend a lot of time with them outside of work. I would strictly advise against this, because the closer the friendship, the higher the probability of a conflict. When we get more intimate, we discover new, annoying traits. This is why a lot of relationships in college are destroyed when two buddies move into the same apartment. The best example I heard about this phenomenon in the workplace came from an interviewee who had started to play squash with a senior official in his firm after a few months on the job.

> The guy was way too competitive. He played like he was possessed and even ran into me really hard at times. I didn't know what I was supposed to do. Should I lose so he won't get upset? Even worse, he would ask me to join him for a snack afterwards, where he ordered the most expensive stuff and never let me pay. I didn't enjoy the occasion at all and it showed. Then, he asked intrusive questions about my girlfriend, how I invested my savings, and so on. Looking back, it would have been better not to hang out with him at all. There are too many things that can go wrong. In the end, I had to cancel my membership and join another gym. Imagine how ugly it would have been to say that I wasn't going to play when he asked for a game, and then be seen in the gym playing someone else.

There really are too many things that can go wrong. On the other hand, when everything goes well, the superior may feel that he is losing his formal authority due to your closeness. Sometimes superiors will need to harshly criticize you, which becomes especially difficult if you are friends. Unfortunately, many bosses realize this phenomenon too late and distance themselves from the employee abruptly. Finally, your manager may feel uncomfortable if he suspects that you are trying gain an advantage in the office by making friends with him, which may not be your intention at all. This suspicion, too, may set in suddenly and produce dramatic changes in his attitude, leaving you wondering what you did wrong.

Despite the risks of becoming friends with top managers, the benefits are very limited. Most people cannot enjoy the time they spend with top managers outside of work, as they constantly watch themselves. In addition, most executives feel uncomfortable promoting a person that everyone thinks of as their friend. Top managers place a lot of emphasis on being seen as fair. Promoting a friend is the easiest way to damage this reputation. The bottom line is do not get too friendly with top managers. Feel free to share a few jokes, but don't try to buddy up with them.

If you cannot get their attention no matter what, try this

Sometimes life becomes so hectic for top managers that it may be simply impossible to get their attention. If you cannot get on the radar screen of a top official, "pulsing" can be a solution. Pulsing is an advertising strategy that is particularly effective in reaching swamped consumers. The theory is that an occasional burst of advertising can be more effective than spreading the same budget thinly over the entire year. A working mother, for example, may never really notice your ad if she sees it once a day. A better approach can be to show her the ad five times a day for a week and then stop for four weeks. This way, you can pound your message into her head at least for a full week, no matter how loudly the kids are screaming in the background.

The same strategy can work well with top officials who are constantly bothered by an army of screaming people around them. Consequently, these high-ranked managers may not notice your accomplishments. Pick a relatively uncluttered period and bombard the target manager for a week or two. Give him all the good news about your projects, present in meetings, and hand him printouts he can use in different occasions. No matter how preoccupied he is, he will notice the significance of at least some of your messages. But don't overdo it. Once you get your point across, step back, or you will quickly annoy your audience. Remember that master performers leave the stage before the applause dies down.

5 Key Points You Should Remember

- Have 30-second mental summaries of your projects for top management
- Understand what top management is trying to communicate to the world, and speak with the same voice to help them do so
- Never make excuses in front of top managers
- Only provide easy-to-understand, bite-sized information to top managers
- Rely on quality work, not speed, to impress top managers

CHAPTER 8

Teaching Your Boss to Leave You Alone

While most of what we saw on managing top executives still applies, you face additional constraints when working with your direct supervisor. First, you spend much more time with your boss, and he knows the details of your job much better. He also observes you under a variety of circumstances, and his opinions heavily impact how other top managers see you.

Most importantly, your boss has the formal authority to assign you any work he wants. When another superior asks for something, you can always try to dodge it by convincing your boss that the request is inappropriate. There is no such buffer zone, however, between you and your direct boss. You have little choice but to do whatever he asks of you, so it is well worth studying how to keep his demands under control.

The four stages of freedom
Earlier, we saw how the trust of coworkers leads to greater freedom in every area and reduces your workload. The person who has the biggest influence on your freedom is your immediate boss. The more he empowers you, in other words the less he interferes in your job, the fewer inefficiencies you will deal with and the less stress you will endure. Regardless of your rank and experience, obtaining this freedom progresses through four distinct steps.

First, your boss will dump all the boring tasks that require little skill and creativity on you. In the second stage, you will be given more critical assignments, but will be asked to perform them exactly as your boss wants. After displaying reliability and attention to detail, you will gradually be given more freedom to do the tasks, still decided upon by your boss, as you want. In the final stage, you will be able to decide not only how you carry out the tasks, but may choose what tasks to carry out to achieve your objectives. As you move through these stages, your freedom will increase exponentially. As a result, your workload will diminish greatly.

These steps are like the four stages of maturity—childhood, adolescence, adulthood, and old age. Just as one cannot truly become an adult before his childhood needs are met, a manager cannot gain full independence before he demonstrates that he can perform drudgery and follow directions to the letter.

The same way psychological maturity is independent from chronological age, the degree of empowerment is independent from rank and experience. Senior managers who are given almost no freedom and must obey every direction of their superiors are as common as children who walk around in adult bodies. You should closely study every step below, because you might be stuck at one of the stages without realizing it.

I) The "donkeywork" stage

This stage starts as soon as you accept a position and continues until you can muscle your way out of it, which can last a lifetime. Your superior's urgent need to unload the boring tasks, the fact that you don't know enough to make important decisions, and the lack of trust between you and your boss give him no choice but to dump the lowliest work on you.

Ranging from updating presentations to scheduling meetings, these chores are the fire in which new hires must be baptized before they can truly gain admission into the organization. Since these duties frustrate the freshly hired manager who was hoping to perform much more creative functions, this phase can also be called the "reality shock stage." Unfortunately, successful completion of these boring duties is mandatory before one can move to the next level.

This phenomenon is observed in all large organizations. In fact, the person who summarized it best was a police officer who heard from his daughter that I was studying the subject and wanted to meet me. At well over six feet tall and 250 pounds, this ex-wrestler certainly had the build to scare the bad guys. When he entered the police force back in the seventies, he thought that he would be chasing criminals in a week or two. But he soon realized that the life of a young officer is not what we see in movies. At first, he was so bored that he seriously considered leaving to work as a bouncer in bars.

> There isn't just a lot of drudgery to be done. As a young officer, you do your own drudgery plus that of two or three senior officers. By the time you're promoted, you're so tired of it that you ruthlessly dump it all on the new guy. People say they'll remember how they felt and go easy on the new guys, but you can't help yourself, because you are so sick of it by the time you're promoted. Therefore, new officers spend months drowning in paperwork before they see any action.

It is no different in a consulting company or auditing firm. The new hire, eager to show his skills by building financial models or repositioning brands, finds himself formatting presentations. His boss will be so eager to get rid of the brainless stuff after all those years, that he will dump it on the new hire all at once. The frustration builds up until the new guy is assigned an assistant a few years down the road, and mercilessly dumps it all on his new employee. To add insult to injury, the new hire is also discouraged, or sometimes outright prohibited, from touching any critical work at this stage. For example, the assistant finance manager we previously saw may be asked not to touch critical fields in financial models or talk directly to top managers about budgets.

Although you may not have such a bad experience if you join at the middle management level, the basic rule always holds. Superiors will first transfer the worst tasks and closely supervise you before they give you more substantial assignments. Even if you are the VP of finance, in the beginning the CEO will not only tell you to calm down angry bankers who really want to talk to him directly, but also tell you precisely how to do it. As a result, you may have to fly to New York when a conference call would suffice. Therefore, having an efficient strategy for dealing with this situation is a basic necessity of work life.

Most managers respond to this challenge in the worst possible way. When faced with donkeywork, they take it personally and show contempt towards those tasks. They feel that unless they can display more strategic skills, they will be updating presentations forever. But the "Don't give me this stuff, I am here to do creative managerial work" attitude makes a bad situation worse. The only reasonable response for the supervisor is to further restrict the freedom of such a disillusioned individual, who will surely make mistakes if left alone. And as you well know, less freedom always means more work and more stress.

Although young people are more susceptible to this mistake, experienced managers also fall into this trap. Remember the example in Chapter 6, where an interviewee described how the new division manager attempted to turn the world upside down right away. Even such a high-ranked official can easily lose the trust of superiors and attract unnecessary scrutiny with this attitude. If you wish to spend less time doing the brainless, uncreative donkeywork and move to the next stage as quickly as possible, do the opposite of what your instincts tell you and embrace those tasks with great enthusiasm. Here is why:

> At first, I was fighting with my boss all the time, and the more I fought the more I ended up working. He gave me lots of clerical work, which I considered an insult. I'd say, "Can't we hire a part-timer for that?" or "Can't a secretary schedule this meeting?" and frustrated him so much. I should've known that he would never do this stuff for me, so I just had to shut up and get it over with. The more I bitched, the longer these chores took because he constantly checked up on me. I had to CC him on e-mails and get his approval for everything, because he didn't trust me. In my third month, I finally came to my senses. I apologized for complaining so much and promised to handle the chores smoothly. Without my boss breathing down my neck, every-

thing became easier. Since he stopped checking on me, I do things my way and stopped doing some things altogether. For example, he would make me call all the field offices to make sure they would send in the numbers on time. When I work on my own, I only call half of them, because I know where the slackers are.

As this interviewee points out, not only can you do the chores more easily when your boss isn't breathing down your neck, but you can also completely eliminate many of them. This leads to tremendous productivity gains. Do not worry that by doing the brainless work with enthusiasm you will get stuck at that level. Instead, pay attention to detail and prove that you can do those things well. In addition to reducing your workload, this gives your supervisor the breathing room and confidence to share more strategic matters with you.

Furthermore, by focusing on less important matters in the beginning, you gain valuable time to observe the organization. This break-in period will significantly improve the quality of your suggestions later on, and make it much more likely that your supervisor will listen to your strategic opinions. If, on the other hand, you immediately try to save the world while the budget is waiting to be updated and you don't know the business, you may appear ignorant and naive.

2) The "do as I say" stage

After demonstrating that you can handle the donkeywork, your superior will start to pull you into bigger projects but continue to give very specific directions. Our famous financial assistant will now start to do substantial work during the budgeting process, but the boss will dictate every detail. Consequently, the work will take much longer than it needs to. The assistant might now be allowed to deliver a presentation to marketing, but the boss will determine the content of each slide, their order, and how much time to spend on each of them. Naturally, the boss may not know exactly how long each slide takes to prepare. Hence, when faced with more than one alternative to tell the same story to marketing, he will often pick the harder method.

On top of it all, the assistant will continue to do the donkeywork at this stage. But by learning to do it faster, eliminating certain tasks when the boss stops watching him too closely, and delegating some of them to newer managers or support personnel such as secretaries, he will now spend much less time on them.

This is usually the most delicate stage and the key word here is patience. Whereas previously you wouldn't see what was going on behind closed doors, you will now witness the process and develop your own theories about the job. But you must wait a little longer before you can put those theories into action. In the prior stage, you were typing a presentation for the boss and, perhaps, wouldn't care so much about the content. In the end, it was someone else's ideas and you were just asked to put them down on paper. Now, however, you must present those words as if they were your own ideas, and it will probably matter to you whether you agree with them or not. This is where it becomes painful to follow the directions, since you may feel that your integrity is being compromised.

The worst thing you can do during this phase is to start a premature argument with your boss. Trying to prove that you have better ideas will only prolong the road to freedom. Keep in mind that the boss is still testing you for the fundamentals. When the boss asks you to deliver his presentation, for example, he just wants to see if you can address a crowd and keep listeners awake for 15 minutes. Without seeing that you have this capability, he cannot let you develop and present your own theories. One must look at only one variable in an experiment, while everything else remains constant. Hence, your boss must first assess your ability to implement a strategy before he can gauge your skill in developing a strategy on your own. Do not take it personally; patiently follow the orders. Once you have built sufficient trust, launch an attack to move to the next phase, where most of your problems will be remedied.

3) The "do as you want" stage

After demonstrating sufficient skill in implementing the strategies dictated by your boss, the next step is to gain the freedom to accomplish his end goals by using your own methods. This mode of operation will provide more satisfaction, while dramatically cutting your workload.

Let's see how our assistant accountant can do this when the budget season arrives again. His mission is to shift the focus of discussions between him and his boss from how the task will be carried out to what exactly needs to be accomplished—from the means to the ends. Last year, the unspoken message he had to communicate was "I am detail-oriented and careful. Tell me how to do it and I will." This year, he must communicate a different message: "I passed the first test and showed you can trust me. Tell me what exactly I need to do and let me decide how to do it. I can work faster on my own, and you will have one less thing to worry about."

This message will be delivered with actions as opposed to words. The key is to understand the boss's priorities by continuously communicating, in other words, "getting into his head." Does he want speed or would he rather be late to achieve accuracy? Does he think that we were too tough on marketing last year or too soft, doing too much of their work? Armed with this knowledge, the assistant can go to the boss and present a game plan that demonstrates an in-depth understanding of the situation. The superior should think, "He gets it. I no longer need to tell him how to do every little thing." The game plan could sound as follows:

I know you were unhappy with the brand managers last year. This year, I suggest we contact BMs earlier and make it clear that we won't be as picky about details, but we want them to respect deadlines. We don't want to stretch the calendar again. Maybe we can provide the templates next week and have a meeting to show them how to fill in the numbers. I can take care of that and be ready with the budgets for the board meeting on the 15th. Actually, I already did the first drafts. Please take a look at them and let me know what you think.

What would you think if you heard such a pitch that addressed your concerns? You would probably be impressed and leave the person alone, wouldn't you? Once free to do the job as he wishes, the assistant's work hours will drop like a rock. Yet, he can do even better by advancing to the fourth stage.

4) The "do what you want" stage

Let us suppose that the process above runs smoothly and, the following year, the assistant wants to take it to the next level. The goal is to go beyond deciding how to do things, so you influence what things will be done. The objectives above were the supervisor's wish list. Since he didn't have sufficient leverage, our assistant had to take these as given even if he disagreed with them, or even if they made his life too difficult. This year, his mission is to end up with easier goals.

This requires a deeper understanding of the supervisor. The assistant must know not only what the boss wants, but also why he wants it. Let's say the boss insists on a hard-to-meet deadline so he can present the numbers before the CEO takes a vacation. If the assistant realizes that the CEO never goes over the entire budget, he can propose a top-level analysis that only shows sales and profits for broad categories rather than for every product. Such a project can be completed without fighting with BMs or correcting their mistakes caused by the time pressure. The rest can be filled in comfortably later on.

The amount of time you will need to gain this flexibility will greatly vary depending on the organizational culture, the boss, and your skill level. Although I have used annual increments for simplicity in the above example and went through two years, you will probably need much less time. It is always important, though, not to rush. If you ask for too much and fail to handle the challenge, you will be sent back to square one, where the boss dictates everything.

Where you are along this continuum is independent of your seniority. You may have been stuck at an early stage without realizing it. If you are the VP of public relations in a giant firm and the CEO won't let you appear on any TV channel without first approving your speech and the program you will appear in, you are stuck at the "do as I say" stage. Your problem is essentially the same as that of the financial assistant who must deliver the boss's presentations, and so is your remedy.

By avoiding premature conflicts and paying attention to detail, you can move to the next step, where you only need an approval for the general message to be delivered through the media. This will significantly reduce your burden. You can choose the TV station whose studio is closest to you, and prepare your own speech the night before without having to show it to anyone. To further reduce your workload, you can then gradually switch to a media strategy that relies less on your personal media appearances, and more on the public relations department.

Never forget who the boss is

Like every good thing, the above process can be overdone. In the extreme fifth stage, you become so good at this game that you gain more freedom than the boss is comfortable with. At that point, your supervisor can no longer influence you and must bend to your requests, instead of the other way round. Although this may not sound so bad, it will hurt your boss's pride and open you up to retaliation. Even if you are delivering terrific results, some kind of tension may develop. In the long-term, this leads to conflicts, communication gaps, and inefficiencies.

No matter how much freedom you gain, always remember who the boss is and make a sincere effort to accommodate his personal preferences. Do not impose your own style on him. He may insist on silly things, such as sending handwritten thank-you-notes to every single client. Although these habits do not make any business sense, and may be inconvenient for you, remember that most humans are proud of their peculiarities. Supervisors find pleasure in seeing their people make the effort to respond to their needs. One interviewee likened this to ordering french-fries in his favorite restaurant and getting barbecue sauce on the side without asking for it.

> I'm touched on a personal level when a waiter remembers what I like with fries, because in this age most people don't even remember your name. Similarly, I feel special when an employee remembers and respects my need to see all e-mails going to the legal department, because it shows me he cares. This makes me feel understood, and I will make the extra effort to make such a guy happy, too.

Remember, the more willing you are to operate as your boss wants, the more freedom you will be given and the less work you will do. If, however, you insist on doing things your way, you will not only be given less freedom but your performance evaluation will also suffer. Top management would rather see a coherent unit implementing a passable plan than a boss and a subordinate fighting over the scientific truth. You and your boss must speak with one voice. Even if such a team falls short of achieving its goals, you will have proven your ability to work with people. This is a much more important skill than formulating a policy. In fact, you may become the perfect candidate for your boss's spot if top management sees that you have better ideas than the current plan, which you are only supporting for the sake of continuity.

If you are spending time on something, make sure that your boss sees it

If you want to leave the office at a reasonable hour, you cannot waste time on projects that the boss won't notice. We all face the dilemma of having to respond to minor requests that take a lot of effort but are not worthy of the boss's attention. The problem is that such donkeywork will delay other tasks that the boss actually cares about. If you cannot find a way to communicate what you are doing, your boss will inevitably think that you are slacking off. Even worse, he will dump more work on you when you cannot handle it. Here is a subtle and non-invasive method for making your boss aware of what you're doing.

> We get a lot of requests for simple but time-consuming files. The trouble is that the boss won't know about these and will think that you are a slacker. In the end, you get zero credit for the most painful work. Here is how a guy I work with solved this problem. When people call with a request he says, "Can you please send me an e-mail and CC my boss? If I am tied up or something, he can help you." This will tell the boss what you are doing. If you got the e-mail and sent it to the boss, you would look silly to be wasting his time with such a minor issue. But here someone else is sending the e-mail, so it's okay.

When you cannot resort to this method because the person sends an e-mail without calling first, there are other options. If the report is going to an important recipient, it is reasonable to show the final version to your boss before sending it out. This looks better than asking questions about a simple file, but will still explain what you have been doing for the last two hours. For a less important recipient, you could CC him on the outgoing e-mail, but you shouldn't abuse this method. If your boss gets dozens of CCs from you every day, he will start to send them straight to the trash. This will lead to a serious communication breakdown.

Instead, try to casually mention the work you did: "By the way, I sent a chart of factory orders to the warehouse manager. If you ever need this data, it is under the FACTORY folder." You can also leave a printout on his desk, preferably with a note to pique his interest: "Prepared this for the warehouse manager. Check out the jump in volume last week!" Finally, you can ask an innocent question: "I am charting weekly factory orders and recall seeing a similar file. Do you remember sending something like this?" It is much better, of course, to switch back and forth between these methods, as opposed to sticking to just one of them.

Never let your boss push you into fights

Naturally, you will handle most of your boss's unpleasant duties, but one thing you should not do on behalf of superiors is fight with others. The inefficiencies you will create in your relationships will far outweigh any favors you might gain from your boss. Every person you fight with will try to make you miserable. Just a few such enemies can add hours to your workweek by sending the files late, calling you at bad hours, and badmouthing you.

Supervisors face a dilemma when they must pressure an unresponsive colleague, but they worry about getting labeled as troublemakers. The tendency in such situations is to ask the subordinate to take care of it. Most managers know that they can push their people into a conflict and then step in to calm the scene, getting the best of both worlds. They obtain what they want while earning the honor to end a fight—basically a variation of the "good cop, bad cop" theme.

The interviews show that this drama is staged in a similar way across all organizations. First, the boss provokes his subordinate: "These _____s are treating us like fools. Tell them to send that damn file by tomorrow or else _____" Next, the subordinate's aggression escalates the conflict, and the risk that senior management could get involved frightens both sides. Just like an elementary school teacher, top management rarely has the time or patience to investigate who started the fight. Consequently, everyone associated with trouble gets hurt.

Finally, the boss resolves the problem he was originally responsible for by calming everyone down: "If my subordinate sounded harsh, I apologize. It was only because he needed your help desperately. Let's put it all behind us, shall we?" In exchange for a mild apology, he usually gets what he wants, since the file—or whatever—will now look like a small price to pay to put an end to this misery. Furthermore, he is remembered as extending the olive branch.

This is a shortsighted approach, because tarnishing the image of a subordinate for a small gain undermines the efficiency of the team, leading to workload inflation for both the boss and the subordinate. So do not feel that you must take part in this act. While it can be difficult to simply say "no" to your boss, you do have options.

Whenever my boss wants me to fight someone, I get him involved. This forces him to be more diplomatic. If the other person is in the same building, I tell him to stop by when I know my boss will be around. Then I walk into my boss's office with that guy and say, "So-and-so stopped by and wanted to get your opinion, since you are here." If I am on the phone, I tell that my authority is limited and ask if they want to talk to my boss. Then I conference my boss in saying, "He wanted to talk to you." Once involved, he is forced to compromise and things are often resolved quickly.

An alternative is to delay the resolution until the next meeting, when both your boss and the other party will be present. He will usually be forced to confront the issue, instead of pushing you into a fight.

When all of this fails and you must deal with the problem on your own, remain calm and do not let your boss aggravate you. It is not worth damaging your relationships to get a file a few days earlier. If the conflict escalates despite your best efforts and you don't know how to handle it, step away. Tell your boss that the tension has risen too much and focus on pure business concerns, such as the probability of reaching a deadlock or jeopardizing your long-term projects.

Respect the expertise of your supervisor and let him coach you

In a fast moving world, managerial knowledge can become obsolete very quickly, and senior officials may seem like they belong to a different era. While it is natural to be irritated by the outdated suggestions of your boss, remember that like all people managers desire to teach. So respect his need to coach you. Even if his advice sounds like nonsense, you will make your life easier by listening and trying to follow the instructions, instead of showing him a better way.

My boss has been here for 20 years, but hasn't evolved. He still tells me to do what would have worked 20 years ago. I used to get mad when he told me to call certain people, and I would try to explain why that person would not be the right one to call for that issue. Now I approach it differently. Instead of spending five minutes discussing why I shouldn't call the research department, I just spend 30 seconds making the call. Or if he wants me to do a spreadsheet the old-fashioned way, I ask myself if it will be faster to explain my way or to do it as he wants. This saves me time and makes him feel so much better.

You will also better grasp your boss's worldview by listening to his advice. Be especially alert when he gives career guidance, because such counsel will clearly expose his mentality.

Another easy way to annoy your boss is to make him feel like an idiot by understanding his explanations too quickly. If he is educating you about something that took him two months to learn, you should not get it in 30 seconds. Suppose your supervisor is drawing diagrams and providing elaborate examples to describe what he believes to be a complicated financial structuring model.

You, however, are familiar with the concept from your accounting classes. To save him the effort, you jump right in and tell him that you already know it.

What can he possibly think? He will probably not be impressed. His first reaction will likely be denial: "Wait a minute, it took me two months to get it and this guy understood it in 30 seconds? Either he is a genius or I am an idiot." This will only give him an incentive to constantly check on you to catch your mistakes. He might also think that you don't respect his knowledge. The sad thing is that you may be doing this to give him a chance to put your skills to good use.

Even if you understand what he thinks is a complicated subject right away, do not make him feel like he is talking to the wall. Be especially careful if he implies that you won't be able to grasp it at first: "I know it's confusing but you will see what I mean after you work on the file." Tell him that the explanations were helpful and that you will spend more time on it until it really sinks in. If possible, ask further questions after a few days. This will show that you have been thinking about the topic and his effort wasn't wasted. Keep in mind that it is human nature to pass on our prized knowledge. The world has become so confusing that most of us only know one subject—our jobs—well enough to teach it. Do not deny your boss this great pleasure.

Try this if your boss is stifling you

A boss who is all over you all day long is one of the worst disasters in an office. Supervisors who come over every five minutes with a question or comment will keep you on your toes at all times and have a devastating effect on your efficiency. They not only prevent you from concentrating on the task at hand, but also cause a lot of psychological stress.

The best thing you can do in such a situation is to propose a weekly or even daily meeting to update your boss about ongoing matters. If the supervisor knows that you will meet at a set time every day, he is much more likely to save his questions until then. This will give you some breathing room. Even if you are interrogated about a matter that you aren't prepared to discuss, you can often say that you will provide a detailed update in your meeting later during the day.

If your boss is not willing to hold such meetings, group together multiple issues and go to him only a few times a day with thoughtful answers, and preferably printouts, instead of knocking on his door every ten minutes. The message is "You can constantly bother me and get incomplete answers, or you can be patient and let me come to you with proper solutions when I'm ready." While you cannot prevent all ad hoc questions, this will at least reduce their frequency. Also, you will sound much more credible when you are cornered and say "I was going to talk to you about that and a couple other things in half an hour." Furthermore, your boss may see how much better this mode of operation is and, after a while, propose to meet periodically for updates.

Recurring commitments, such as daily conference calls or files that must be sent by a certain time, can be used to accelerate this process. By gently but consistently reminding him of when you will be unavailable, you may be able teach your boss to come to you during a narrow time frame. Even if there is no formal agreement to hold a daily meeting at a set time, you will feel much less pressured if you can roughly anticipate when he will come to you.

Another benefit of presenting multiple issues is that you can achieve a neutral or positive balance in most conversations. You can save the favors you must ask for, as well as the bad news, for the meetings where you also have good news to give. This enables you to cash in your chips before they depreciate with time. Politicians do this frequently. By bundling the good and the bad, they dilute the negative impact of announcements such as tax hikes or budget cuts.

Before we conclude this chapter, here is one more tactic to ease the pressure of an irritating boss:

Bosses who constantly check the status of your work usually suffer from chronic anxiety. All they want is some reassurance that you're doing something. When I must work for such people, I open a file as soon as I get the assignment and do 10% of the job. This way, I can at least say that I have started working on it. This soothes the boss's fears and buys me some breathing room.

5 Key Points You Should Remember

- Do not seek too much responsibility too soon
- Adopt your boss's work-style wherever feasible
- When stuck with a piece of unproductive work, let your boss know about it
- Do not fight with others on behalf of your boss
- Have a few well-planned meetings with your boss instead of knocking on his door whenever you have a simple matter to discuss

CHAPTER 9

Getting What You Want from Peers

A black belt Judoka (Judo expert) who had the pleasure of breaking one of my ribs once said:

> In Judo, your true finesse shows against an opponent of similar physical strength. A much stronger opponent will test your speed and courage. When fighting an opponent who is much weaker, you see if you can finish the match without wasting much energy. This is critical in tournaments. But when faced with someone whose strength is more or less equal to you, it's the grace, the harmony, and the refinement in your movement that brings you the victory.

The same is true in management. When working with the top, knowing how to condense large amounts of information and making an impact in a brief period of time are key. When dealing with subordinates, your capability to nurture and support another individual is demonstrated. Relationships with peers, on the other hand, demand true finesse. When there is more or less a balance in power and position, you need the flair of a diplomat to get what you want.

Like a diplomat, you must build alliances to promote mutual interests. Alliances tremendously improve your efficiency. By getting that file early and done right the first time or by having your calls returned in a timely manner, you will achieve better results with much less work. Results obtained with the help of others will also be perceived as more valuable by top management. Ironically, doing something alone won't improve your image in an organization. On the contrary, it will raise questions about your leadership qualities. Now, let us take a closer look at how the finest diplomats build those valuable alliances to cut their workloads.

Help others look good
What ultimately matters for a manager is how he is perceived. He might have moved mountains, but if people whose opinions matter are not aware of the feat or if they fail to grasp its significance, the manager will obtain little in return. So if you want others to go out of their way to help you, think about how you can make them look good.

In the previous chapter, I explained the importance of letting your boss know that you are stuck helping someone. When you ask a coworker for help, keep in mind that he will be in the same situation and try to notify his supervisor about the request. One solution is to send an e-mail to both the manager and his boss. While this will work, it is unwise to clutter the mailbox of a busy executive, especially if you ask for help frequently. A better approach is to stop by the superior's office briefly and thank him for the work of his subordinate in front of the person who did the job. In addition to being practical, this gesture means a lot more than an e-mail.

If you get regular assistance from someone, you can thank his boss with an occasional e-mail and sum up the recent activity of the subordinate. If the supervisor is a hands-on manager who wishes to retain control over everything his assistant gives out, you can also call and briefly discuss the issue to kill two birds with one stone. A question such as "In tomorrow's meeting, I'm showing a chart about the growth in soft drink sales; actually your assistant is sending me the data later today. Do you think I should include bottled coffee products?" will both inform him about the work that his assistant is doing and reassure him that you wouldn't alter his data without asking first. Another solution is quoting both the subordinate and the boss in reports or presentations. In addition to informing the boss that his subordinate helped you, this also advertises the team's work. One interviewee explained as follows:

> Putting someone's name in a presentation makes them so much happier than simply thanking them in a meeting. I often credit individuals or departments at the bottom of my slides. If you just say, "thanks a lot to so-and-so" in the meeting when the person is there, they think that you saw them and felt the pressure to say it. But if they see their names on the screen, it means that you really planned the gesture. Besides, it is more glamorous to have your name displayed on the screen.

When asked if this would make it look like others did all the work, the interviewee said,

> No way. Showing that three of my twenty slides were done by others won't hurt me at all. Plus, people will be more willing to help me the next time.

Another interviewee noticed the value of distributing certain information through other people.

> I compile a lot of data from different sources and forward them to big mail lists. But when I get something that has more to do with some-

body else's job than mine, I send it to only that person and let him forward it. If a survey shows quality improvements, you can bet that the factory manager will be interested. A few hours after I forward him the file he sends a mass e-mail with graphs and charts, talking about how much progress we made. That makes the factory manager happy and is a better use of resources. If I send the data without the commentary, it wouldn't even get noticed. Besides, I already send too many e-mails.

Finally, avoid making others look bad. If you spot an error in a presentation or e-mail, do not draw everyone's attention to it. When people need to be aware, contact the author first. Even if everyone already noticed the error, it looks much better for the author to send a second e-mail, where he can make it look like a typo. But if you announce the issue, the author will look like he wasn't aware of the mistake.

Also, be careful with questions in meetings. Do not let anyone feel attacked in front of others. Make your criticism constructive. Always start with a positive comment, as opposed to telling the person that he was flat-out wrong. Instead of asking someone why he used the Dow Jones Industrial Average and not the broader S&P 500 index, tell him that you like the Dow because it is widely followed but that the S&P could provide further information.

If possible, sell your solution as an addition, rather than a replacement. For example, suggest charting the Dow and S&P on the same graph. The old trick of turning comments into questions may also help. In this same example you can ask: "Is it worth charting the S&P also, or does it always run in tandem with the Dow?" These questions can not only help the other person, but also reduce the risk of a counterattack, where he pulls out a chart that you were unaware of to make you look terrible in front of everyone.

Know about people's jobs, but don't overstep your boundaries

Others must feel that you can be helpful to them when needed, and to be able to help people, you must understand what they do for a living. But due to extreme specialization, today's managers hardly know what their colleagues do on a typical day.

When I was a brand manager, for example, I always wondered what the production line manager did. I understood his basic objectives, such as improving productivity and reducing defects. I also knew what I had to call him for and when I had to contact the quality control department instead. Still, I had no idea what such a person actually dealt with ten hours a day. Whenever I went to the factory, the technicians would be running the production line. This ignorance made it difficult to optimize our relationship. Despite my best intentions, I would end up harassing him at the worst moments and often made him look bad with inappropriate questions in meetings. (In case you're wondering, I still don't know what exactly a production manager does.)

As always, your tools are observation and continuous communication. Talk to colleagues frequently. Do not wait for a meeting or until you spend a day at the factory. Instead, call and chat briefly when you have a question or suggestion. Stop by their desks if you are in the same building, or make short but frequent visits as opposed to long and infrequent ones. You cannot see the production manager's typical day if you go to the factory only for the quarterly meeting, since he will delegate and reschedule his work to be free on that day.

But no matter how much you know, do not overstep your boundaries. Do not be so involved that colleagues feel like you are watching over their shoulders. A sales person had just this sort of experience with an ex-salesman, who had become a brand manager.

> The guy drives me crazy. Whenever I tell him that something cannot be done by a certain date or within that budget, he tells me how he did it when he was in sales and then starts giving me advice. He doesn't supervise me in any way. I already had a serious talk with him about this, but he doesn't get it. I don't think he is bad at heart. He's probably trying to make my life easier, but I don't need this. Dealing with one boss is hard enough. I really cannot handle a second one.

The issue is not how much you know about people's jobs. Problems start when you aggressively demonstrate this knowledge. Do not utilize your wisdom as a bargaining tool; use it to smooth the workflow. Instead of criticizing another department's way of getting things done or giving them instructions, note when they will be busy and avoid calling them at those times.

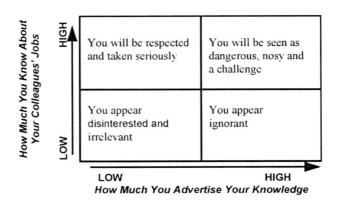

Make their lives easier

Anything you can do to reduce the workload of colleagues is a step in the right direction to reduce your own workload. This can be done in many ways, but the prerequisite is effective communication. Be curious and ask non-intrusive questions to ensure continuous information flow. When sending a file, for example, ask what it is needed for. I am often asked for data in an Excel file. I get the information from presentations, then copy and paste it into a spreadsheet. When I later see the same data in a presentation, I wonder how much time we wasted by changing formats twice just because the person didn't ask me if I had a PowerPoint slide.

Another way to make the coworkers' lives easier is to shift the workload from those whom you need to please to those who need to please you. Many of us have access to people with unscheduled time such as secretaries, support staff, or interns. You can perform a great service to your organization by shifting some of your colleagues' tasks to these people. In addition to providing a benefit to a coworker, you may also help the support person in the process. Interns, in particular, need a chance to demonstrate their skills to get a permanent offer or a good reference letter.

External parties constitute another great resource. Many organizations buy the services of outsiders with a binding contract and, to be safe, pay for slightly more than they expect to use. Consequently, you may find yourself with an under-utilized data vendor or consultant who could help your coworkers. As usual, asking the right questions is key. If you request a price quote from the purchasing department and are told that this isn't a good time, find out why. You may be able to send over someone to help your colleague, and in turn get the prices a day early.

Finally, a simple step that can save colleagues a lot of time is putting a subject on e-mails. It amazes me how people spend twenty minutes to write a perfect message, but don't take ten seconds to type a title. As a result, those messages become impossible to retrieve after a month. The only way to find them is to recall their date or search for an unusual word you remember from the message. If there is an attachment but no text, the second option won't work, and you will have to go through almost every e-mail from that person. Even worse, such messages are often deleted by mistake.

In addition to torturing other people, you will encounter the same problem when trying to find your own message in your "sent" folder. To make everybody's life easier, take a few seconds and type a self-explanatory subject. Make sure that the title will mean something after a long time has passed. Instead of "Regarding Your Request During the Meeting," use idiot-proof lines such as "2003 Profit Analysis Breakdown by Customer Type."

To get things moving, talk to the correct people in the hierarchy

Most managers mistakenly believe that they must use their most senior contacts to accelerate processes. The worst example I have seen was calling the global head of HR for an employment verification letter. That is like lighting a cigarette with a hand grenade, and rarely saves you time.

When people need something simple from my division, like a price quote, they assume that calling my boss will speed things up. It never does. First, it'll take longer for me to respond, because you will probably not catch my boss and have to leave a voice mail, which he'll tell me about later. Second, mistakes are more likely if you don't contact the right person. My boss may not tell me every detail, whereas if you call me I can ask questions to clarify. Third, you annoy me by going to my boss for every little thing, which tells me that you don't trust me. Fourth, after a while, my boss will start to ignore you. If you come to me for minor requests, and talk to him only when he needs to be involved, he'll take you more seriously.

To prevent details getting lost while information is relayed, talk directly to the individual who will do the work. If you must contact the supervisor to pressure an unresponsive employee, follow up by calling the person who will perform the job, after you talk to the boss.

3 Key Points You Should Remember

- Be aware of who your colleagues are trying to impress, and help them do so
- Know about the jobs of your colleagues, but do not advertise this knowledge
- When you need something done, try to talk to the person who will actually do the job, as opposed to the most senior person you can catch

CHAPTER 10

Getting the Most Out of Subordinates

During the interviews, I met some of the most fascinating people I have ever known. One such gentleman, who was legendary for his speed and efficiency, had the following quote on his wall:

"If I had eight hours to chop down a tree, I'd spend six sharpening my axe."—Abraham Lincoln

When I asked how this quote was relevant for him, he said,

A manager's axe is his people. I give myself at most eight hours every day to chop down whatever tree they put in front of me. So I spend six hours working with my people and sharpening their skills to do the work that I am accountable for. Thanks to this mentality, I have left the office in eight hours, or less, almost every day over the last ten years.

This brilliant analogy pinpoints the direct relationship between your effectiveness and that of your subordinates. Your contributions to the efficiency of peers and top managers have an indirect impact on your work hours. However, any improvement in the efficiency of subordinates will directly and immediately reduce your workload. In other words, if you save your people an hour of work, you can hand over one hour's worth of your duties. But you cannot do the same with peers or top managers.

Furthermore, how you manage your staff is one of the most important criterion for promotions. If you reach business objectives at the expense of your staff, you will leave a wreck behind you. Low morale and internal struggles will make it impossible to repeat the achievement, and you will be seen as a threat to the organization's long-term success. If, however, your people build good relationships with other departments, enjoy their work, and know their jobs, you will probably be considered a competent manager, even if you fail to deliver the best numbers.

In spite of this, managers pay very little attention to subordinates. This is because your people rarely give you instant feedback the way superiors do. When you offend the boss, you will probably know right away. But if you anger your assistant, you may not hear the complaint until after he hands you a resignation letter, because it is too risky to criticize superiors. Consequently, most managers assume that they are doing a great job.

Although this chapter is primarily about managing subordinates, most of these points apply to all individuals below you in the organizational hierarchy. So even if you have no one reporting to you, pay attention to the following discussion. Not only will this help you to manage support staff, interns, and secretaries, but you will also be a better supervisor if you study the basics well before you are promoted. Finally, knowing what an ideal boss would do will help you to nurture those qualities in your own supervisor.

Select employees based on personality / expectations, instead of skills

Remember that nobody is right for everybody and everybody is right for somebody. You should staff your team with people you can get along with. When making a career decision, always pick the option that will give you the most flexibility in selecting subordinates. For example, taking over a department where numerous people are scheduled to retire or leave soon is often a golden opportunity. It provides a chance to hand pick most of your employees.

When selecting subordinates, however, do not make the mistake of only looking for a skill set, while ignoring the personality of the individual. There are very few skills that cannot be learned on the job. Although certain positions require a particular background, such as an accounting degree, all candidates will probably satisfy these conditions. In fact, inexperienced people are sometimes better, as they come in with fewer rigid opinions. In other words, the skill set of the person can be changed. Personality traits, on the other hand, are almost impossible to change. When it comes to character, what you see is what you get.

Most importantly, assess if the candidate will be happy with the amount of freedom you wish to provide. Not everyone prefers more liberty, because freedom must be paid for with responsibility. Being told what to do at every step may be boring and result in longer hours, but it also eliminates liability. After all, no one can blame you if you were just following orders. Be candid during interviews. Communicate how much freedom you will grant and give candidates a feel for what their daily lives will look like. If you want to teach someone to "do what he wants," but he desires to always "do as you tell him" (recall Chapter 8), you will have serious problems.

Try to understand how much responsibility candidates have taken in the past. However, remember that someone who never had a chance to show his capabilities under a control-freak may be hungry for more. Although you can find out a lot by asking the right questions in an interview, keep in mind that an internal transfer can be safer, as it involves fewer unknowns.

You must also assess how the candidate handles people. Most of us have a dominant style of people management. If your employee's style is incompatible with yours, you will frustrate colleagues by sending conflicting signals. You will look like a basketball team where three players do full-court press and two play man-to-man defense. Pay attention to how the candidate negotiates, how he communicates, how high his expectations are when dealing with people, and what behaviors he finds intolerable.

> My boss is a former salesman and, like most salesman in our firm, he is too tough a negotiator. For example, when someone says that he can be ready for a meeting in three days, my boss will immediately ask to meet tomorrow, even if three days is fine. No matter what you offer, he will always push for more. I am not like that at all. I believe in treating people like adults and letting them do their jobs the way they want, if I can live with the results. Consequently, I am finding it very hard to work with my boss. We always argue about what to say to others and leave people completely confused as to what we want.

Your career expectations must also be compatible. If you only have a year left before you retire and just want to take it easy, you will probably have issues with an ambitious associate. Risk tolerance is another key area. One interviewee had tremendous problems with his boss who had just drawn a big loan for a new house. While the interviewee wanted to take what he considered to be calculated risks, the boss couldn't afford to risk anything at all and strongly resisted.

You will have similar headaches, of course, if your expectations are incompatible with those of your own boss. Unfortunately, most managers only assess technical skills and background when recruiting. So even if a prospective boss thinks that you are the perfect candidate, you should make sure that he and you are on the same wavelength before accepting the job.

Demonstrate a strong commitment to your subordinates

To bring out the best in your subordinates, you must assume full responsibility for their activities. Make it clear that you and your people are a unified team and you are willing to be held fully accountable for their actions. Such a commitment will send a clear message to the top. It assures them that you will step forward with your head high when things don't work out, as opposed to wasting time by finger-pointing. This will give superiors a strong sense of control.

More importantly, you will communicate to your employees that you are in this game with them and need to help them for your own survival. This gives them tremendous confidence and motivation. If all of this sounds a bit abstract, the following suggestions will clarify what I mean. These principles apply whether you have only one assistant or supervise a team of thirty.

- Encourage others to treat your group as a single entity. Say, "Call someone from the group when you need help" as opposed to, "Call me, or if I am not there, try my assistant."
- Include everybody's name and contact information at the bottom of group projects, even if a few haven't contributed. This will show that you are a team and you win or lose together.
- *De-emphasize* rank and seniority within the group. Do not to refer to junior people as "assistants," or "juniors," but treat them as equals in front of others (how about "my colleague"?) List names of team members in alphabetical order, not by seniority.
- Treat other people's subordinates with the same respect. Do not automatically go to the most senior person if a lower-ranked individual can help you. In e-mails, do not CC people just because they are ranked lower. Relevance, not rank, should determine TO vs. CC.
- Never compete with your people for attention. If you do, you must ensure that they are no more successful than you are. In turn, they will do the same to you, leading to a vicious circle. If, however, you attribute all results to the team, your employees will strive to make you look good because they will get some of the credit. Even if you get none of the praise for the success of subordinates, your stock will go up if people flourish under your supervision.
- Encourage your people to help each other when someone is feeling overwhelmed, even if the task at hand is the responsibility of a particular individual.
- Do not allow one member of the group to rise to stardom at the expense of the others. Reward achievement and competence, but do not let anyone—you included—dominate the stage. If you do, the team will soon start to disintegrate.
- Provide opportunities for junior members to improve their skills. Let them represent your group in meetings and other occasions, but do not adopt a sink or swim mentality. Help them prepare and, if possible, stand by to jump in if they crack under pressure.
- Never criticize your people in front of others, and never use their mistakes or incompetence as an excuse for failure, even behind closed doors. As we will see later, this will only hurt you as a manager. Do not make a public affair out of problems between team members.
- Never start a fight with another division, thinking that you can later distance yourself by pushing in a subordinate. Side with your people in conflicts. It is better to anger another department than to abandon

an employee in a battle. Remember that your employees do the work that you wouldn't want to touch and allow you to have a life outside the office.

If you want your people to learn the game, let them touch the ball

Most supervisors mistakenly believe that they can teach the job by just talking about it. After lots of verbal instruction, they hand over certain responsibilities, but are then forced to take back most of those tasks when they realize that the subordinate is not yet ready. Nothing comes for free. The price you must pay for handing over part of the job is allowing your people to make mistakes under your supervision. Good judgment comes from experience, which can only come from bad judgment. If you dominate the relationship and make every judgment on your own, your people will never get up to speed.

The short-term gain—a smoother operation as a result of being in charge of every aspect of the job—will come at the expense of long-term efficiency. Although everything will be done exactly as you want, you will always have to be involved and will never be able to completely delegate anything. The results will likely be lack of focus, mental fatigue, and time-famine.

I learned how to develop people the hard way. At first, I was such a perfectionist that I would make every decision on my own and would use my people only for implementation. As a result, they never learned the work and I couldn't delegate anything to them. It was ridiculous. I would be stuck in the office, but would have to tell my people to go home because I couldn't trust them to do any of the work sitting on my desk. Today, I delegate things to them even when I know they are not 100% ready. I accept their low-risk proposals to give them a sense of what it feels like to be in the driver's seat. Even if I am sure that their ideas will fail, I let them go ahead if it isn't a big deal. This is the only way to show why certain things that look great on paper won't work in real life. The last person I want to delegate to is someone who has never made a dumb move. I remember how as a kid I always wanted to touch the hot iron. Eventually, my mom set it on medium temperature and let me touch it. Naturally, I never asked again. In a way, this is what I am doing with my people here before I let them use the iron.

Another costly mistake is to overwhelm subordinates with your knowledge, as we saw in Chapter 6. If you constantly ask your people to express their ideas but cannot get much out of them, your know-it-all attitude could be to blame. In addition to being intimidating, this style also makes your aides think that they are supposed to know everything. Most managers complain that their people are afraid to say, "I don't know," but fail to see that the subordinates are only copying the boss. As we will see below, losing touch with subordinates can not only inflate your workload, but also lead to much bigger disasters.

Encourage your subordinates to redefine their jobs, just like you do

The central message of this book is that you can change the amount of work you must do to be successful at your job. By now, you can probably see the difference between redefining your job to maximize efficiency and slacking off when superiors are looking the other way. If so, you should have no problem encouraging your subordinates to do the former.

To get the most out of your people, tell them openly that you have no interest in seeing them trapped in the office. Discourage them from staying around for face time. Do whatever you can to streamline their jobs. If you help them to save time, you will have the right to ask for some of the savings to be returned to you. When the employee is the one solely responsible for the efficiency improvements, however, he will not be nearly as happy to share the fruits of his labor.

When I first started here, I was putting in over sixty hours a week, mainly because my boss was so unproductive. As I learned the job and took over some of his tasks, we both started to leave earlier. But instead of being grateful, he said that we had a lot of free time and could do more. This made me sick to my stomach. I felt like he was stealing something from me. We had free time because I had killed myself to get the place in order, but the pay-off was even more work. The lesson is: If someone can get his job done faster because he is a more efficient worker now, let him enjoy at least some of the free time. Otherwise he'll have no incentive to improve further. If you save him time, then you can delegate some duties. But don't confiscate his newfound free time if he created it.

Recall the steps that led to less work in Chapter 8 and teach subordinates how to progress along this path. They must understand why one starts with boring and monotonous things before assuming bigger responsibilities. They should also know that if they prove themselves by doing those things well, they will graduate to more exciting tasks. This will greatly motivate them. But be careful never to promise more responsibility than they can handle, even if they ask for it. Remember that, as their guardian angel, you must sometimes protect them from what they want.

Do not lose touch with the donkeywork that you dump on your people

You will naturally hand over most of the tedious tasks to subordinates. It is not advisable, however, to completely lose touch with those duties. First, this leads to major inefficiencies. Numerous interviewees mentioned how the ignorance of their bosses multiplied their workload.

> I prepare a monthly report for which my boss tells me what graphs to include, but never bothers to ask where I get them. As a result, we fight all the time. Recently, he came to me at 6 PM and told me to add the occupancy figures. I couldn't reach the lodging manager at that time, but my boss didn't want to understand. I probably spent half an hour explaining why I couldn't pull the numbers from the Web or get them from the junior lodging manager. I go through this every day because my boss is so uninformed about what I am doing and how I am doing it.

In addition to wasting your people's time with unrealistic demands, you will be lost when you must operate on your own. You probably have seen people desperately trying to reach a subordinate who was on a camping trip, just to ask where a file was saved. Imagine what can happen to someone like this if his subordinate unexpectedly resigns. Furthermore, these supervisors can look horrible by promising to send a report, "before the end of the day," only to find out that the assistant has to get it from the East Coast where it is already 9:00 PM.

You also lose control over your people when you are totally detached from their jobs. Although the relationship should be based on mutual trust, you still must have an idea about how your employees are spending their time. Otherwise, you will have no choice but to take their word when they say, "I can't handle anything else, I'm swamped."

Know where key files are located and help a little with the donkeywork. If you spot a minor mistake in a file, for example, correct it yourself instead of dictating the change to your assistant. This way, you can at least learn where files are saved. I have had supervisors drive me insane, asking me to change a single word in a file when it was already open in front of them.

For the health of the relationship, it is especially important to get involved when a subordinate is suffering. If he gets stuck in the office on his birthday because of a system crash, do not leave at five to play golf. Even if you cannot do much, stay around for at least a while to demonstrate that it is a team game, not a slave-master relationship. In addition, give a hand when physical labor is needed. If you are moving the office, do not just shout out instructions from your desk on how to label the boxes. Get up and do something. Similarly, if your assistant is carrying thirty binders to a meeting, do not walk next to him with just a cell phone.

Do not overestimate your ability to deceive subordinates

As paradoxical as it may sound, superiors are easier to deceive than subordinates. Most managers never realize this because the compliance of subordinates creates an illusion of power. Since those below us must do what we tell them, we mistakenly assume that we can also manipulate what they believe. Nothing could be further from the truth. Like it or not, your subordinates can influence your beliefs much more easily than you can influence theirs.

Most supervisors have no option but to blindly trust their people. An interviewee working as a quality control manager at a large warehouse was a typical example. After two decades in the business, this person knew exactly how to check the quality of thirty tons of chicken breasts in half an hour. He could look at a truckload of melons and magically tell that the grower had stashed a bunch of unripe ones at the bottom of the pile. In other words, he knew everything that takes extraordinary passion for your job and twenty years to learn. On the other hand, he didn't know how to enter the number of defective products into the electronic database. Since punching in a bunch of numbers and navigating through all the menus took no special skill, he had delegated these tasks years ago. He even admitted that when he tried to do these himself while his assistant was out sick, he couldn't figure it out for over an hour and had to call for help.

Such an assistant can enter almost any figure into the database and artificially skew the quality record. The only person who knows what the real numbers should be has no clue how to check the entries. As you rise through the ranks, such situations are inevitable. To perform the high value-added tasks better, you must delegate most data gathering, record keeping, and regulatory functions to your subordinates. Even if you don't lose touch with these tasks completely, like the interviewee in the prior example did, you will simply not have the time to monitor the details. Therefore, a disgruntled or lazy subordinate can often feed you incorrect information.

It is much more difficult, however, for the boss to lie to the assistant. The subordinate will do all the donkeywork and be so familiar with the details of the project, that sooner or later he will find out. While the boss will only see the end result of most of the subordinate's work, the assistant will update every spreadsheet, make all the boring phone calls, and chase all the secretaries. Therefore, somewhere, somehow, he will uncover the fraud. To make an analogy it is easier to hide the skeleton in the closet from your spouse than from the cleaning lady.

As a result, the anatomy of a scandal in a large organization is almost always the same. An individual or a group makes a bad move and thinks that it can be kept a secret. But inevitably, the information leaks downwards. The little accountant who files the receipts, the young officer who counts confiscated weapons every night, or the unimportant clerk who checks transaction records finds out. Then that person either joins in or is threatened to not reveal the scam.

As the crisis grows, it gets harder to expose. Since the news travels downward, each new level of the organization involved in the scandal becomes progressively weaker. And the weaker they are, the easier they will be to silence. Also, as the scandal evolves more people get involved, and the potential enemy base of the whistleblower grows substantially. By the time it is revealed by a brave soul who risks his career, and sometimes even his life, it is usually big enough to end up on the front pages of newspapers. Every time it is the subordinates pulling the wool over the eyes of the bosses, almost never the other way round. And every time, the public is yet again shocked to learn how the all-mighty CEO or VP was so clueless about the matter.

Since it is so difficult to deceive the people below you, just don't try. If you tell them that the file is due for a meeting at two, when in reality the meeting is at three, they will probably find out. In addition to losing credibility, you also give subordinates a reason to retaliate. Believe me, this is a game you cannot win. If your assistant tells you that he cannot be ready by two, because Sue in finance, who gives those numbers to Andy, who calculates the figures in your slides, is sick, there is very little you can do short of firing him. You simply won't have time to check the accuracy of such a story. Even worse, this can soon result in a complete loss of trust between you and your subordinate, prompting both sides to be dishonest whenever they are confident of not getting caught. Needles to say such a fight can devastate your efficiency.

Reveal true deadlines, as well as limitations such as budgets. It is acceptable not to discuss everything with your subordinates. Feel free to tell them from time to time that you do not want to talk about a certain issue. In the long-term, this will work much better than distorting the facts.

5 Key Points You Should Remember

- Select subordinates based more on personality than on work experience
- Make people around you aware of how much you care for your subordinates
- Allow your people to leave their comfort zones and, if necessary, to fail in controlled environments
- Encourage your people to reshape their jobs to suit their personalities and preferences
- Never forget the disastrous consequences of trying to deceive your subordinates

CHAPTER 11

Dealing with Troublemakers

The previous five chapters emphasized the importance of building positive relationships at all levels. The interviews show that extending the olive branch is the best opening strategy. Like the well-documented correlation between the beliefs of a teacher about a student and the child's grades, there is a connection between what we assume about coworkers and how they treat us. So unless you know someone, assume that he is a nice guy.

However, every strategy has its limitations and even your best efforts will fail against egotistical individuals who simply refuse to cooperate. I will refer to these people as "troublemakers." Troublemakers come in all shapes and sizes and can appear at any level within an organization. They are solely concerned with their own needs and don't even want to know about your situation. If they need a file, they couldn't care less how long it will take you to produce it. Meetings must start when they want, and conferences have to be held in their favorite hotels.

It shouldn't be surprising that a book that talks about workload reduction dedicates a chapter to troublemakers. These people not only try to shift a disproportionate amount of their own work to you, but also increase the total workload in the organization with their inflexibility.

As a general rule, avoid troublemakers whenever possible, because a fight can leave scars on your image regardless of who started it. A conflict can also lead to a lot of inefficiencies if future interactions with the individual are unavoidable, since he will make your life difficult whenever you need his input. A fight with a more top official can have even bigger ramifications.

On the other hand, if a number of conditions are met, you can gently retaliate to defend yourself. First, the person should not be above you or be a candidate for rapid advancement. Also, the pain he causes must be high enough to justify the confrontation, and you should have other options if he refuses to cooperate in the future. Finally, never fight with a personal friend of your boss.

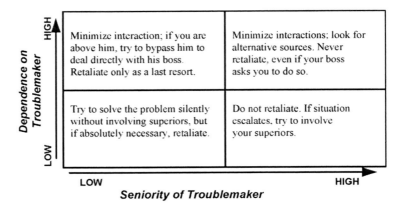

When dealing with these people, you can be caught on either side of the equation. You may be harassed for a particular task or conversely, you may badly need the input of an unresponsive troublemaker. Before we look at each case in detail, I must repeat that unless you know the individual, you should assume that he is a reasonable fellow. Always wait until you are attacked. If you must constantly resort to the tactics below, you are probably the chief troublemaker.

When the troublemaker is chasing you

When a troublemaker has an unfair request, delay your response as much as possible without appearing too uncooperative. This provides numerous advantages. First, he may just give up. He could simply conclude that it isn't worth the hassle, or his deadline may pass. Troublemakers are usually very badly organized. It is rare for someone who cannot work with others to be able to sort out his own thoughts. Therefore, they usually panic as deadlines approach and are forced to rethink priorities. If the troublemaker needs a dozen charts for the appendix of a report before Friday, you may only need to keep him on hold until Thursday. By then, he may very well have a major crisis with half of the pages still missing and skip the appendix altogether.

Second, delaying the process will minimize follow-up requests. If you send everything right away to get him off your back, the troublemaker may conclude that you barely did any work and feel entitled to ask for more. Also, troublemakers tend to be over-analytical and often harass you with follow-up questions. They want to know why profits went up while sales were down or why the data goes back only two years. The faster you respond, the more time you give the troublemaker to go over the information with a microscope and find questions to ask.

Finally, delaying the process will reduce future expectations. If he can obtain what he wants only after a battle, he may either look for another victim the next time or scale back his requests. But if you reply too fast, the troublemaker will gain an advantage in future negotiations by saying that he knows you could help him quickly if you wanted to cooperate.

The challenge here is to delay your response without looking too bad. You must always pay attention to this because even if you don't realize it, important people, such as the troublemaker's boss, may be observing you. Your first defense is to postpone the initial contact as much as possible. If he calls you, try not to pick up the phone; if he sends an e-mail, respond later rather than sooner; if he tries to catch up with you by the coffee machine, make an excuse to talk later.

The troublemaker may leave long voice mails to detail what he wants. In response, call back when he cannot pick up and leave a message. If he is always in the office, call late at night from your cell phone and say that you are sorry that the two of you could not yet talk. However, if the message system displays time and phone number for voice mails, this may not work so well. The time or the phone number you are calling form might show that you are trying to avoid him. When leaving such voice mails, be prepared for the phone to be picked up half-way through. Do not say "Hi, it's 9 PM, sorry I couldn't call earlier but I just got back to my desk," when in fact you are calling from home at 8. If he picks up the phone after you have said all this, you may find yourself in a very embarrassing situation. Just say that you got his message and will try him again.

It is also crucial to bring all the complications to his attention. This will naturally slow down the process. When he asks for inflation figures, for example, tell him that you can provide consumer or producer price inflation, or exclude the volatile food and energy components. Always conclude the message or e-mail by saying that you must talk to clarify. Do not list all possible alternatives. If you do, the troublemaker can pick one of them in his next e-mail and clear up the confusion.

When you finally talk, your first priority is to avoid setting a deadline. Unless he asks when you will get back to him, do not bring up the subject. If he pushes you, try not to make a commitment. Tell him that you will call him or send an e-mail once you find out what is available. Do not put yourself in a situation where you will look like a failure unless you reply by a certain date.

If the troublemaker does not give up after all this and you have to send him something, provide only what he asked for and absolutely nothing else. Assume that in the previous example it is agreed that consumer inflation figures are the best choice. The biggest mistake you can make is to forward a file with all possible inflation figures. You may do this in order not to lose time with copying and pasting cells in Excel or, think that you will get rid of the troublemaker for good by giving him everything you have. At best, this will reveal that you have a lot of data and encourage him to call you whenever he has a question that is remotely related to you. At worst, it will restart the whole cycle. He may find new information he likes better and force you to redo the graphs or request additional ones, maybe even blaming you for having misled him by recommending something else.

A final point you must consider is the update time of files. When you delay sending information to the troublemaker, always open up the file and resave it so that its last update time matches the time of the e-mail. Otherwise it will become clear that the files were ready in their final form long before you sent them.

When you are chasing the troublemaker

If you are caught on the other side and need something from an unresponsive troublemaker, do the opposite of what I describe above. Talk to him in person as soon as you can to prevent him from slowing down the process. Do not leave a voice message, because you will look pushy after a few unanswered voice mails. Call when you know he is available. If he says that he will call you back, tell him that you are hard to reach and ask for a specific time to call him. If he is in the same building, make an appointment to see him in his office. When cornered, he can always make up an excuse and walk out of your room, but it is much harder to kick you out of his office.

Once you get hold of him, do not give him too many details that can be used against you. Assume that you are working for an automobile manufacturer and want the economist to present at the dealer conference. If you ask for a speech about consumer spending, inflation, and the impact of exchange rates on the auto market, you will provide too much raw material for excuses. He could say "I'm not the exchange rate expert, give __ a call" or "Those topics are too complex, we'll confuse the dealers. Let me get back to you with other ideas" and stall the game.

Instead, just get his commitment to talk by making the task sound as easy as possible. Say that you only need a brief economic overview. Even if you have specific subjects in mind, do not bring them up at this stage. Once he agrees to talk, you can involve your boss or find other ways to influence the topics of the presentation. It also helps to point to a precedent of what you want. If a similar presentation was delivered in the past, go to him with a copy and say that you want the same. Since it has been done before, it will be much more difficult to argue why it is impossible now. Additionally, this clarifies what you want and makes it harder for him to prolong the process by faking confusion over minute details. One interviewee uses a variation of this tactic for all of his requests.

> Instead of explaining the job via e-mail or talking on the phone forever, I just forward a file and ask them to fill in the red cells. I don't

give people a chance to say, "I got your file but couldn't figure out what you wanted." Nobody can receive one of my idiot-proof files and say he couldn't figure out what I wanted.

Once you agree on what the troublemaker will do, even if only broadly, set a deadline. Do not let him tell you that he will call you in a few days or when his computer is fixed. If he resists against a firm deadline, provide a reason beyond your control. In the above example, the conference team may need the presentation in a week to produce handouts. Such reasons are easy to find, since in large organizations someone will need something by almost any day on the calendar.

Now that we covered the basics of dealing with annoying people, let us turn our attention to specific types of troublemakers. A complete typological analysis is beyond the scope of this book. The discussion is thus limited to the most common types mentioned during interviews. Also, note that I intentionally selected extreme examples to better demonstrate the principles. The study of a tyrannical dictator, as opposed to the ten-year-old who beats up his classmates, can reveal much more about the inferiority complex—even if dictators are less common. Similarly, the chronic cases over the coming pages will expose the minds of these troublemakers.

The Thief

The thief is the parasite of the organizational ecosystem. By producing very little, but specializing in stealing intellectual property, he can get by for years until top management wakes up. The thief regularly takes someone else's work and forwards it to important end users, such as clients or top managers, or presents it in meetings or conferences as if it was his own product.

A peculiar characteristic of the thief is his excessive interest in your work. He constantly wants to know what you are working on or when you will publish the next big report, but rarely has a good reason for this curiosity. The easiest way to recognize a thief is to simply ask what he will do with the information. If he gets upset and provides evasive answers such as "I may need it when you're not around," he could have unethical intentions. You can also recognize him by his e-mails and presentations, where he uses lots of information that have nothing to do with his area. If a sales manager makes a long speech about raw material manufacturers followed by a discussion of the new accounting laws, but barely talks about sales, be suspicious. Especially if he talks about these when the purchasing and accounting people are not around, you are almost certainly dealing with a thief.

There are many counterattacks you can employ against this type. Although you should always exercise caution, his actions will rarely be approved by top management and therefore it is relatively safe to challenge him. Your first defense is to make the thief uncomfortable. Every time he requests information, even for a legitimate reason, ask what he needs it for. Dig deeper and provide alternatives or make suggestions, instead of sending him everything you have. He will soon realize that your curiosity can expose his intentions, and he will feel threatened.

Suppose that a client asks the thief for labor productivity figures. Instead of referring the client to the firm's economist, the thief tries to get this data from the economist so he can send it himself as if he produced the file alone. The economist could easily expose the plan by simply asking if the thief wants the manufacturing or service sector productivity, as opposed to forwarding a file with both sets of figures right away. It will likely become evident that the thief does not even understand the concept of labor productivity and couldn't possibly do anything with the file other than forwarding it to someone else.

The second line of defense is to make the data more difficult to use. This was suggested by an interviewee who observed how most thieves will tell you that the data is "just for my own information." You can respond to this by saying "OK, I've got something which is sort of incomplete. I wouldn't send it to a client, but it'll certainly give you an idea," and send him the most rudimentary version of what you have. After all, it isn't like he will send it to someone important, right? You can provide slightly outdated information or something that would require substantial formatting to make it presentable. The idea is to make it difficult for him to steal your data, so he looks for other victims in the future.

Sometimes the thief will admit that he will forward the data but won't say to whom. He may say that he is meeting some clients in a conference but that the list of attendees is yet to be confirmed. Dig deeper and make him uncomfortable. Say "OK, let me give you a call when you return. I'd like to put whoever gets this file on my e-mail list for updates" and call him later on.

In addition to being disrespectful, most thieves are also lazy, which is the main reason they steal. They seldom review your files in detail before sending them out. This gives you the chance to brand your data so that people find out where it came from. As we will see in Chapter 17, you should brand all your work for easy recognition. By inserting your name and contact information at the corner of your files and using consistent fonts and colors, you can ensure that much less of your work is attributed to others. An added benefit is that these may work like a booby trap if your files are abused. Imagine a thief sending your spreadsheet to a client and apologizing for being late, adding that it took him a couple of hours to calculate the numbers. At the very least, the client will get suspicious when he opens the file and sees someone else's name at the bottom.

The final and most intelligent defense suggested during the interviews involves a strong counterattack. If you have an idea whom the file might be forwarded to, send the data to the thief and, after a few days, send the same information to these potential recipients. The e-mail can say that your division recently prepared the attached analysis and that you wanted to share it with people who might find it useful. If you guessed correctly and the thief presented it as his own work, he will look really bad. If you were wrong and the thief never contacted these people, at worst they will ignore the message. So you have nothing to lose other than the thief's sympathy.

The Data Fetishist

This type cannot make a decision unless virtually everything points in the same direction, presenting a black-and-white picture. For example, the data fetishist must see a growing market, weak competition, and declining cost base before he can launch a new product. Since it is almost impossible to have that many odds in one's favor, the data fetishist has to dig really deep for the bits of information that may relieve his fears. The deeper he digs, the harder the data becomes to obtain. You can probably imagine how annoying this can be, if you are the one who must dig on his behalf.

It is important not to confuse the data fetishist with the thief. Although both always ask for more information, the data fetishist does so to confirm his ill-conceived hypotheses and to soothe his fears, while the thief wants more alternatives to steal from. The data fetishist is always puzzled and drowns you in questions. He cannot accept the fact that things won't be black-and-white all the time. The thief, however, lacks a good justification for requesting more. He fears that a conversation may reveal his objective and doesn't want to talk. Therefore, the same litmus test that exposes the thief—asking what he needs the data for—is equally effective in identifying the data fetishist.

Also note that the data fetishist is usually not as evil as the thief. His obsession often hurts him as much as it harms others. While the thief is usually the first one to go home at the end of the day, the data fetishist is among the last. The behavioral pattern of this poor fellow perfectly fits the definition of addiction; he could also be called a "data addict."

If someone grins from ear to ear when you give him a two-inch thick report, you are probably facing a data fetishist. While most managers would be turned off by the vast quantity of data, the fetishist will be seduced by the immense volume. For him, more is always better. He can also be recognized by his office, which is often a mess because he cannot throw anything away. His electronic folders are even worse. Since he saves the same figures under a different name after every modification, he will have files with such names as "2005 Budget Version 8."

Your first priority when working with the data fetishist should be to understand what he is trying to prove. Ask as many questions as possible. Most of them are talkative academic types, so this should be fairly easy. After that, go back to your desk and look specifically for facts and figures that prove him right. If the information comes as a package, remove the pieces that contradict his views. The more everything points in the same direction, the better. If, for example, you find an article supplemented with many graphs, give him only the figure that supports his theories. Otherwise, he may find minute inconsistencies and ask for more information. In addition, don't forget to put the right spin on the data. If teddy bear sales have not grown as much as he'd like to see, mention that steady sales, despite the declining birth rate, are nevertheless impressive.

Next, make the supporting data as difficult to analyze as you can. Since he has immense amounts of information, the data fetishist rarely has the time to go through everything. Just knowing that he has a ton of data at hand gives him reassurance, although he is very unlikely to use it in any meaningful way. The data fetishist is like the driver who uses an ultra-rugged sport utility vehicle to drive to the mall. The driver may never utilize the off-road capabilities of his truck, but still needs to know that he could if he wanted to. Similarly, most data fetishists will only read the conclusions, but need to have the numbers, figures, and appendices "just in case."

Your objective is to further encourage him to skip the analysis by making that portion harder to decipher. When providing financial comparisons, include different currencies so it becomes impossible to use them without a history of exchange rates. When analyzing a company, mention the complications arising from the tax shelters in Bahamas and the accounting rules changes. If you also provide a juicy management summary that supports his view, he will probably not go through the balance sheet data to find inconsistencies and make further demands.

In addition, prevent the data fetishist from discovering new information sources. If he finds a new Web site, database, or library, he will try to extract as much from that source as possible. When he must know where the data came from, provide a general answer without getting into the specifics. If, for example, you obtain a few graphs on cottage cheese from a report by the Dairy Manufacturers Association (DMA) and are questioned about the source, just say that you got the data from DMA. While most managers would feel more confident about the information after learning that it is from a specific report about the subject and stop inquiring further, the data fetishist will do the opposite. You will get comments such as "I didn't know there was a report on cottage cheese. What else is in there?" or "Can you find a similar report on yogurt?"

The Prosecutor
The prosecutor often suffers from acute anxiety, which in extreme cases can border on paranoia. He cannot accept the risks of working for a large organization, where top managers have a hard time tracing results back to a single person and often accuse the wrong people when something goes wrong. The prosecutor

is paranoid about being singled out as a source of failure. He avoids responsibility at any cost. When working with other groups or departments, he strives to find someone he can hold responsible in case of trouble.

He is happiest when he can locate an official document outlining responsibilities. He regards these as his insurance policy and goes to great lengths to find them. While others rarely know about "interoffice code of conduct" documents or "departmental workflow charts", the prosecutor is intimately familiar with these. You will hear questions from him such as "Who is supposed to update the prices?" or "Who is responsible for publishing the warranties?" When he cannot obtain clear answers to these questions, he gets nervous and holds his only contact person responsible for the unclaimed task. He can make this individual feel like he was put on trial with endless questions and accusations, hence the name prosecutor.

Unfortunately, the prosecutor tends to select his victims among those who try to be helpful. Imagine the following scenario: The phone rings at 7:00 PM when most people have already gone home. The caller is desperately searching for something, and you happen to be the only one he can reach. You kindly tell him that you are not the right person to talk to, but will do your best and provide whatever information you have.

His questions are too detailed and his attitude gets worse by the moment. When you remind him that you are not the right contact and therefore are unaware of details, he implies that you must help him. He asks how you can work in logistics and not know such matters or why you cannot justify the numbers in your e-mail. He is desperately in need of someone who is responsible, and loses his temper when he cannot find such a person. When it is over, your reaction is "What a _____, I am just trying to help the guy." Does this sound familiar?

When someone asks for things that you are not supposed to do or have but could still help with, make it clear that you are not the one to talk to. Then see if he gets it. While a reasonable person will apologize for the irrelevant request and kindly ask if you can still help, a prosecutor will barely be impressed. Other warning flags include a disrespect for your time (in his mind it is your duty to help him, so he can take as much of your time as he wants) and the need to cover his back. If he constantly tells you that the information must be correct because he is sending it to so-and-so or because his name will appear on the report, alarm bells should be ringing in your head.

The best defense against the prosecutor is to use his own weapon against him. If he asks you for help regarding something that is not your responsibility and you have received a few of the above signals, just end the interaction. Say that you do not have the information because it is someone else's job (nothing you can do, that's the rule.) This may not sound like the nicest thing, but if there is no way he can find out that you actually had access to the data, it is the best choice. By helping him when you don't need to, you will put yourself at risk for nothing. He won't appreciate the effort, but can make you miserable.

The more relevant question, of course, is what to do if the prosecutor asks for something that you are supposed to have. In this case, communicate your responsibilities very clearly so he doesn't hold you accountable for someone else's work. If you took the budget figures from accounting, for example, make sure that he understands this. Define the boundaries very strictly and never step forward as the representative of your entire division.

Should his questions drift into extraneous subjects that you are not obliged to know, gently remind him of your exact duties. Just as you do with the data fetishist, do not give the prosecutor more than he absolutely needs. If necessary, delete parts of a file before you forward it. But always include a detailed list of sources and references. He will he feel safer and walk away sooner when he has a clear source to blame. In addition, you will cover your own back.

3 Key Points You Should Remember
- Minimize your interactions with potential troublemakers
- Do not engage in a fight with anyone without carefully weighting the consequences
- Learn how to identify and avoid the major types of troublemakers in large organizations

And a word of caution...
Do not over-mechanize your relationships
In this part, we saw how the needs of individuals vary based on their positions in the organization and analyzed different strategies for different hierarchical clusters. This mentality, however, should not be taken to extremes. You will severely compromise your efficiency if all you see of people is their ranks and titles. Such a worldview makes it impossible to recognize the peculiarities of coworkers and optimize every relationship.

Catching a morning person at the wrong time or offending your boss with a bad joke can wipe out an entire week's work. Remember that business literature is full of multimillion-dollar deals that were closed only because the two CEOs enjoyed the same pastime. So do not treat people as just a box in the organizational chart. Make a sincere effort to understand their unique personalities and, if necessary, override any of the rules explained over the last six chapters.

PART 3

Polishing Up Your Image To Cut Your Workload

The word image tends to have a rather poor image. Especially in the minds of most managers, it refers to the sum of all undeserved impressions we have of something or somebody. In reality, however, image is simply what we think of an object, an abstraction, or an individual. When, intentionally or accidentally, false information is transmitted, image deviates from reality. The problem is that when we ignore our image, we almost always transmit the wrong information and create a worse image than we deserve. And this inevitably inflates our workload.

A favorable image, on the other hand, will reduce your workload in two ways. When coworkers have a good impression of you, not only can you achieve better results with less work, but also people will attribute a greater proportion of those results to your managerial aptitude, instead of other individuals or simply luck. In other words, you will more easily move from the first to the second and from the third to the fourth stage in the managerial value chain.

Although most people can readily see the connection between a better image and more appreciation, few can understand how a positive image leads to greater productivity. If others think highly of you, they will applaud you harder, but how can their perception help you to do more in less time? The answer is quite simple; when people expect something to happen, they help it to happen. This phenomenon is known as the placebo effect in medicine and is widely encountered in all areas of life. When an obese patient is given a fake weight loss drug, i.e. a placebo, he often regards this as a chance to finally shed the excessive pounds and, knowingly or inadvertently, "helps" the drug. Just one less bite of food at every meal and taking the stairs as opposed to the elevator twice a day can soon add up and result in weight loss.

The placebo effect is also observed in social settings. To properly assess the impact of an after-school program on student's grades, researchers must ensure that the teacher doesn't know which students are taking those extra classes. Otherwise, the teacher might give more attention to these kids, so they get the most out of the program, and unintentionally lift up their grades.

Similar dynamics evolve in large organizations. If you have the aura of a winner, the organization will make it easier for you to win. Take a moment to think of the latest round of budget cuts in your own company. Who got the bigger hit? Managers widely expected to succeed or the ones who didn't look very promising? Likewise, it is not too difficult to guess whom top management will pay more attention to or send to the expensive training sessions. In addition, peers will be more willing to lend a helping hand if they believe that you will succeed. The motivation to be part of a winning team is among the biggest drivers in large organizations. In short, the better your image, the less effort you will have to expend in order to make something important happen.

Before going further, let me address potential concerns regarding the ethical consequences of working on your image. Some managers think that advertising one's merits is essentially bragging. They say that this gives one an unfair advantage over one's dignified peers who refuse to engage in the same practice. Others, such as the following interviewee, claim that promoting your achievements and skills is a waste of resources and, therefore, an unethical act.

My prior achievements already boosted the bottom line of the company, and they will not have a bigger effect if I go out and tell the whole world about them. My sales figures from last year aren't going to double just because I make people aware of them. By using my time to promote what I did last year, instead of working on the here and now, I would be wasting the company's resources.

I have a slightly different view. Like every employee, your mission is to add as much value to your organization as possible (without inflicting harm on the outside world, of course.) This is the only way to justify your salary and ensure that the transaction between you and your employer remains fair. If you were a manual laborer, you could maximize your added value by remaining silent and simply doing what you were told. You would hardly need to advertise yourself. But as a manager, things are a bit more complicated. In order to do the best job you are capable of, you need more than just a drill or a jackhammer. You need a sufficient budget, enough subordinates, time, and a host of other resources. As Napoleon Bonaparte said, "Ability is of little account without opportunity," and you, too, need an opportunity to make the most out of your abilities and create added value.

If you don't show people what you are capable of doing, you will not be given the opportunity you deserve and will underachieve. If, God forbid, everybody in the organization adopts the "silence is golden" attitude, refusing to talk about their achievements or potential, the entity will suffer immensely. Top management won't be able to properly allocate limited resources; they'll put too much in the hands of ineffective managers, while starving the competent business units. Consequently, the shareholders will lose money, the consumers/clients will pay too much for inferior products, and the company's future will be jeopardized. Does this sound ethical?

Do not operate under the mistaken assumption that "good results speak for themselves." In a small company where the boss can see every result produced by his eight people, this may be true. But in a giant, turbulent, and ever-changing organization, you often have to put a microphone in front of your results to help them speak a little louder. Otherwise, their voices will get lost in the chaos. Over the next six chapters, we will see how you can do this in a just, fair, and dignified manner.

CHAPTER 12

Gaining Freedom by Inspiring Confidence

In both Chapter 6 and 7, we saw how the trust of your coworkers can cut your workload by boosting your freedom to operate as you see fit. Since this concept is so critical for efficiency, we will analyze it in greater detail in this chapter. To be more precise, we will see how you can go beyond gaining the trust of coworkers and inspire a sense of confidence in them.

To trust someone means to believe that the person will keep his promise and treat you fairly. Confidence, on the other hand, is a broader concept. It denotes both trust as well as a belief that the other person is capable of making the right decisions. For instance, a close friend of mine, who is an avid investor in the stock market, suggested on many occasions that we open a joint account. I have known this person for almost twenty years and never doubted his integrity. In other words, I trust him. The problem is that I don't see how someone sitting alone in front of a computer can outsmart the pros with a wealth of information at their fingertips. Put another way, I do not have confidence in his ability to manage my money well. Therefore, I chose to invest in a mutual fund, where I think the portfolio managers are both trustworthy and competent.

Below, we will see how you can gain the confidence of coworkers by demonstrating that you are both trustworthy and capable of making the right decisions. Your goal is to give them the peace of mind to leave you completely free, so you can operate in the most efficient manner.

As an added bonus, these strategies will also help you get more credit for the results that you produce. If people trust you enough to let you make critical decisions on your own, they will also be more inclined to give you the credit you deserve. If, however, they feel that you cannot do a proper job alone, they will underestimate your contributions to the outcome. What happened to me under the supervision of my first boss is a good example. The newly appointed R&D coordinator invited all the brand managers to lunch, where we would give a brief presentation about consumer habits. Since my boss had to attend another meeting, she sent me to represent our product. However, she was so certain that I would mess up that she asked another senior brand manager to jump in and help me when necessary.

Luckily, all went well. Later, the R&D coordinator sent individual e-mails to thank the brand managers for their time. Guess what my boss did when she received an e-mail where the coordinator praised my presentation. She immediately called the other senior brand manager and thanked her for her help—without even asking me what actually happened during the meeting. In reality, the senior brand manager did not move a finger. The rationale of my boss was simple: since, in her mind, I was unable to do a good job on my own, someone must have helped me. So I didn't deserve much credit for the result. If, however, I had been able to inspire confidence in my boss, she wouldn't have interfered by asking someone else to help me, and she would also have given me the respect I deserved.

Know your numbers

An experienced supermarket manager I used to work with always said, "You can only manage what you can measure." Without a doubt, quantifying results, objectives, and future projections is a big part of every executive's life. Therefore, we think highly of managers who are aware of key numbers. Few things are as impressive as a salesman who can quote from memory how many units he sold from each of a dozen products and how much more he must move to meet his quotas.

> I have a love for numbers because of my background in engineering, so I calculate a lot of statistics and can quote them off the top of my head. Although this doesn't make me a better manager than someone who reads them from a spreadsheet, it always charms people. The coordinator recently saw me in the hallway and asked me how sales were going. When I quoted her the exact figure for the different product lines, she almost fainted. Hard to believe that you can get so much credit for knowing a handful of numbers, but it works every time. I guess people somehow assume that if you know key numbers, such as profits or shipments, you must also know how to improve them.

As the interviewee points out, knowing key numbers by heart somehow creates the impression that you also have control over those very parameters. Perhaps, this shows that you took the time to think about them in great detail. Therefore, accessing the same figures from a handheld computer or ultra-light laptop—even if you can do so at blinding speeds—won't have the same impact.

Knowing key numbers is even more critical when dealing with top managers because they tend to ask questions when you don't have any documents with you. They quiz you in elevators, hallways, or during business dinners. Since you will only have a handful of opportunities to talk to these people, every occasion can make a big difference. Always take the time to go over important figures in reports, e-mails, and presentations. Underline or flag them so you can skim those numbers quickly before meetings or discussions with top managers. The above interviewee uses another great tactic.

> Carry the most important numbers with you. I produce a weekly page by printing key data from our Web site and always keep this page handy. This enables me to do three things. First, I go over these numbers on the train, so by Tuesday night I often know them by heart. Second, if my boss or his bosses need a summary, I just give them the appropriate page. This scores a home run. Imagine expecting to get only a ballpark number after you storm into someone's room before a meeting, but getting this perfect summary instead. Finally, this cheat sheet is a huge help in meetings. Suppose a subject comes up in a meeting unexpectedly and nobody has precise numbers on it. Pulling up a sheet with the most up to date figures and reading the numbers to the third decimal point knocks them out. People think that you either brilliantly predicted that the subject would come up, or that you are fully prepared to talk about every single issue. Regardless, it gets you a standing ovation.

Whether you use such a cheat sheet is up to you, but you will derive a huge benefit from knowing important figures. Read them before going to bed, write them on your bathroom mirror, or do whatever used to work for you while studying for the history exam, but learn your numbers. Posting important figures and charts on your wall can also help. In addition to making it easier to memorize the data, this will show that you are really into your job.

Know the lingo

In addition to key figures, we want experts to know the jargon in their fields. Therefore, doctors, engineers, auto mechanics, and even plumbers throw all sorts of terms at us, even when they can explain the same concepts with much simpler phrases. A physician I talked to while working on this book said,

> When you go to the doctor and understand everything he says, you'll probably doubt his knowledge. People are so used to being confused by medical jargon in a doctor's office that when it doesn't happen, they think that either the doctor isn't proficient or doesn't take them seriously. To satisfy this need, we tell you to reduce your LDL or risk a myocardial infarction, when we could simply say that you may get a heart attack unless you lower your cholesterol.

Furthermore, the jargon works as a membership pass to the club. An advertiser must talk about such things as the "big idea," or at least be able to respond to these terms when others throw them at him. If top officials are unfamiliar with the lingo and customers or other outsiders use those terms, your knowledge will become even more valuable. You will not only translate the foreign language for the top officials, but also show to outsiders that your company understands the slang and that it should be taken seriously.

Keep in mind, though, that excessive use of specialized terms will get on everyone's nerves. People who try to demonstrate how much they know are universally disliked; we all take great pleasure in seeing these know-it-alls trip up. Instead of using the lingo all the time, resort to it when there really is not a simpler alternative. Few people will be irritated when you say "penetration" instead of "Percentage of retailers carrying the product," because the latter is too long. This is another reason it pays to know the lingo well: the more terms you know, the better you can spot proper uses for them and show your knowledge without annoying people.

It is also important to explain the terms. This will convince your audience that the jargon is not intended to make them look ignorant. But do not insult the expertise of the professionals during this process by explaining concepts that are second nature to these people. A good solution is to clarify, as opposed to explaining. A comment such as "Just to clarify: we use the term 'penetration' to refer to the ratio of retailers who sell our brand, as opposed to the percentage of consumers who use the product" is much better than a straightforward lecture. It educates the novice without insulting the expertise of the professionals in the audience.

To be able to accomplish this, you must first know the lingo, of course. Although learning the key terms requires only minimal effort, very few managers take the time to do so. Start by asking questions in low-risk environments. If your boss uses a new term, make note of it and ask him to explain it when the two of you are alone. More than likely, he will be glad that you acknowledge his expertise. Similarly, ask questions to colleagues when a large audience is not watching.

The best way to learn the lingo, however, is to get a good reference guide, such as a financial or marketing dictionary, and study it. The ones published by industry associations tend to be best. You will be surprised how few terms there actually are and how fast you can learn them. Just as one can appear to be an authority in French cuisine by memorizing the names of 15 unusual dishes and a dozen expensive wines, many experts have an "exotic vocabulary" that doesn't exceed thirty words. Do not let these people outshine you only because you're too lazy to invest a day or two to learn a few words.

Know the news

Society wants to hear major developments from the most prominent figures. For example, after a major earthquake, especially if there is lack of reliable information, the Prime Minister or President is expected to get in front of the news cameras right away. Similarly, most employees expect to get the first confirmation of a merger from the CEO. If the leader acts too late, allowing rumors to spread too far before he speaks, he will give the impression that things are slipping away from him. On the other hand, being the first to make a serious announcement sends the message that the leader is on top of the matter. Particularly if he can reveal new information during his statement, the leader shows that he has a firm grip on the situation.

As a manager, you will probably be the most prominent figure regarding something, no matter what your role is. So, if you want people to know that you are in charge, even if it is only of managing a brand of ballpoint pen, be the first to discover and announce key events in your area. Give an added insight that they cannot get elsewhere. Like a good journalist, go beyond "what," "where," and "when." Also cover "why" and "what next."

If Congress increases taxes on your product category, for instance, be ready to explain the real motivation behind this move and how it will impact the market. If most people have already heard about the news, providing this further insight becomes even more critical. Otherwise, you will appear to be merely repeating what you saw on the Internet and look helpless. Remember that most crises will give you an opportunity to shine by showing that you were two steps ahead of the curve. In other words, proving that things had been under control all along.

The bigger the event, the more senior people will get in touch with you directly to get the "inside scoop," and the more will be at stake for you. When a couple of consumers get sick from the soft drink you are responsible for, the probability of receiving a call from the CEO or plant manager is very high. While it is often impossible to obtain perfect information in such a crisis, find out as many details and confirm the news from as many sources as you can. Try to learn how many people are having symptoms, where they are treated, where they bought the product, and exactly what time they reported to the medical facilities.

Although some of this may not appear critical to you, someone else could find it very useful. When the CEO calls and realizes that you've got such information, he will be greatly relieved. Do you remember the prosecutor who drowns people in endless questions due to his borderline paranoia? Well, in times of crisis, everyone becomes a bit paranoid. So the more questions you can answer, the better. In addition, the CEO can direct other key managers to you, since you have the most comprehensive facts and figures. This way, you can control the information flow and optimize the use of resources, while improving your image. So dig out the details.

However, never communicate rumors as facts. Remember that nothing is worth risking your credibility for. If the rumor is worth people's attention, despite being unproven, say so or no one will hear the next time you cry wolf. Since conservatism is the hallmark of leaders, being overcautious with public statements will only lift up your public profile.

To access key information efficiently, set aside a full day to perform a very thorough search on the Internet. Look for sites that provide e-mail news alerts. If good news alerts are unavailable and you must regularly scan several sites, try to share the work with coworkers or subordinates. I met two salespeople in the financial services industry who divided up the major financial sites. After going through the headlines every morning, they get together and exchange information. In addition, make the most out of the information systems in your own organization. Get on other departments' distribution lists and learn to use internal databases such as sales tracking tools. The bottom line: know more about what is going in your area and know it sooner than anyone else.

Know what your people are up to

The most important and often the most expensive resource that is entrusted to a manager is his subordinates. Therefore, managers are first and foremost expected to be in charge of their own people. Unless you can demonstrate effective control of your subordinates, you can never hope to give the impression that you are on top of the situation.

As I said in Chapter 10, being detached from the daily tasks of your people can create embarrassing situations. Promising to submit a document to the CEO in thirty minutes, only to find out that it will take your assistant two hours to get it, will devastate your image. This shows clearly that you are unaware of what is going on under your nose. If you cannot properly manage someone who is obliged to obey your orders, how will you manage others who don't have to even listen to you? One interviewee favors a very structured approach to avoid such blunders.

> I have four subordinates, and sometimes it gets very difficult for me to keep an eye on what is sent to clients. We had a lot of problems in the past with the wrong information getting out. I recently sat down with my people and had a meeting to agree on what can be communicated without my knowledge. We made a list of things that I must see before they get out, things that I don't need to see, and things that I want to see only if I am in the office. I am no longer caught off guard when a client calls about a file that has my name at the bottom. In the

past, my response would be "Did I prepare that file?" and that looked really bad.

Whether you want to be that strict about the information flow is a personal decision, but the interviewee has a great point: You must know what your people communicate to the world.

Speak with one voice

Synchronizing the verbal messages that your team sends out presents an even bigger challenge than coordinating written information flow. One of the most important functions of a manager is to unite people behind a cause. This process must start with your subordinates. Quite simply, if your own people do not buy in to your arguments, nobody will. You and your staff must speak with one voice. Superiors should walk away with the same impression of your strategies and worldview regardless of whether they talk to you or your subordinates.

This is easier said than done. Your people cannot provide a transcript of every comment they make in a meeting or send a carbon copy of conversations. Besides, even if they give an honest account, you will rarely get a good sense of what they are communicating to the world. Gauging the impression we leave on others is an extremely rare skill. To avoid sending inconsistent signals to the world, you must identify the discrepancies between what you and your people say and bridge the gap with one of the three tactics we will see below.

Although direct communication is crucial for identifying discrepancies, it is rarely enough. By all means ask your people where they disagree with you and let them freely state their views. But do not stop there. Observe them in front of others, because they may not be fully aware of what they are communicating. A subordinate may officially agree with your position but have minor doubts and therefore come across as skeptical when promoting the game plan. Let your people speak regularly in meetings, and listen to them from the stands. This will enhance their skills and provide a great opportunity to see where the two of you might be playing different tunes.

Once you identify any dissonance, you can change your subordinate's views, change your own views, or agree to keep the matter private. Do not rely excessively on the first tactic by adopting what one interviewee calls the "gorilla approach." If you forcefully silence the opposition of your people to present a coherent picture, they will start to say one thing when you are around and another when you cannot hear them. This demonstrates a total loss of control over your subordinates and will harm your image much more than respectfully disagreeing. It is better to bend a little and occasionally accept the opposing view to preserve a balance in the relationship.

If the difference cannot be resolved in one of these two ways, the right solution might be to agree to disagree behind closed doors. Just as you wouldn't announce every dispute in a marriage to the neighbors, some differences with your coworkers or subordinates are better kept private.

When people ask us what we think about the desktop printer market, we talk about many things. One of these is wireless connectivity between printers and devices like handheld computers. Unfortunately, my assistant and I disagree about this little detail and used to send conflicting messages. What I realized is that people don't care about wireless connectivity like we do. We eat, sleep, and breathe this thing and analyze every detail, but others don't. When people ask about market trends, they just want a broad overview, which you can easily give without talking about wireless connectivity. So we simply agreed not to bring it up unless people want to hear about it. Since then, maybe 5% of the people did. If a disagreement can remain an internal matter, why make it public or force a resolution?

Never blame your people for mistakes

Never, ever blame your people for a failure. As we saw, it is your responsibility to select, motivate, and coordinate the work of the people who report to you. Therefore, blaming them will only be an admission of the fact that you lost control over what you have been put in charge of.

Naturally you will disagree with employees at times, and may even have to fire someone. If you must go down this path, do so in the most professional manner, or your image can suffer more than that of the person you are firing. Most managers badmouth a fired worker, thinking that this is a chance to lay the blame for past mistakes on him. They think that since the employee was let go, the accusations will be credible. Unfortunately, it doesn't work that way.

First, no one will want to work for you after hearing your degrading comments. Although the employee will be gone, your attitude will send a horrible message to prospective subordinates. Second, such comments raise serious questions about your managerial aptitude. If the person was so bad, why did you hire him? More importantly, if he made so many mistakes, why didn't you step in earlier to prevent damage to the company? Be a professional and do not talk about the past. If confronted, say that you respect the person, but that your styles were different.

Use your crystal ball wisely

One of the most delicate situations you can find yourself in is having to forecast a parameter that you cannot control, such as the size of the disposable paper cup market next year or the growth in credit card debt. The problem is that those who ask such questions will rarely be aware of all the factors involved in the forecast and grossly oversimplify the process of predicting the future. Remember that as long as you are performing a managerial function, the people around you will always be unaware of the complexities of your job.

Furthermore, the world is changing so rapidly that even the best experts can no longer foresee the future. In January 2002, fifty-four economists working for the world's most prestigious financial institutions were asked to estimate the U.S. economic growth during the fourth quarter of 2001. These experts provided an average estimate of—1.1%. When a group of authorities is asked such a question, you expect roughly half of them to underestimate and half of them to overestimate the variable. This would mean that, on average, the group tends to be correct. If most forecasts are under or over the real number, you conclude that the group did a poor job.

When the actual figure of 0.2% came out, fifty-one of the experts realized that they had underestimated the strength of the economy, while one of them was dead on and only two were above the real number. Keep in mind that these people are paid to do nothing but forecast economic parameters. In addition, the estimates were collected after the end of the fourth quarter (but shortly before official figures were released), so technically this is not even a forecast. If they are doing such a horrible job with all the data at their disposal, how can you expect to do much better about something as obscure as the size of the paper cup market?

Unfortunately, trying to communicate the impossibility of the task is not a proper solution. Although nobody may be able to forecast the parameter at hand, you cannot use that as an excuse if the variable will profoundly impact you. You will only be seen as lacking direction and as a victim of fate, as opposed to the master of your destiny. On the other hand, simply going with your hunch and hoping that you will be right in the end is hardly a better idea. Few will give you the credit you deserve when you are right, but most people will not hesitate to blame you if you are way off, and you very well may be. So what is the solution?

i) Present a scenario analysis, instead of numbers pulled out of thin air

Your top priority is to steer the discussion away from a single figure towards a scenario or situation analysis. First, this gives you a chance to demonstrate an understanding of the subject matter and gain respect, even if your estimates turn out to be incorrect. When you are asked how much the shampoo market will grow and reply with a single number such as "3%," it will look like you are trying your hand at the roulette table. Even if the prediction is dead on, people probably will not be impressed because they will be unaware of the detailed analysis behind it.

If, however, you present a clear scenario analysis, telling people how much the market could grow under each different condition and explain why, they will realize that you are doing a lot more than simply graphing the past and extrapolating a line. Furthermore, you will appear to have a grasp of all possible outcomes and seem ready to respond to changing circumstances. You may be asked which scenario is most likely. But if you do a good job of explaining your rationale, you will look in charge of the situation even if your final estimate turns out to be incorrect.

Second, a scenario analysis is more quotable, and thus more useful to others, than a single number. People rarely ask your forecast because they are desperate for an exact figure. Usually they just want to get a few bits of information that will make them appear knowledgeable. A number in isolation will never serve that purpose no matter how well thought out it is. While the sales manager could get away with saying "the market will grow by 3%" without explaining why, the production manager cannot. The sales manager's expertise will lend credibility to a figure pulled out of thin air. But the production manager must explain why 3% is reasonable.

An explanation of why 3% is more likely, as opposed to 4%, which is only feasible if raw material prices drop and the growth in rural areas continues at the same pace, will make the production manager look much more informed. This will also ensure that more people in the organization get exposed to key information and make better decisions. Finally, a scenario analysis will show how difficult it is to forecast the future, easing the pressure to put a single number on the table.

> In the tire business, one of the critical factors effecting sales is the SUV to automobile ownership ratio. And one of the critical things that determines this ratio is the price of oil. Because people are not aware of this relationship, they expect me to magically forecast tire sales by sector, which no one can do with great accuracy. So when asked for an estimate, I first explain what factors I feed into my models and present different scenarios based on oil prices. Once people see the role of oil, they usually stop pressing me for a single number, because anyone who ever drove a car or truck knows how fickle oil prices are.

ii) Focus on the indisputable

As we saw, most people will be more interested in understanding the forces that impact your organization than a single number that predicts the future. However, they may not know how to phrase such a query and resort to the more conventional "what's your estimate for next year's numbers?" type of question. So do not automatically assume that the other person is looking for a number to plug into a budget. He may not need a forecast at all. A thoughtful analysis of the big stories driving the market, past trends, and a few interesting figures will often do the job. Needless to say, such an analysis is also risk free. Easy to remember but fascinating facts and figures will provide the most useful ammunition to your colleagues, because they will make them appear informed with minimal effort. An amazing piece of data such as "more supermarkets were opened last year than during the past nine years combined" is easy to recall and highly quotable. Expert opinions can also work, provided that you summarize them in a few sentences and make them interesting. If colleagues continue to insist on a numeric forecast after hearing all of this, the battle is still not lost.

iii) If you must provide a forecast, at least make it a range or direction

Although the above steps will reduce the pressure to provide a numerical estimate, sometimes it may be inevitable. Those steps should, however, enable you to communicate the difficulty of the task and make it acceptable to provide a range, instead of a single number. To further reinforce this message, show how the parameter moves wildly and why a specific estimate such as "3%" is unrealistic. Even if the other party does not understand statistical concepts such as standard deviation, a simple five-year chart of past trends will prove how unpredictable the variable is.

Sometimes you will be tempted to take a risk by giving a specific estimate, feeling that your image will get a big boost if you are dead on. Resist the temptation and go with a range such as "3 to 5%" or direction such as "significantly higher" or "down quite a bit," without specifying by how much. As statisticians say, it is better to be approximately right than to be precisely wrong. If you confidently provide an exact estimate and end up way off, you will look like you do not even understand the risks in your area.

A trick that can make it permissible to give a direction instead of a point estimate is to throw in added parameters. While it may sound naïve to just say "We expect SUV tire sales to go up" when asked for the number of units for next year, it is often OK to say "We are predicting an increase in luxury SUV sales, especially in the Midwest. This, combined with smaller rebates on sports cars and a decline in the share of Asian auto makers, leads us to predict higher sales for SUV tires." Although you are predicting more parameters, you can chose what variables to add into the equation and can therefore pick the safest ones. This tactic is a favorite of top managers and is frequently employed when confronting the press or the investor community.

If you will get emotionally involved, do so in private

In Chapter 7, we saw why appearing stressed, overworked, or frustrated to gain the sympathy of top managers is a bad idea. It almost always backfires and, instead of making things easier, it provides a legitimate excuse for superiors to get more involved in your life.

In fact, it is not only the expression of negative emotions that will hurt your image. Displays of excessive excitement or joy will also work against you. We want leaders to be, first and foremost, in charge of their own emotions. We do not wish to see them depressed during crises or ecstatic after a victory. They must balance extreme sentiments by showing us the brighter side of things when we lose hope and bring us back to reality when our egos grow too much. Leaders are expected to remain calm and not get carried away in either situation.

Keep this principle in mind even if you are not responsible for anyone who looks to you for a sense of direction. Remember that top managers use your ability to keep your feelings in check as a proxy for how well you can control the other variables of success. So if you must punch the wall or pop a champagne cork, wait until you go home.

5 Key Points You Should Remember

- Make sure that you can quote at least some key facts and figures from memory
- Be the first to know and distribute the major news about your area of expertise
- Make sure that you and your subordinates communicate the same message to the world
- Never blame your subordinates in front of other people
- When asked to make a prediction, focus on factors beyond the hard figures

CHAPTER 13

Showing How Busy You Are

Most people, particularly those you are likely to meet in business life, are conditioned to associate activity with productivity. The constant ringing of the cash register in a grocery store or long lines in front of a bakery produce an image of profitability and success. We are so accustomed to drawing a link between volume and value that few of us realize how the discounts of the grocer or baker might actually be eating into the profits.

In his book *The Art of the Deal*, Donald Trump explains how he told his workers to convert "two acres of nearly vacant property into the most active construction site in the history of the world" for a visit by the Holiday Inn Board of Directors. In Trump's words, "What the bulldozers and dump trucks did wasn't important, I said, so long as they did a lot of it. If they got some actual work accomplished, all the better, but if necessary, he should have the bulldozers dig up dirt from one side of the site and dump it on the other...It looked as if we were in the midst of building the Grand Coulee Dam...These distinguished corporate leaders looked on, some of them visibly awed...The board walked away from the site absolutely convinced that it was the perfect choice."

As this anecdote shows, subjective perceptions heavily impact even the most critical business decisions. The ethical values of Mr. Trump are questionable, but the good news is that there are much more decent ways to show people how much you are doing. This chapter is not about making people think that you are working when in reality you are playing video games on your computer. My goal is to help you demonstrate the kinds of things you do that may not be easily visible from the outside. As I explained in Chapter 5, certain duties are less visible than others. Continuing on the previous analogy, it would be unfair for the nearby grocery store to get more respect just because you are doing most of your business online, and thus have many fewer people walking into your shop. The online purchases that may be invisible to the outsiders must be somehow promoted to put things on equal footing.

There are many advantages to subtly demonstrating how busy you are. First, the inflow of excessive work will slow down significantly if people realize how much you have on your plate. To maximize speed and quality, top managers strive to retain some balance in the workloads of the people under them. This may sound ridiculous, given the gross injustice around you. But keep in mind that the workload distribution in your area may appear fair from the perspective of top management. Some people might be much better than you are in showing how much work they have. If that is the case, this chapter will help you to level the playing field.

Second, your results will be appreciated much more, because it is human nature to treasure the products of great toil. The better people understand that the new design or advertising campaign involved substantial work, the more value they will attach to it. Finally, heavy activity on your end will work as a natural troublemaker repellant. These individuals instinctively know that busy people are harder to exploit and prefer to select idle managers.

However, keep in mind that you wish to display a state of controlled and productive busyness. I am not talking about being overwhelmed here. There is a big difference between the two. As we saw, the second will only lead to loss of freedom. You must communicate that you are working a lot because you want to, not because the crushing demands of the job leave no other choice. The following suggestions were formulated with this subtle distinction in mind.

Show them the complexities in your job

Make every effort to show the complexities of your job to other managers. It is natural to oversimplify what we know very little about, and managers often know very little about each other's jobs. As a result, people severely underestimate what the finance guy has to do to calculate cost estimates or how difficult it is to keep a factory running 360 days a year.

Sadly, the more attention you pay to details, the less your work may be appreciated. For example, the flawless work of the programmer may lead the CEO to conclude that "the Web page is running alone anyway" and prompt him to replace the programmer with a cheaper person. You are particularly vulnerable in a support or safety related function because, the better you do these jobs, the less people will see what you do. A bank in Brazil, for instance, fired half of the security guards, because "they didn't have to do anything in years." Not surprisingly, the bank got robbed the following week when there were no longer enough guards to scare the criminals. Legal positions or liaison functions where you ensure compliance with regulations can also be very slippery, because when these jobs are done well, nothing will happen.

Your goal is not to turn people into experts about your job. In fact, I strongly advise against this, as it will restrict your freedom by creating "pseudo supervisors." You simply need to make them aware that there are complicated processes behind the intellectual or physical results that you produce. This will demonstrate both how critical your role is and how busy you are.

A good starting point is to break down medium and long-term projects into smaller bits when communicating budgets, deadlines, and the like. When the IT person mentioned above is asked for a deadline to redesign the Web site, his first instinct may be to provide only a date, so as not to confuse his technically illiterate coworkers. This, however, makes the process look too easy and unimportant. On the other hand, a seven-step action plan summing up each stage in one sentence will show that the redesign isn't a walk in the park. It is even better to show people how those steps will impact them. For example, indicate that e-mail might go off for an hour during the server update for the redesign. This proves that you are making big changes that will have external consequences. We will return to this point in Chapter 19.

Educational workshops or entertaining visits to a facility are other ways to communicate the complexities of your job. These work much better than a long, boring conference because people are more likely to listen if they can benefit or have fun in the process. Here is how a manager in charge of calculating asset valuations for a financial institution does it.

> People always ask me to send them figures that they could download on their own from the database. But most don't know how, because our system isn't very user-friendly. Although I can easily send the numbers, I prefer to educate people. I organize monthly workshops and personally teach higher ranked guys on their own PCs. This saves me time in the long run but, more importantly, it makes people understand that I do a lot more than adding columns in spreadsheets. There is a tendency to look down on what my department does, and I must show people that it is not as easy as it appears. Although in those workshops I don't try to teach them what I do for a living, in the end they say "Man, I had no idea how much information you guys put out." They leave with a better appreciation of what we do. As a result, they respect us a lot more and put less pressure on us.

A trip to a specialized facility can have the same impact. It is hard to see a petrochemical plant or a giant shipment center and not be impressed by the people in charge of such a huge operation. If you work in a place like this, host one of the meetings and give a brief tour of the facility afterwards. Do not forget to throw in some amazing facts and figures about your operation. Not only will visitors be impressed, but they will share these numbers with others and advertise you.

Keep in mind that even if your position isn't very technical or unique, others will still be ignorant about what you do. Therefore you always have room for educating colleagues. A brand manager could show a compilation of funny TV ads from around the world, followed by a brief explanation of the steps involved in making advertising spots. If you never do anything that others may find interesting, just invite other departments over for a small Christmas celebration. Introducing the major players in your department and very briefly explaining what they do is often enough to make your coworkers realize how many complex tasks your division handles.

In short, do not confuse colleagues with unnecessary details about your job, but do not oversimplify your function, either. As Albert Einstein said, "Everything should be made as simple as possible, but not simpler."

Have brief and frequent public meetings

Meetings are inherently inefficient and often lead to a lot of waste. But since they are inevitable, you may as well get the most publicity out of them by maximizing their visibility. (Please note that this brief section addresses how to impress the outsiders who are not part of the meeting. How to handle the actual participants will be discussed in great detail in Chapter 16.) This will clearly communicate how busy you are. Although everyone knows that little gets done in meetings, people realize that one often walks away from these gatherings with a long to-do list. Managers who are seen in lots of meetings are therefore considered very busy and active.

To amplify this effect, hold brief and frequent meeting in visible locations such as your desk or a central conference room, ideally with glass doors. Since participants won't be as comfortable in such places, these meetings also last shorter. This requires talking again soon, leading to a series of short and efficient meetings with great publicity value. Finally, such gatherings show that you are getting out of your corner and reaching out to other parts of the company.

Whenever possible, meet colleagues at your desk or walk over to their offices instead of waiting for the next marathon meeting. Talking at your desk gives you maximum visibility within your own department and is particularly effective in impressing your immediate boss. Meetings at the desks of colleagues, on the other hand, provide more flexibility. While it is very difficult to kick someone out of your own room or cubicle, it is much easier to walk out of their territory.

To improve the visibility of larger meetings, use conference rooms on your floor and avoid daylong off-site events. When you must meet with customers or suppliers, invite them to your territory, as opposed to going to theirs, where none of your coworkers can see you. When outsiders come over, serve them well and try to coordinate the transportation. Arrange a room where they can work in peace before or after the meeting. In short, give them a reason to come to you.

Make the most out of business trips

In an ideal world, nobody would care about the number of hours we spend in the office, how we dress, or whether we put people's names on the cover or the last page of reports. Unfortunately, we live in a world where these things matter. In this world, being away on a business trip is usually associated with slacking off. Visiting another city or country and dining out on the organization's budget sounds exciting, at least in theory. People tend to assume that you will be taking advantage of the opportunity, instead of working while away. This, however, is not inevitable. In fact, a well-planned business trip can be a great way to show how busy you are.

The first rule is to not disappear altogether while you are away. At least, send a few e-mails every day, which can be composed and saved as drafts before your trip. Saving important messages as drafts, then reading them once more during your trip prior to hitting the send button, will also enhance the quality of your written communication. Perhaps the worst e-mails I've written were those that I composed and sent in a hurry at midnight before flying out to a meeting the next morning. Messages sent from outside the office are also ideal for introducing people to controversial ideas. By asking to talk about the matter when you return, you can keep the issue open for an extended period of time and ensure that the other side doesn't prematurely reject the concept. We will return to this topic in Chapter 20. If e-mail is not an option, you can send a few notes through secretaries. Whether in a client's office or a conference, you can probably find someone to fax or e-mail a brief note to your coworkers on your behalf.

Also, check your voice mail and return important calls—preferably later in the day. If you are still working at 7 PM during a business trip, you may wish to subtly get this message across, because most coworkers will likely expect you to be at the hotel bar or the swimming pool by that time. But do not inflate expectations by leaving a greeting message on your phone saying "I'll check voice mail occasionally during next week." Instead, surprise people with a returned call when they weren't expecting you to respond until after your trip.

Another great way to show how active you have been is to bring back something useful, such as samples or hardcopies from presentations. When I was a brand manager, I would pick up interesting products from supermarkets in other countries to share with colleagues. Even if their value is limited, these gestures demonstrate that you were thinking about your job while away, just as a gift picked up for your spouse will demonstrate that you were thinking about him or her.

Bringing back useful contact information by initiating relationships on behalf of colleagues is even better. You probably know the kind of people and information your coworkers are interested in. Keep your eyes open to obtain business cards and try to talk to the prospective contact to get him interested in meeting your colleague. This kind act, which often takes just a few minutes, will lift up your image both within your organization and in the other entity.

Finally, you can send out a brief but interesting e-mail about your trip.

If, for example, you observe an intelligent use of new handheld computers on the factory floor, other factory supervisors might find this information useful. Again, this must not be too time-consuming. If you have something good to say, you only need a few sentences and maybe a contact name.

When things are getting out of hand, consider this as a last resort

When an organization is going through tough times and the pace of change is dizzying, information flow can be seriously hampered. If the company is fighting to stay alive and gets reorganized every month, top officials worry about saving their own skins and often lose touch with subordinates. Consequently, fairness will fly out the window. In such situations, a lot of good managers can be fired, while others with barely anything to do might hold on to their jobs. If you end up in such a situation, you may find the following interview valuable. This strategy is indeed risky, as well as ethically questionable. Nevertheless, some of the people I talked to believe that the gross injustices that may arise during restructuring operations could justify such a move; obviously, it is a personal decision. Furthermore, your subordinates or coworkers might resort to such tactics, and it is always better to be aware of what is happening around you.

> A guy I work with believed that he'd be laid off in the restructuring. He kept telling me that his boss had no idea how critical his function was, since everyone was taking the division's smooth performance for granted. To make people realize his worth, he decided to take a week off in the busiest season. He announced on a Friday that he couldn't come in next week due to a family reason. As expected, there was chaos. They had to call him every day and even asked him to come in couple of times because it was impossible to get things done without him. This, of course, was exactly what he wanted. By announcing his absence just three days in advance, he ensured that nobody had time to learn his job. The boss then realized how critical this guy was, and he kept his job when tons of people got fired.

A milder version of this strategy is to encourage colleagues to call you while you are on vacation, as opposed to asking one person to cover everything you do. If your contributions are not appreciated, do not invest a lot of time to train someone to do your job while you are out. Instead of being grateful, people may conclude that, since operations weren't impacted during your absence, they can do without you. Given that these individuals failed to see what you normally do, it is unlikely that they will notice the extra trouble you went through prior to your vacation. If they have to constantly call you, however, it will become blatantly obvious that you are needed.

3 Key Points You Should Remember

- Make people aware of the "invisible obstacles" in your job
- Hold your meetings out in the open whenever possible
- Do not lose touch with the office during business trips

CHAPTER 14

Beating the Last Quarter with Ease

It never ceases to amaze me how the most profound philosophical conversations emerge when you least intend to have them. Although I tried to stay as focused as possible during the interviews for this book, the discussions would often drift into extraneous subjects ranging from the meaning of life to American foreign policy. Naturally, the best conversations took place when I could least afford them. At one such moment—while operating under tremendous pressure to finish the manuscript for this book—I decided to meet briefly with a brilliant manager. The conversation was supposed to be about managing customers and was scheduled to last thirty minutes. Instead, we spent two hours discussing everything else on earth, including love. At one point, he said,

> Men are competitive by nature and often make the mistake of competing with others when they should be competing with themselves. This is nowhere as evident as in relationships. Most men mistakenly think that they are in some sort of contest with all the other guys who loved that woman before and try to love her more than those men did. But they are missing the point. Every relationship is so different that this would be a totally unfair comparison. Women intuitively know this and will not judge you against the other guys. What they want is that you simply love them more than you did yesterday. Failing to see this, most men give the woman all they have right away, and then they cannot keep up the same level of passion. No wonder the biggest complaint among women is "He doesn't love me as much as he used to."

What makes this analysis unique is that not only the phenomenon, but also the dynamics behind it are analyzed so brilliantly. When judging if we are loved enough, we have no reasonable yardstick other than how much we were loved by the same person yesterday. Perhaps this is why it feels so great in the beginning; even a little love is infinitely more than nothing at all.

Just as we cannot compare different lovers, we cannot reasonably measure one manager against his predecessors or against others in similar positions. As we saw, the complexity of large organizations makes it very hard to judge even one manager, let alone compare two vastly different individuals working under ever-changing conditions. So we mostly evaluate managers by how they fare versus their own past. Learning how to beat the last month, quarter, or year with the least effort will therefore greatly reduce your workload. In this chapter, you will find the elements of this fine art.

Step 1: Select an environment where you can outperform predecessors

Above, I pointed out that it is rarely sensible to compare a manager to others, including his predecessors. I wish I could also say that you will only work with sensible people, but I cannot. Unfortunately some superiors will compare you against forerunners even when circumstances are immensely different. To hedge against this possibility, start by selecting projects, tasks, and, if possible, even jobs that you can do better than your predecessors did.

Factors that determine the difficulty of beating the past can be separated into two categories: the previous person who performed the task, and the constraints such as market conditions and budgets. Try to get assignments where the previous person failed to take advantage of the opportunities or where new opportunities are sprouting that were previously unavailable. If both factors are present at the same time, you may have a great future ahead of you.

Conditions improving	OK	Best place to be
Conditions deteriorating	Worst place to be	OK
	Predecessor did a good job	**Predecessor did a poor job**

In my earlier experience as a brand manager, for example, my boss was so inefficient that after she left—when I had to do both my own job and hers—I was able to do better than the two of us combined. If she had been a great manager, this would have been simply impossible.

Before going further, I must warn you against overestimating so-called revolutionary changes, which are in fact, nothing more than window-dressing. Since change is such a buzzword, we see a lot of useless or even harmful change in large organizations. It is common to dismiss a department head to cover up deeper issues or to buy new computers instead of teaching employees how to do their jobs. Since these minor fixes are often sold as major transformations, you may be lured in to replace a deposed ex-manager in what is now "a different and exciting place to be." In reality, little may have changed and the situation may in fact be deteriorating, with most employees losing a bit more hope after every reform.

Also, do not accept a job or a duty only because you believe that things cannot get worse. The problems just may be too severe. A complete lack of trust in a department or product, subordinates who have given up all hope, or a lack of organizational expertise against giant competitors are issues you don't want to grapple with. Even if things cannot be worse, probably nothing short of a total turnaround would satisfy your superiors, which may be impossible under such circumstances.

Finally, avoid positions where you will be one of numerous managers in a standard role. Although every managerial position is different, and cross-sectional comparisons are almost always meaningless, such jobs can prompt bosses to measure you against peers. In addition to the disadvantages we saw in Chapter 5, this will also prevent you from getting the credit you deserve for doing better than predecessors. The more people you are compared to, the worse off you will be because you will have to outdo the best practice in every field. This is like comparing a real woman to what you see in fashion magazines, where best body parts appear in close-up shots page after page and produce the image of a superhuman physique that does not exist.

Once in the right place, you need a game plan to run fast enough to please spectators near the starting line, but not so fast that you burn out halfway through the marathon.

Step 2: Manage expectations and buy time
After you find out what problems you must tackle, reduce the expectations and negotiate for more time to improve the results. To do so, show the darker side of things that the prior manager will certainly have de-emphasized. This is not to imply that the prior person lied. But he will naturally have talked more about his achievements than the problems (there are always problems, no matter how rosy things look from the outside.) You, too, will do the same after you spend a few months on the job and start to "own" it. So when you are first assigned to the position, show your superiors what those problems are and buy some breathing room. You will need this room and time when putting out the fires later on. This is especially important if you had to accept a job where the predecessor did well. Unless you can show why past results will be very difficult to duplicate due to the problems that you have inherited, supervisors will expect an immediate improvement. Even if past results have been exceptionally bad and you could do better right away, do not pass on the opportunity to lower expectations. But do not demoralize your subordinates during this process. Talk to your bosses privately when emphasizing the difficulties.

Depending on circumstances, you can buy anywhere from a few weeks to a year. During this ease-in period, focus on structural changes as opposed to short-term results, so you can sustain the momentum for much longer later on. Let's look at a textbook example of this maneuver.

> When I was appointed as key account manager, I realized that the previous person had pushed retailers in my area pretty hard and damaged relationships. We also had insufficient support personnel in some locations, but were overstaffed in others. Although I could improve sales quickly by correcting the basic mistakes and pocket a good bonus, I decided against it. Instead, I put my energy into explaining the deeper problems to the head of sales and showing why I needed more than a few weeks to resolve the issues. It wasn't easy. I had to visit the worst supermarkets with him over and over to demonstrate what I was grappling with. This relieved the immediate pressure and greatly reduced his expectations. Had I skipped this stage and tried to jack up the volume right away as he wanted me to, I'd be in deep trouble after six months. The momentum would have further inflated expectations, yet the deep-rooted problems would have remained intact.

If you cannot buy more time, at least put more of your energy into long-term solutions during the first few months. It is usually OK to slightly compromise short-term results at this stage. A slow start is always better tolerated than stalling after a spectacular opening.

Step 3: Make long-term investments that will pay off over time
In the third step, use the window of opportunity that you opened during step two in order to make meaningful long-term changes that will have a lasting impact. The same manager describes his progress.

> Once I relieved the pressure for short-term results, I held meetings with all my people to decide on the best course of action. We agreed that a lot of support personnel had to be moved around and trained extensively to match the needs of retailers. In addition, the promotion budget had to be used more prudently. Next, I visited every supermarket to decide how many of my staff to assign to each location and how much of my budget to allocate to them. None of this would have been possible if I was desperately trying to beat last quarter's results.

While the long-term investments you will make at this stage can involve major changes such as R&D projects, developing new client relationships, or educating your personnel, they can also be much simpler. If you believe that a good structure is already in place, invest your time into learning the details of the job and understanding the organization.

When I started to work in advertising, my boss decided to keep me away from big projects for a few weeks because I was in the process of moving. This slow start made a huge difference. I spent many hours studying old campaigns and reading extensively about the brands I would later work on. If you are new in the organization, you will also need to study databases, learn lots of new names, and even figure out the transportation. The more time you can invest into preparing yourself for the challenges ahead, the easier it will be to deliver solid results later on.

Step 4: Pace the results

In the fourth stage, when you must finally show the fruits of your labor, think a few steps ahead to keep up the momentum for the foreseeable future. Since people will compare you to your past, be careful about setting a benchmark that you cannot beat later. As the interviewee states below, you are much better off starting with the hardest targets and progressively moving towards easier ones. This may sound counterintuitive; the instinct is to reach for the low-hanging fruit first. But by resisting the temptation, you can present an upward trend for much longer.

> After the reorganization, I didn't want to send the wrong message by bombarding the easiest accounts with promotions and showing the boss a huge spike up in sales. This would have created the impression that all problems were solved and it would be all downhill from there. The quotas would have jumped up and we would likely fail to meet those pumped-up targets two months down the road. So we decided to hit the toughest accounts first. Obviously, results improved gradually in those places, but this was actually better. It was to our advantage to go slow and build a strong foundation when the expectations were still low in this transition phase. If anything went wrong later on, we could turn our attention to the easier accounts to make up for the deficits elsewhere. By thinking ahead, we have improved sales every single quarter since I took over.

As an added bonus for the firm, this approach also maximizes total sales in the long run, because you attack the biggest accounts only after experimenting with the smaller ones and gaining sufficient experience.

Corporate America is a master at the game of presenting an upward trend.

By using the strategies we saw above, as well as a variety of accounting treatments, they consistently beat their past results. Notice the smooth and steady improvement in the progression of Net Income for The General Electric Company.

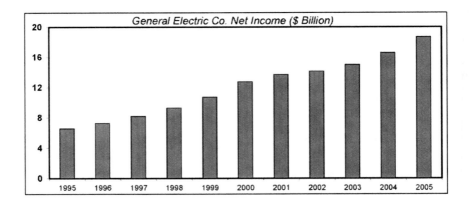

The steps outlined above are relevant not only for long-term projects or when you change careers. If you develop the habit of looking several moves ahead and thinking of today's results as tomorrow's benchmarks, you will find many opportunities to apply these principles.

Assume that you need to prepare an internal report. Start by picking a subject that was analyzed badly in the past. The research could have been poor, deadlines might have been missed, or the conclusion could have angered top management. Then show why it will now take longer to prepare the same thing and buy some time. Make long-term investments to produce that report or similar ones faster and better in the future. You can spend a day in the library to build an archive, teach a secretary how to format this type of data, or negotiate with an outside consultant for a yearlong deal to help you with subsequent projects. When you finally deliver the report, try to beat your predecessor by a significant yet reasonable margin, as opposed to making the analysis so comprehensive that anything you submit in the future will pale in comparison.

Just as you would do in a long-term project, start with the hardest targets; try to sell your study to the least passionate supporters. Regardless of whether they buy your ideas or not, you can go to your allies the next time and produce a larger and stronger fan base for your subsequent work. Remember, as the British author Samuel Johnson said, the future is purchased by the present.

3 Key Points You Should Remember

- Seek assignments that were performed poorly in the past
- When faced with a long-term project, start by managing expectations
- In long-term assignments, make long-term investments early on

CHAPTER 15

Filling Your "Face Time" Quota

The mission of this book is to help you reduce the number of hours you spend and the amount of stress you endure while doing your job. In other words, to help you become a more efficient worker. As I have repeatedly stressed, doing so will not diminish your contributions to the organization. On the contrary, it will enhance the productivity and competitiveness of your employer in a variety of ways. Unfortunately, this relationship is very hard to grasp for some individuals whom I call "hour counters."

The hour counter is a close relative of the bean counter and has a similar impact on the organization. The bean counter lacks the sophistication to assess deeper concepts such as the brand equity, customer service, or innovative capabilities of a business unit. Instead, he simply pulls up a profit-and-loss statement. How sustainable this profit is or whether it came at the expense of another product line's fortunes matters little. The bean counter is simply not willing or able to think in those complicated terms. He can hold only one single number in mind. Similarly, the hour counter finds it extremely difficult to evaluate a manager in multidimensional terms. He cannot easily assess your creativity, communication skills, or strategic insight. Instead, he reduces your managerial contributions to a single factor: the number of hours you work. In addition to spending a disproportionate amount of mental effort keeping a time log for everybody around him, the hour counter also likes to boast about how much he works. He constantly talks about how he has been getting by with four hours of sleep a night for the last two weeks or describes the breathtaking sunrise he witnessed from his desk the other day.

Hour counters do terrible damage to the company. As they say, what you measure is what you get. Therefore, the more hour counters you have in an organization, the more people will hang out in the office only for face time. Not only will creativity take a nosedive, but it will also become impossible to assess who is adding more value and thereby compensate people fairly. As we will see later, some managers may even resort to deceptive tactics, trying to look like they are in the office when in fact they are not. These dynamics will make it extremely challenging to create an atmosphere of trust, and the organizational culture will quickly degenerate.

In this chapter, we will see how you can defend yourself against hour counters by making it either impossible or very difficult for them to keep track of your work hours. This will compel them to use more legitimate yardsticks to evaluate your performance, such as sales, client satisfaction, or profits, hence easing the pressure on you to stay in the office longer than you need to. Before we go further, let me point out what this chapter is *not* about. It is not about deceiving hour counters by creating the impression that you are working when in fact you are doing something else. At the end of this chapter, I analyze the long-term damage that such dishonest tactics can inflict on your career and help you identify the subordinates and coworkers who resort to these methods. Our goal here is to simply hamper the hour counter's ability to calculate the number of hours you spend working, thus forcing him to base your promotion and compensation on other, more meaningful criteria. The first advice below will clarify how this seemingly unachievable goal is, in fact, very feasible.

Whenever possible, work away from your desk
An extremely effective solution that has already liberated millions of managers from hour counters is to work from home. Such arrangements where you meet coworkers only for rare face-to-face meetings, but otherwise do all of your work at home—or any place where you can have Internet access—make it simply impossible for hour counters to know how much time you spend doing your job. Consequently, these people are forced to evolve and find more relevant measures to appraise their subordinates as well as coworkers.

If you do not have the option to work from home, perform as much of your work away from your desk as you can. If your colleagues know that you can get a lot done even while you are away from the office, they cannot count the number of hours you work unless they stalk you.

The most critical step is to get a laptop and obtain remote access to the e-mail system. While most employers now encourage this practice, your boss may not want to pay for a portable computer. If not, buy your own. Even the cheapest models will handle your basic e-mail needs and can be purchased for a very reasonable price. Always on, wireless internet connection is a plus, but old fashioned dial-up modems generally work well enough if you can afford to send and receive messages in batches. You can simply compose your messages offline, then get on the network a couple of times a day to send and receive e-mail.

To make the most out of your laptop (or remotely connected PC), get into the habit of frequently using the draft function in your e-mail software. If you are not sure how to conclude an important e-mail, do not waste ten minutes finding the perfect punch line; just save it as a draft. Later that night when you have a ten minutes while waiting for your spouse to get ready for dinner, you can go over the unfinished message, find a more creative conclusion, and send it out from home. If you don't have such draft messages to work on, you will probably not be able to use those spare moments outside the office as productively. Such e-mails sent late at night, early in the morning, or while you are on a business trip prove that you don't need to be at your desk to do work and discourage hour counters from keeping track of how many hours you sit at your desk each day.

Late night e-mails are also extremely effective in impressing workaholics (there is some overlap between workaholics and hour counters but they are not always the same people.) All managers quickly scan their inboxes before they leave the office at the end of the day. As a result, most can easily spot the e-mails that were sent between their departure the day before and their arrival the next morning. Those who leave relatively early will find numerous new e-mails the next morning. Lots of people will stay in and continue to send messages long after these managers leave. Since these individuals won't be surprised by the large number of new messages, they rarely check the exact time of each e-mail. Consequently, they can rarely distinguish a message that was sent five minutes after they left at 5:30 from one that was sent at midnight.

Workaholics, on the other hand, find many fewer new messages when they arrive in the office. If you leave at 11 and come in at 8 the next morning, you will have just a few messages from real people working in your time zone. Most e-mails sent between 11:00 PM and 8:00 AM will be from either automated systems such as news updates or people who work in another time zone. An e-mail from a coworker in the same office that was not there the prior evening will really stand out. Even if the workaholic does not check the time of the message, he will be impressed (though he will most likely check the time to see by how much you beat him.)

Another way to do more of your work while you are away from your desk is to use teleconferences instead of face-to-face meetings. Propose such meetings whenever hour counters are around and, if possible, dial into the conference from outside the office. Imagine how the hour counter would feel if he hears you in one of these meetings, then stops by your desk five minutes later to ask a follow-up question, only to find out from the secretary that you have been out for the last two hours. He will clearly realize that you have different work habits and tallying the number of hours you spend in front of your office computer is meaningless.

Do not allow the hour counter to use your cell phone to track you

Like many high-tech devices, cell phones can be highly dangerous in the wrong hands. Whenever you are out, be prepared for an hour counter to dial your cell phone to locate you. A typical line is "I just wanted to stop by and have a chat with you in half an hour. Are you going to be around?" Some people do not even bother to make up such a lie and simply call you on your cell phone to ask if you got their last e-mail. These calls usually conclude with an annoying question such as "By the way, haven't seen you in a while. Are you in today?"

To neutralize this weapon of hour counters, you need to teach them not to dial your cell phone unless absolutely necessary. This involves several steps. First of all, get into the habit of forwarding your office line to your cell phone before leaving the office for an extended period. When you are in the office, however, simply switch off your cell phone. (If there are important clients or colleagues who have only your cell phone number, look at the caller ID and do not pick up if that caller also has the number for your office line.) Consequently, you will almost always be reachable at your landline, but significantly harder to catch on your cell phone. Furthermore, callers will not know where you are when picking up the phone. Thus, the cell phone will lose its efficiency as a tracking device. This should deter most hour counters from calling your mobile number. Finally, remove your cell phone number from your business card and standard e-mail signatures if your job does not require you to be reachable at all times.

One thing that you should not do, however, is to take a call when outside the office and act as if you were at your desk. Remember, you are not trying to deceive the hour counter. You are only trying to eliminate his ability to use your cell phone to find out where you are. Pick up forwarded calls just as you would answer any incoming call. If the caller should ask where you are, simply tell him that you are outside the office, as opposed to saying something like "I am in a meeting" or "I just stepped outside for five minutes to get a sandwich." At the end of this chapter, we will talk about such deceptive tactics and their potentially devastating impacts.

One potential inconvenience of this method is that forwarded calls may appear as "unknown ID," on your cell phone and you won't see who is trying to reach you. But this problem is relatively easy to solve. If you receive a lot of personal calls from unknown caller IDs, and thus cannot tell if the incoming call is a forwarded business call or a personal one, getting two lines on your cell phone will provide a lot of relief. Most cell phones can be programmed with different ring tones for each line. By using one of those numbers exclusively to forward your office phone to, you can tell, just from the ring tone, if the incoming call is business related. If you are unable to talk, you can simply check your voice mail a bit later and return the call from a quiet location.

Choose a job / location where the hour counter cannot see you

If you don't want hour counters to be able to quantify your work habits, select a job and physical location where they cannot easily notice you. First of all, avoid jobs with routine duties that must be performed at a certain time every day, especially if colleagues depend on this routine input. Typical examples would be entering stock prices into a database daily by 4:00 PM or having to approve sales numbers every morning before they can be sent to accounting. The problem is that even a slight delay in these things, no matter how legitimate the reason, will disrupt a large operation, immediately telegraphing your absence to a large audience. Even if you work until midnight every day, saving the prices five minutes late will get you labeled as either absent or negligent. Timely delivery of routine results, on the other hand, will be taken for granted and go unnoticed.

In addition, such duties will severely restrict your freedom by forcing you to schedule your day around them. If these functions cannot be delegated, at least try to obtain more flexibility in how you handle them. You can fight for a larger time window (entering prices between 4 and 6, instead of strictly at 4), or try to reduce the frequency of the task (entering prices once a week for the prior five days.)

It is even more important that you select a physical location where you are seen by as few hour counters as possible. This advice, too, may sound odd at first. After all, most of the hour counters whose opinions matter are senior executives, and classical management books tell you to occupy a central spot in the office where such people can see you. In addition, you may think that selecting a peripheral seat is unethical, since it is a way of hiding. My view is slightly different. I think that you are only trying to keep your work hours a private matter, just as you would keep your salary confidential. Here is what can happen if hour counters can easily see you all the time.

> My boss comes in at 10:30 and stays in the office until 8 at night so she can avoid the rush-hour traffic.* Like most bosses, she wants me around when she's in and I don't really have a problem with working from 10:30 to 8. Actually, it was great until last month. I'd go out almost every night and sleep until 9 in the morning. The problem is that I am sitting in the middle of the floor and everybody sees me. A month ago, my boss's boss asked why I came much later than other juniors. Now I must stay from 8:30 to 8:00. Another junior works for someone who comes in at 6:30 and leaves at 4:00. But he sits in a corner where nobody can see him and works ten hours a day without any issues. Could you have imagined that the location of your desk would add an hour and a half to your workday?
> (*Author's note: This office is located in downtown Los Angeles, forcing most managers to use such strategies to avoid the horrendous rush-hour traffic.)

If several senior hour counters can see your desk, you may have to satisfy all of them at the same time. Imagine sitting between a field supervisor who spends most of the day out in supermarkets and is in the office 7 to 9 PM and a single mom—another senior hour counter—who comes in at 7 AM and leaves at 4 PM to pick up her kids from school. If both want to see you around most of the time, you may as well sleep in the office on weeknights.

Another problem with a central position is that people will stop by your desk to talk. It will often be for trivial issues that would never have been brought up if the person had not seen your face. In addition, such locations can be very noisy, making it difficult to concentrate.

If your current desk puts you at a disadvantage, remember that seating arrangements change frequently in today's organizations. The key to getting a good seat when people move around is to act early. Do not wait for an announcement. Talk to your boss or the HR department now, and tell them that you want to sit at a particular spot if the opportunity arises. Be ready to give up some prestige and comfort for greater freedom and better concentration. But even if you must sit right in front of everyone and have recurring daily duties, there is still a lot you can do, as we will see below.

Vary your schedule constantly

Can you tell me—in less than a minute—how much you spent on rent (or mortgage) during the last year? You probably can, because chances are you know what you pay every month and only need to multiply that number by twelve. Even if you moved recently, your rent probably changed only once over the last year and the calculation will become only marginally more difficult. Now let's see if you know how much you spent on food last year. Can't you figure it out in under a minute? You probably couldn't come up with an even remotely accurate figure even if you had an hour. Your total rent is simple to calculate because it is stable. To find out your annual food expenses, however, you would have to add up hundreds of different numbers.

The hour counter's challenge is no different. If you come and go at basically the same time every day, he will soon get a perfect tally of how many hours you are working. Having found the gold standard for performance evaluation, he will then pay much less attention to anything else that you do. What you don't want the hour counter to say is, "Jim comes in at 8:30, catches the 6:15 train home, and takes approximately 45 minutes for lunch every day. Damn! I've been in this company for twelve years and this rookie is working less than I do."

As if this wasn't enough, another disadvantage of sticking to a routine schedule is that you soon become a prisoner of your self-imposed curfew. When you start to come in a little later than usual or leave a bit earlier because of your improving efficiency, people will immediately notice the difference. Chances are they will attribute the change to a decline in your motivation.

To avoid these issues, come and go at different times as much as possible. Blend long and short days in an unpredictable pattern, confusing the hour counter and forcing him to give up trying to figure out how long you stay in the office.

Instead of always leaving early on Mondays and Wednesdays to play tennis, and working late on Tuesdays and Thursdays to prepare for the weekly meetings, mix things up a little. Stay really late two days in a row and then come in at noon for a few days. The next week, send a few e-mails from home on Monday as soon as you wake up and schedule a meeting for 7:30 PM on Tuesday. Do not be like the sun, which arrives and leaves in a perfectly predictable pattern. Be like the rainbow, which can magically materialize or disappear anytime.

If you must stick to a schedule, make sure it is unconventional

If you must stick to a schedule (or wish to do so to have a more orderly life outside the office), routinely avoid the hour counters either at the beginning or at the end of most days. For example, if you always come at 10:30 and leave at 7, while the hour counter works from 8 to 6:30, he simply cannot count how long you are in the office. He will always see you around when he walks out the door in the afternoon, and will have no way of knowing how much longer you stay.

A variation of this strategy is to come in half an hour before everybody else arrives and leave substantially earlier than they do. Again, hour counters won't be able to keep track of your hours. This is the favorite tactic of managers who want to spend quality time with their young children at night. An early cycle also gives you a quiet and productive period in the morning, when you can work with minimal interruptions. Furthermore, traffic is usually better early in the morning than in the late afternoon. Another approach, which is particularly popular with athletes, is to leave early while everyone is still working, do some exercise, and then briefly stop by later to wrap up the unfinished tasks of the day. This tactic yields the best results if the hour counter works late. You could leave the office at 5:00, train at a nearby gym, and come back at 6:30 (or anytime as long as the hour counter is still in the office) to work for another hour.

If the hour counter demands your presence both early in the morning and late in the afternoon, but doesn't care as much about what you do in between, try to make the most out of your lunch breaks. You can pick up your dry cleaning, do some of your shopping, or even go home to cook dinner if you live nearby. As before, the key is irregularity. You cannot stick to a standard midday schedule where you routinely leave at noon and return at 1:15. This will get you labeled as the person who always disappears in the middle of the day. Instead, alternate between long and short breaks. Another solution is to divide your lunch breaks in two. You can leave at noon, have a quick lunch to come back at 12:30, and then leave again between 1 and 1:45. Although you will still be out for 75 minutes, this is much less likely to attract attention. Besides, if the hour counter happens to need you urgently, you will be getting back to him in no more than 45 minutes, which is not unreasonable. But in the first scenario, he may have to wait for 75 minutes to hear back from you and get really agitated as a result.

If work hours are very strict in your industry (for example, you have to be in the office while the stock exchange is open), and you therefore find these tactics difficult to apply, get into the habit of coming in just a little before everyone else on most days, and arriving really late when you need the extra time in the morning. By routinely showing up slightly after your coworkers, you will gain a negligible amount of sleep time, yet still get labeled as the latecomer. Be disciplined and get out of bed when the alarm rings. If you need to be late, however, take your time and make the most out of it by having breakfast in bed or cuddling with the kids. In most workplaces, doing this a few times a month is tolerated much better than consistently being five minutes late.

Do not allow the hour counter to lower your moral standards

In this chapter, I have outlined what I consider to be moral methods to deal with hour counters. This advice is unlikely to inflict damage on the organization or your career. Some of your coworkers, however, will likely go a step further and try to give the impression that they are working, when in fact they are either engaged in another activity or are not even in the office at all. I believe you should be aware of these methods for several reasons. First, some of your subordinates may try to impress you in this manner, even if you tell them that you don't care about face time as long as they do a proper job. Second, certain coworkers with whom you compete for a promotion may employ these tactics, gaining an unfair advantage if the promotion or compensation committees include hour counters. Watch out for such people. They will likely have lower moral standards and might hit below the belt in other ways.

Finally, you should refrain from ever resorting to such fraudulent tactics because, if discovered, your credibility will take a tremendous blow. Furthermore, your own subordinates will easily notice such actions. Remember, it is extremely difficult to hide anything from them. You will essentially communicate to your people that window dressing is more important than adding real value to the organization and will soon lose control over them. Here are some of the things that you or your subordinates should _not_ do and watch out for in others. If nothing else, some of these will probably give you a good laugh.

i) Leaving a ghost behind

Some managers go to great lengths to create the impression that they are still somewhere in the office long after they are gone. One way is to leave a personal item, such as a purse or a briefcase (empty), at a visible location in the office. When someone sees this, he will probably think that you couldn't have forgotten such an important article and must be in a meeting or the restroom. One dishonest interviewee even keeps an extra umbrella, which he leaves on his chair before going home on rainy days. The rationale is that you wouldn't forget an umbrella on a rainy day; even if you did, you would have come back to get it. Therefore, you must still be around.

Leaving some unfinished work on the desk can serve the same purpose. A bunch of papers and an open pen scattered on an otherwise tidy desk, especially when there is also an open file on the computer screen, will create a similar impact. Some people who are worried about sensitive documents even use a screen-saver that activates only when the mouse or keyboard are touched. Yet another tactic is to lock the computer and leave the lights and a small fan on.

Another strategy is to be seen leaving the office without a coat in winter. Imagine freezing temperatures outside and a colleague walking out with nothing but a shirt on. What would you think? Most people assume that he must be going downstairs or to the cafeteria. The trick usually involves either leaving your coat in the car or using a closet far away from your office, possibly one located on another floor, to hang your stuff. For greater impact, some illusionists keep a second coat on their chairs when they go home. Isn't it amazing how much effort some people put into the planning and execution of these things?

ii) Controlling your computer remotely

Certain software programs give you the ability to operate your computer remotely, sometimes with a handheld organizer, from outside the office. This can look really spooky. The mouse pointer will float around the screen, opening and running applications as if an invisible hand was guiding your mouse. The hope is that people will think that you are working from home when they see the activity on your PC. I personally find this rationale ridiculous, because there are much more efficient ways to work from home. Someone trying to remotely steer his mouse via a handheld device needs to visit a computer store and discover better technologies. If you must operate your office computer remotely, at least turn off your screen before you go home. Otherwise, you may look dishonest even if you really are doing work from outside the office.

iii) Relying on delayed e-mail delivery to deceive the recipient

Composing an e-mail at noon and setting up your software to automatically deliver it at midnight might sound clever. But at some point, people will realize what is going on. Sooner or later, someone will get a message from you when he knows that you are not anywhere near a computer. As a result, the delivery times of all your e-mails will become irrelevant, and your image will be tarnished. Sending late e-mails from home is perfectly fine, and can even enhance the quality of written communication, as we saw. But timing an e-mail to be delivered when you are asleep is just not a good idea.

iv) Making shopping excursions appear like meetings

Since the advent of ultralight laptops, some managers have realized that, by taking these machines and a bunch of papers, they can make any trip outside the office look like a meeting. The scam goes something like this: Pick up your laptop and 15 copies of a heavy presentation, then leave the office in a rush. Remember to turn off your cell phone; after all, you are in a meeting. When you are done with shopping or finished your two-hour lunch, return to the office with two copies of the presentation (you always take extra copies and bring the unused ones back to the office to save on printing supplies), a few business cards, and a triumphant smile on your face—another day, another productive meeting.

v) Proposing unrealistic dates/times for meetings

When asked for a convenient meeting time, some managers habitually propose outrageous hours such as, "anytime after 8:30 PM Monday through Wednesday is fine," or say things like "I must call a client tomorrow at 7:30 in the morning, can we meet before then?" The goal is to demonstrate that they always work such long hours and don't mind it. Naturally, hardly anyone will agree to meet at those times, and most bluffers get away with this show of dedication. Still, this is a highly frustrating behavior and will do little for you in the long-term. At some point, people will realize that you don't work those kinds of hours and discover your true motivation.

vi) Pretending to be in a meeting when you are not

Another sleazy tactic is to pick up the phone (either cellular or conventional) as if you were in a meeting. This works by answering the call relatively late—perhaps after the fourth or the fifth ring—covering up your mouth with your hand, speaking softly, and abruptly cutting off the conversation by asking to call the person back later. The idea is that even if you don't say that you are in a meeting, your attitude and the way you sound with your hand in front of your mouth will create the impression that you are surrounded by people and are doing something important—extremely rude and distasteful.

If you must stay in the office, at least do something useful

Sometimes, nothing will help and you will have to stay in the office with absolutely no work to do. You may have to wait for your boss to get out of a meeting, or the people around you may be dealing with such a big crisis that you need to stick around to give them moral support. To make the most out of these occasions, always carry some personal files you can work on. A great habit is to keep such things as checks, bills, or mortgage forms with you so you can get those boring things out of the way instead of surfing the Internet for hours. Keeping those documents in one folder will also help you to find them quickly at home. Finally, this will make it easier to grab your errand folder when going on business trips and keep busy in planes or cabs. But never bring this folder to a meeting, hoping that you can fill out a mortgage application while an irrelevant topic is being discussed. If this is how much attention you pay to the average meeting, read on. In the next chapter, I will explain how much this attitude can harm you.

3 Key Points You Should Remember

- Learn to work from a variety of physical locations
- Seek jobs and assignments with few regular, recurring duties
- Try not to stick to a highly regular and predictable daily schedule

CHAPTER 16

Shining in Meetings with Less Effort

Meetings are like politicians: we dislike them because they waste resources, we do all we can to avoid them, but nobody has yet found a way to get rid of them. Since meetings are inevitable and play a critical role in workload distribution, let us see how to handle this necessary evil.

Meetings influence your workload in two ways. First, there is a direct effect. In most meetings, you are assigned duties to complete by a certain date or before the next gathering. Especially when formalized with meeting minutes, these assignments become very hard to avoid—even if they are unfair or unnecessary. In fact, meetings were the biggest workload generator for most of the managers I interviewed.

The indirect effect, however, is just as important. Meetings have a tremendous influence on your image as well as your power, and thus they determine your general efficiency. Usually, meetings expose you to the highest ranked officials you will meet. Just as apparel manufacturers decide on next year's styles in fashion shows, these top officials decide on next year's promotions in meetings. Such occasions provide an excellent display of managerial aptitude. When working alone, you can cover up inadequate interpersonal skills by working unnecessarily hard, like the assistant finance manager who was doing other people's spreadsheets because he could not convince them to send the files on time. In meetings, however, such flaws are easily exposed. All attendants will see whether you can win people over, handle the pressure of being put on the spot, or distill the essence of a complex argument into a few simple sentences. If you lack these abilities, no amount of effort or preparation can save you.

Meetings also serve as a barometer of diplomatic skills. If you fail to properly address a crowd of coworkers in meetings, you will attract extraordinary scrutiny whenever you are sent out to represent the organization. Superiors will watch you with a strong pair of binoculars to ensure that you don't tarnish the image of your organization during contacts with external parties, such as clients or the press. Their demands to see anything you send out and heavy interrogations before and after client contacts will dramatically inflate your workload.

Show that you are taking the meeting seriously

In small entities, such as a company with only seven employees, everybody will be involved in almost every task. Therefore, most topics in meetings will be relevant for every participant. In bigger entities, however, jobs are much more specialized. Everything in a meeting is no longer of great interest to everyone. Consequently, meetings are much more boring. In a board meeting of a huge corporation, for instance, the factory manager will have to sit through a discussion about the new tax code, while the head of the quality control department may be forced to comment on the latest consumer promotion featuring Mickey Mouse. Should you find yourself in such an unexciting situation, realize that you aren't the only one getting bored to tears. Do not appear frustrated. Instead, try to show that you are taking the meeting seriously. This requires only marginal effort, yet it really helps you stand out in a sea of yawning faces.

If available, read the minutes of the previous meeting. With an effective archiving system that lets you easily access them, this will take just a few minutes. One creative interviewee copies and pastes meeting minutes into the scheduling software on his PC. Once inserted as a note accompanying the appointment, the minutes automatically pop up on the screen when you look up the time or place of the meeting. You can make a quick printout or even read them on your way to the conference room if you are keeping your agenda on a handheld organizer.

In addition, "process" the meeting minutes or anything distributed beforehand. Simply highlighting a few lines in the printouts and attaching some Post-Its proves that you read them carefully and puts you in a different league. If you suspect that reference materials might be helpful during the meeting, you should also bring these along. When the discussion will involve the aging consumer base in your geographical area, for instance, you may want to print out a copy of the latest Census Survey. Although they take mere minutes, such gestures show a much higher level of commitment than simply opening up the last meeting minutes and hitting the print button. They prove that you took the time to think about and prepare for the meeting.

Finally, always take notes during meetings, even if it is just a couple of scribbled lines. If you dislike writing, take notes on printouts. While just two lines on an empty notepad might look weak, even a few exclamation marks can significantly transform a graph or table. It is extremely tiring to demonstrate attentiveness with only facial expressions, especially if the meeting runs long. You can achieve the same impact much more easily by taking a few lines of notes.

Do whatever you can to talk later rather than sooner

Perhaps the most important source of power and prestige in a meeting is the speaking order. Management books make a big deal out of where you sit and for how long you occupy the stage. When you address the attendees, however, is much more critical. The later you speak, the more counter-arguments you can hear and tackle. You can also introduce new arguments that were not preempted by the prior speakers and conclude the meeting with an unanswered blow. Remember that a mediocre but unchallenged argument will impress the audience a lot more than a perfect pitch that was attacked from all angles. It is hardly surprising that the lawyer who makes the final closing argument in the courtroom has a better chance of winning the case.

Another advantage of talking later is that you can scale your demands up or down depending on the climate in the meeting, only asking for what you can realistically obtain. As we saw, you can only change people's ideas one step at a time and must therefore consider what your audience currently believes in when trying to persuade them. By speaking later, you can gauge the mood of the participants and refrain from asking for anything that will likely be rejected.

Any idea that has been refused in the past starts the race in last position the next time it is put on the table. Therefore, never push your ideas into the ring until they are strong enough to properly defend themselves. Otherwise, they can get permanently crippled in the battle. (This is another advantage of having proper meetings with your boss, instead of popping your head into his office whenever you need to talk to him. By saving critical issues to the end of a meeting, you can get a better feel for whether or not that is the right time to ask him for a concession or favor.)

Furthermore, the last-speaker advantage is magnified in larger meetings. Small and informal gatherings resemble casual conversations. Since people routinely interrupt each other in these meetings, you can always jump in to say just one more thing and prevent your opponent from having the last word. This, however, would result in utter chaos in a big meeting. In such gatherings speakers are given only a few opportunities to talk and cannot jump in at will. The bigger the crowd and more senior the participants, the more strictly this order is enforced and the more critical it becomes to talk later. Of course, such meetings also have the biggest impact on your career. In other words, knowing how to speak later is one of those neat skills that will help you when you need it the most.

i) E-mail a little something before the meeting

Simply committing to talk later without a good strategy does more harm than good. Taking a step back and insisting that your colleagues go first may work in an elevator, but it looks horrible in a meeting. You will be seen as manipulative and even those who would naturally speak before you will push you forward. A much stronger yet subtle tactic is to simply e-mail a page or two for people to look at before the meeting. This way, you can kick off the discussion by asking others what they think about the material, pressing them to reveal their positions first.

Worried that nobody will bother to read the material beforehand? Even better. Ask if you should sum up the information "in case some people didn't get a chance to look at it." Then briefly go over the exact same material without revealing anything new. This should give you the justification to ask others what they think. Since you prepared those documents in advance and kindly presented them, it will be very difficult for someone who has not even read your work to ask you to talk more. After the opposition takes the stage, you can almost certainly speak once again to make your closing arguments, because the opening speech was obviously a "warm-up drill."

The best material to circulate or present is objective information spiced up with a few light questions. You don't need to disclose groundbreaking news. Giving a brief account of what happened on the East Coast and asking the West Coast guy to sum up his situation will get the ball rolling. Especially if you distribute this on paper, having taken the initiative to prepare printouts will give you the upper hand, forcing the West Coast person to reveal more than you did. In most cases, you will need to do zero additional work for the handouts since you will almost always have something relevant in your computer that you can simply print out for the meeting. Handing something out also has a symbolic impact. Standing up and distributing those papers while everyone else is sitting makes it look like you are running the show. Distribute printouts whenever possible, even if you are sure that the audience read your pre-meeting notes.

ii) Relay someone else's message

Another way to get the ball rolling is to relay a message from someone who cannot join the meeting. Ask sales what they would like you to pass on and kick things off with their message. By doing so, you can start the cycle without giving away your position on critical matters or using up your turn. Afterwards, you can easily take the stage again for your own remarks.

iii) Remind them of the overfilled agenda

If the agenda is overly busy, you may only need to remind the participants of all the topics that need to be discussed. Fearing that they may not get to talk at length if they wait too long, most managers will likely jump in right away. While you may have less time by speaking later in a crowded meeting, this is usually a profitable tradeoff. Especially if numerous competing proposals will be presented, try to talk last even if it means having half as much time as other participants. Your speech will stick in your audience's mind much better and, since you were cut off prematurely, you will have justification to see some of the attendees later in person. This will give you yet another chance to drive home your most important points.

iv) Make a daring opening speech

When you cannot distribute something on paper, make an opening speech. This should be more of a situation summary and serves the same purpose as handouts. The idea is to kick things off without using up your actual turn.

You could also stir things up a little with a controversial comment to prompt someone in the audience to start talking. A comment such as "XYZ Company's last study shows that we have one of the worst consumer satisfaction records. I know that their surveys are not perfect, but I just wanted to bring this to your attention" will probably make the consumer service department take the stage immediately to give a lengthy presentation.

v) Observe the chairman of the meeting

Sometimes the speaking order will be strictly dictated by an authoritative top manager. If he is somewhat reasonable, this manager will stick to an objective pattern, such as going clockwise or asking people to talk in the order their names are listed on the last meeting minutes. Observe what process the manager uses so you can end up last or close to last. Luckily, most people employ a fairly consistent methodology for determining the speaking order.

Dictatorial managers, on the other hand, often manipulate the order to sandwich the opposition. They take the stage and open up with a long, biased speech. Then they force the skeptics to talk. After that, they hand the stage to their advocates, sandwiching the skeptics. This dilutes the disbelievers from both sides, while also ensuring that the closing arguments go to supporters. When the meeting is chaired by such an individual, and you know that he won't like your argument, do not reveal your position too early. If he senses where you stand on the issue, he will force you to talk sooner rather than later. Your casual statements before the meeting and your body language during the event need to help create the right impression. In addition, be careful not to give away your position while lobbying before the meeting.

Come prepared to capitalize on opportunities

Imagine this scenario: After a participant talks about cheaper priced Chinese imports, the CEO says that it would be helpful to see a comparison of shelf prices. You immediately start looking through your stack of papers, because you have that chart somewhere. But before you can find it in that mess, the CEO says "Alright, we'll discuss this later, let's move on" and all you can do now is to kick yourself. You lost a great opportunity to show how prepared you were and talk about a subject you that you really wanted to bring up. Other managers will simply obtain a copy of that chart from you before the next meeting, and you will get zero credit. Does this sound familiar?

Another highly irritating situation arises when someone puts out misleading information that makes you look bad. This will rarely be an outright lie. Often, it is a misinterpretation of reality. For example, a colleague could mention how much your sales decreased compared to the same month last year, which is an unfair benchmark because of the consumer promotion during that period.

To properly respond in such situations, come to meetings with lots of well-organized data. If you already have the cheat sheet we saw in Chapter 12, take multiple copies to the meeting. In addition, print out your most important files. Printouts are usually better than handheld or laptop computers, because it is faster to pull a piece of paper out of a stack than to open up a file or even to scroll down on a screen. But do not walk in with a disordered pile, or you will get lost in the mess. Organize the material and make sure that you can pull up any sheet in a few seconds.

True meeting masters are so organized that they can find what they are looking for while addressing the attendees. As soon as the subject opens up, the master will start talking to prevent others from bringing up a different topic. While talking, he will go through his papers and time his sentences so that he can smoothly flow from the opening statements into the more substantial comments when he finds his documents.

Let me explain by continuing with the prior example. After the CEO says that he'd love to see a price comparison, the master politely jumps in to keep the subject alive and says, "I agree." He has already started to go through his notes. It will take him just seconds to locate the data, so he won't need to say much. His eyes are alternating between the audience and the papers. "Since most competitors are priced lower, we may be more vulnerable, especially after the price cuts of ABC Company." He has already found the data and can now start to read. "The last survey shows that, out of 14 brands, we are the fifth most expensive and sell at 21% above the market average."

To do this, you must be confident that you can find the right data quickly. Otherwise, you will ramble on and on while sifting through the papers. But don't worry, it is much easier than it sounds. With a little practice, you can learn to float through your files like a butterfly and sting like a bee at the same time.

Observe the coalitions

There is rarely sufficient time in meetings to thoroughly analyze a problem and make a decision based purely on facts. Outcomes of meetings depend primarily on who is supporting what idea. Top managers, in particular, weight the jockey much more heavily than the horse. Since they rarely have detailed knowledge about every matter and will hand the execution of the decisions to their subordinates anyway, they often go with what their favorite people advocate. Therefore, meetings present an outstanding opportunity to observe the power camps and alliances.

Especially if a coalition forms too soon to be based on facts and holds up very well across various subjects and meetings, you are faced with a solid power camp. Spotting these camps is a tremendous step towards understanding your workplace. You will get a better idea why people make certain decisions and whom they are trying to please. In addition to giving you a chance to tailor your ideas to please power groups, this will also enable you to better forecast the outcomes of discussions. Finally, coalitions expose whose opinions top managers depend on. If you cannot convince top managers directly, their close allies are the ones to go after. Their positive impressions about you will directly translate into the top manager's approval.

3 Key Points You Should Remember

- Try to talk as late during meetings as possible
- Come mentally and physically prepared to make the most out of meetings
- Observe the organizational dynamics that manifest themselves in meetings

CHAPTER 17

Simple Strategies to Preserve Your Brand Image

The tactics we saw over the last five chapters will help you to build a strong brand image. But unfortunately, this image will soon depreciate unless you work on maintaining it. For one thing, the people you have impressed will forget you over time. Especially in a large and chaotic organization, the attention span of the average manager is extremely short. Furthermore, you will be constantly exposed to new faces. This phenomenon too, is much more prevalent in large entities. People working for such organizations are not only more likely to join a competitor, but they also get reassigned to different departments or regions fairly often. It is due to this reason that in a small company you have a much higher chance of meeting an "Uncle George," who has been doing the same job for the last 25 years.

The above mentioned dynamics call for targeted strategies, to remind people of your virtues. Such strategies, however, must involve as little energy as possible because you will have to use them for as long as you work. Let's see if we can find the right solution...

Brand your intellectual products

To get the most bang for their advertising dollars, brand managers rely on easily identifiable cues such as fonts, colors, slogans, and characters. For instance, it is hard to mistake a McDonald's ad for anything else when you see the golden arch. Think how wonderful it would be if your work was that recognizable. Imagine one of your reports or e-mails getting forwarded several times without your name, but at least some of the recipients still knowing at first glance that it belongs to you. Wouldn't you be getting a lot more out of every minute spent in the office?

i) Brand your files

Most of your intellectual investment probably resides in files such as spreadsheets, MS Word documents, or presentations. So let's start by looking at how you can better "copyright" those.

I remember sitting in a meeting where we were going over financial summaries prepared by a few different accountants. When someone wanted to conference in the accountants who had prepared those reports, we noticed that the secretary hadn't pasted names into the PowerPoint file. Still, almost everyone knew right away where one of those pages came from. There was a long disclaimer at the end, and only one person used those disclaimers. This made me realize how easy it can be to brand your work and how much more exposure you can get by doing so. Now, I put similar clauses on my pages—just three standard lines stating the source of the data, plus a legal notice—and make them look different from other people's files in my department. It's working great. Even when my name isn't on those files, people usually know that I did the work.

Brilliant, and so easy to do. While a disclaimer will work, there are many other options. If a legal notice would not apply to your job, you can cite the accounting treatment for inventories or the method used for calculating market share, at the bottom of every page. In addition, include your name and contact information at the same spot in all your files. This is much easier if you prepare a template with this information for each file type such as Word, Excel, or PowerPoint, and open up one of these for new projects. The template can also automatically insert disclaimers. To further enhance branding, use the same fonts, colors, backgrounds, page layouts, and other visual cues across different file formats. Sometimes it may be inappropriate to include your name in files, so these cues will be your only tools to communicate the author's identity.

ii) Brand your e-mails and attachments

The problem with e-mails is that they are extremely easy to modify and forward. Even if your e-mail stays intact, it can get forwarded so many times that one may have to scroll down several pages just to see who composed the original message.

As a first line of defense, change your default settings to make your messages look slightly different. You can use different fonts, colors and slightly narrower margins on the sides. The last tactic will also make your e-mails appear longer. If you receive a lot of long messages and send much shorter responses, this could create a more balanced look. Most importantly, however, you should brand and promote any attachments, which are the most valuable part of many e-mails.

Do not make the mistake of spending an hour preparing a huge file and then attach it to an e-mail that only says "The monthly sales report is attached. Thx." This provides no incentive for the recipients to open the attachment. While those waiting for the file will still open it up, others, especially those who are on the CC list, may save it in a folder and forget about it. If you actively promote the attachment, however, not only will more people open it, but even those who do not will be aware that you prepared it and a lot of work went into the file.

In addition, people will be less likely to lose track of who initiated the message when it gets forwarded. Suppose that you prepare a price analysis but fail to promote your work in the body of the e-mail. A colleague receives the report and forwards it to his VP with a detailed explanation. (Always assume that your work is good enough to be forwarded.) After obtaining a satisfactory explanation from the paragraph on top, the VP will probably not scroll all the way down to read your one line introduction. Hence, he may never know who prepared the report. But if you include a proper description, your colleague will not feel the need to write a whole paragraph. Even if he does, his comments are less likely visually overpower yours or prevent people from seeing your name.

Think of the body of e-mails with important attachments as thirty-second trailers advertising an upcoming pay-per-view program. If you do a good job of promoting what is attached, people will invest the time to open and review your file, just as they would invest $19.95 for a movie promoted by a good commercial. Explain what the file contains and why it is important, as you would do in an executive summary. Such a sales pitch often takes less than a minute to write; it could look as follows for a monthly sales report of soft drinks:

"The sales report for March is attached. You'll notice higher sales to hotels and catering companies and an increase in market share at public schools. In contrast, sales to fast food outlets were down. A discussion of possible reasons and a forecast for April is also included."

Even if recipients do not open the attachment, they will understand that the file has more than just four rows of numbers. They will also realize that it is your own work, as opposed to someone else's forwarded file. When writing such pitches for attachments, use large, bold fonts and bullet points. Remember that this part should stand out even if the message gets forwarded.

iii) Brand your reports

Periodic reports that you send out often lose their appeal after a few issues. Especially if you send these files to a secretary who formats and forwards them to a large list, people may even forget who is preparing them. Better branding will usually solve this problem.

Simply add a few paragraphs to the e-mail containing the report. These paragraphs can highlight important developments and remind people who is preparing the piece. If you cannot find the time to do that, just copy and paste a couple of comments from the report into the body of the e-mail. If even this sounds like too much work, ask a junior or a secretary to pick key sentences from the file. Should he know absolutely nothing about the topic, ask him to copy the side comments or bold sentences from the report. In the end, your e-mail can look as follows:

Your
comments.
This part
should
take under
a minute
to write

> Dear All,
>
> Our monthly distribution report is attached. As seen, we have managed to keep inventory costs under control and expect further declines with the addition of the new warehouse. Please contact me for any questions.
>
> Best regards,
> Stuart

This part
is copied
from the
report by
your
assistant

> *Highlights From Monthly Distribution Report*
>
> Inventories increased by 21% vs. prior month
> 14% of the increase is due to new product launch
>
> Inventory costs declined for 5th straight month, reducing impact of recent increase in inventories
>
> Most shipments were for new orders, backlogs made up 31% of shipments vs. 54% last month
>
> New loading docks to open March 15, as planned

> *Attachment:*
> *Feb 2003 Dist Report.xls*

Such an e-mail will also show that the report contains substantial information, which some recipients may otherwise not realize if they don't read it. Best of all, it should take less than a minute of your time. Another solution is to decorate the graphs by superimposing memorable comments on them such as "The 15% increase in sales is the biggest jump since Jan 1994." These tell the reader that someone thought about the numbers, as opposed to just pasting them in, and also make most people search for the name of the author out of curiosity.

If the brand value of the report has depreciated so much that no one opens it up anymore, a relaunch is your best bet. Make a few changes such as adding a new graph and modifying fonts and colors to give the report a new look. This alone can be enough to revive the interest of your audience. An e-mail to explain the relevance of the additional fields in the "new and updated" report should increase readership and remind people who is putting in the time for the piece.

Remember things you are not supposed to

We all know how good it feels to find a few dollars in the pocket of an old shirt. A little surprise, no matter how cheap, always pleases, because when the expectation is zero, anything will beat it. Therefore, the easiest way to impress someone is to do a small but unexpected favor. One option is to remember little things that you are not supposed to. Such gestures also show that you can keep track of issues on your own and do not need to be harassed constantly to produce results. This motivates coworkers to give you the freedom that is so critical for efficiency.

Let's say someone asks for last quarter's shipment figures, which are scheduled to be released in two weeks. When you tell him that the figures will come out later, he notes the date and says that he will call you then. If he will definitely call back because he must have the numbers, take the initiative and send him the data before he calls. This requires no more work than responding to his request, but will really impress him. How many of your coworkers are kind enough to do this? Probably not many, and chances are they really stand out. But as you see, they may not be doing any additional work. Furthermore, such surprises will make it harder for the other person to annoy you with unnecessary follow-up questions, since you have already gone the extra mile.

To do these things without stressing out yourself excessively, you must find a way to easily remember the request. One way is to insert a prominent reminder into your own file, which you must open to update the information. Give a conservative timing in your first conversation, so that if you are a day late you can still call him before he calls you. What you should not do is let an e-mail sit in your inbox, with the hope that you will remember to reply to it on time. This will not only occupy valuable space in your inbox, but also plant an open loop in your mind. Every time you see the e-mail, you will need a moment to remember what it was for and remind yourself to send out the data on time. This will soon become too annoying and you will just delete the e-mail for good.

Meetings present another great opportunity to pleasantly surprise people. For example, a top manager could mention that it would be nice to see the quality record of competitors, but he might not officially ask for it. If this is a person you wish to impress, or if he has many admirers dying to please him, take the initiative and send him the information. In the first case, the cost-benefit ratio is too favorable to let this opportunity pass. Since he is expecting nothing, even a mediocre study will impress him and earn you praise for having paid attention to his comments. In the second case, a member of his fan club will most likely get the information from you and forward it to him. Under this scenario, you will still put in the same effort, but get almost no credit at all.

However, do not spoil the surprise by revealing it too early. If you publicize in the meeting that you have the data, the impact will be much smaller. This will severely inflate expectations. In addition, the person may not remember if he had asked for the work or you had volunteered. You could also irritate and aggravate colleagues who compete for the attention of the same person.

Keep track of your good deeds

Amazingly, most managers forget about their own achievements and the past work they did for others. This is highly unfortunate because keeping track of your good deeds has enormous advantages.

First, you will appear completely in control if you can effortlessly find a paper document or electronic file that someone urgently needs. Top managers, particularly, tend to lose whatever you give them and race into your office before a meeting to ask for another copy. Keeping a top official waiting while trying to find the file in your electronic junkyard is highly embarrassing. Calmly locating the file and quickly printing a copy for the panicked manager, on the other hand, will absolutely charm him. Like it or not, these demonstrations of control and serenity can make a bigger impact on your career than a Ph.D. In addition, effective archiving helps you advertise yourself, as explained below.

> When a new director came in, we were all asked to make a brief presentation about our sectors. Most presentations were similar, containing sales, profits, forecasts etc. but one guy added a slide that made him stand out like a superstar. He simply put up a list of his recent projects and said that he would be happy to forward any of the listed files for further information. In this job we are asked for sales trends, feasibility studies and so on all the time, and we've all got a bunch of these sitting in our folders. He didn't do anything extra. He was just better organized and had a proper list of the work he had done before. But the director doesn't know that, of course. He now thinks this guy produces much more than anyone else does.

Follow-up e-mails after meetings or information requests present further opportunities to display your work. Make a list of your studies, presentations, and files and update it regularly. It will only take a few seconds to add one line to this list for each major study you complete. When the opportunity arises, you can copy and paste parts of this list into an e-mail to make someone aware of what is available. If a senior official requests a list of top ten clients, for example, you could mention that you also have other related information, such as the kinds of products bought by the biggest clients or their average order volume.

Customize your work

The manager who tailors his work to make it more appealing to the end user is disappearing as quickly as the custom shirt maker. The vast majority of data generated in large organizations is sent out indiscriminately to anyone who may or may not need it. The information is rarely touched up to better suit the needs of recipients. As a result, it appears crude and unrefined. Below, I will address both of these issues and show how easily you can stand out from the pack with just a tiny bit of additional effort.

i) Use numerous small e-mail lists, as opposed to a few large ones

In a large organization, you are only one piece of a giant puzzle. You will inevitably forward most of the information you create down the data chain to another recipient. This flow, however, is often inefficient. A lot of data either reaches its audience too late or gets lost in an overcrowded inbox. Consequently, the producer of the data rarely gets the credit he deserves.

One problem is that we tend to have just a few giant e-mail lists and end up sending a lot of information to people who are not interested in it. After a few irrelevant e-mails, these individuals start to ignore all of your messages. Even if recipients read the message and open all your attachments, this mass marketing strategy diminishes the perceived value of your work. A standard file sent out to fifty people will taste like a mass-produced donut from the corner shop, instead of grandma's apple pie that was baked just the way you like it.

To make your work more appealing, use small and targeted e-mail lists and send things only to the most relevant users. Do not rely on previous mass e-mails by opening them up and replying to all recipients. Instead, take a few minutes to create relevant address books for each major document you periodically send out. E-mail programs can create a lot of fancy lists, but sometimes low-tech solutions may work better, as explained below.

In the past, I used e-mail lists to send each monthly file to a select group of people, but it never worked well. I'd forget to send out the stuff on time or found it hard to remember which file to send to which list. A low-tech solution works much better. Now I simply write the e-mail addresses that I want to send the file to in the left corner cell of my spreadsheets. The names are separated by commas, so I can directly paste them into the e-mail program. Since these cells are painted in flashy colors, I see them as soon as I open the file to update it with new data and never forget to send out the information. By sending each file to a specific group, I can also write customized comments and make it much more useful.

As the interviewee points out, tailoring the mail lists also gives you the chance to add a few lines to further improve the appeal of the attached files. If you are sending the quality survey to the sales department, you can tell them to pay attention to page X, which confirms the problems they brought up in the recent board meeting. This notice will take just seconds to add, but proves that you have taken the time to think about the recipients' interests and are intimately familiar with the report. If the same information goes out to everyone at once, you cannot add this sweet touch.

ii) Give your data a custom-made look

Giving your data a custom-made look is another low-cost, high-benefit habit. It demonstrates how hardworking, meticulous, and attentive you are, but takes very little time. Most people won't know what your raw data looks like or what you receive from automated systems as opposed to what you create from scratch. Consequently, they may not be able to distinguish a file that took you two hours to compile from one that you simply downloaded off the corporate Web page or received from your colleagues in finance. But with tiny modifications, you can show that you created the file specifically for one person.

First, save your files under a unique and meaningful name for each major group of recipients. This will not only show that the file was custom-made, but also make it much easier for them to locate the file in their systems later on. If appropriate, also include your name or the name of your department or division in the file name, for example, "September Quality Survey—J.Smith Oct 9, 2005. xls." If the file is forwarded without mentioning who created it, the label can still communicate the identity of the author.

Minor modifications in the file will reinforce the same messages, while also saving time for the recipients. Highlighting a few rows and inserting a sentence such as "As observed by salespeople, our bottles do leak on the shelves" can completely change the flavor of the information. Similarly, a few Post-Its in a printout will prove that you processed the information for colleagues, instead of simply hitting the print icon. Since you will have to read most of what you distribute anyway, these notes or comments require close to zero additional effort.

When forwarding e-mails to an important recipient, delete the automatically generated "Fwd:" in the title line. Since so many people blindly forward useless messages, anything that arrives with the prefix "Fwd:" generates a great deal of apathy at first sight. Highlight the relevant portions of the original message and, most importantly, point out what is irrelevant so people won't have to read every single line in a long message.

All of this once again underlines the importance of knowing people's priorities and continuous information flow. Unless you know what recipients are interested in, you cannot meaningfully modify your files or e-mails. In addition to talking to people briefly but frequently, also try to take notes whenever they ask for something. This will convince the recipient that you are listening and are going to put together something specifically for him.

Seek the support of key customers; it is priceless

As we will later see, there are few things that will give you as much power as key customers who want to work with nobody but you. It is worth mentioning in this chapter that such support will also greatly boost your image. It shows that an independent party with no vested interest is willing to endorse your performance. While two coworkers can have a lot to gain by building a covert alliance and supporting each other under all circumstances, the appreciation of customers must be earned. Top managers are well aware of this, and find customer approval significantly more credible than a similar backing from internal sources. In Chapter 21, we will see ways to gain this approval.

5 Key Points You Should Remember

- Make your work instantly recognizable by using visual identifiers
- Remember the little things that people expect you to neglect
- Gently and non-invasively remind people of your past accomplishments
- Customize your work for each group of major recipient
- Do whatever you can to get the customer on your side

And a word of caution...
Do not dominate the stage

The tools in this section are so powerful that you can easily overdose on them and make people tired of seeing you too much. Allow me to make another advertising analogy here. No matter how clever or unique an advertising campaign may be, if you overdo it people soon get irritated. They get bored of the same slogan and start to resent the brand for monopolizing their time. Furthermore, the manufacturer's over-enthusiasm may raise doubts about the product's quality. With time, people also start to notice little faults, such as the dirty glasses of the model.

Similar problems will develop if you dominate the organizational scene. If the directors see you much more frequently than they see other people at your level, if you present at most major meetings and send several e-mails a day to senior managers, your image can take a beating before you realize it. People may get tired of you, start to notice small mistakes when there are no more positives to note, and see you as too ambitious. Other managers competing for the same promotion or bonus pool may get nervous, even launching a counterattack.

Step back a little when you feel that you've gotten your points across and give credit to others where it is due. Do not overshadow subordinates. Allow them speak in meetings, instead of always seeking the spotlight. Especially after major victories, when jealously will already run high, be modest and wait for others to declare you the winner, instead of reaching for the trophy. As Tom Brokow said, "Heroes are people who rise to the occasion and slip away quietly."

PART 4

Gaining The Power To Do Less

An old adage in racing is that horsepower is like money, in that you can never have too much of it. With both of these resources, having an excess supply makes everything run faster and smoother, even if you will never use some of what you have.

Assume that two cars, with top speeds of 110 and 80 miles respectively, are racing on a twisty public highway and must stay under 77 mph to avoid the police radar. Although the excess power of the first car appears to be of little use, it can actually make a huge difference. Both at the start and after slowing down for the turns, the first car will hit 77 mph much faster because it will be operating so much below its maximum capacity at that speed. Squeezing the last bit of performance out of anything is always a long and burdensome process, which is exactly what the second car has to accomplish. Furthermore, the engine of the second car will be stressed a great deal more and has a much higher probability to fall apart before the end of the race.

To see how the same phenomenon applies to large organizations, let us compare two managers, both of whom must talk to the Vice President to ask for a favor. Let us assume that the first manager is powerful enough to contact even the President on a regular basis, while the second manager lacks the power to go beyond the VP level.

The first manager can probably catch the VP with one or two phone calls. The second individual, however, will have to send several e-mails, ask the secretary to squeeze him in, and maybe even ask personal friends of the VP for help. So, although both managers have the power to contact the VP, the excess power reserve of the first manager makes things much faster and easier for him. To put it in managerial value chain jargon, power makes the transition from the first to the second step easier, as it enables you to achieve the same result with much less effort.

Power also makes it easier to get more credit for what you accomplish. In other words, it enables you to move from the third to the fourth stage. When people sense that you are not strong enough to make something big happen, they will attribute that big thing to someone else, even if you pull it off alone. For example, politicians, who have strong approval ratings and are seen as capable of solving the country's problems, always get most of the credit for improvements in the economy. But when the same happens during the term of a less liked leader, it is always "the entrepreneurial spirit of the people" that pulls the country out of the recession, because voters cannot comprehend that the incapable administration could do much good in any area.

In other words, the more power you have, the less work you will have to do in order to succeed. Over the next five chapters we will see how you can gain the power to do less.

CHAPTER 18

Giving Up a Little Fame to Gain a Lot of Speed

In his classical masterpiece *The Prince*, Niccolo Machiavelli says, "For as those who draw landscapes set themselves on the plain to examine the character of hills and of high places and set themselves on the summits to examine the lowlands, so in order thoroughly to understand the nature of the populace one must be a prince, and in order to thoroughly understand the nature of a prince one must be of the people."

Just like mountains, large organizations are best viewed from a few miles away. Active members of these entities can rarely see the entire picture, often missing the forest for the trees. So it is hardly surprising that some of the most insightful comments for this book came from retired executives who left big organizations to start their own businesses. When they look back at big companies, the biggest complaint of such people is the lack of independence.

> The worst thing about working for a big company is the dependence on sloppy people. In my whole career, I could do almost nothing entirely on my own. I was always pushing, chasing, or begging somebody to give me something. Nothing moved unless I poked accountants or bugged the sales people. At first, I had the illusion that only junior guys had this problem. I used to dream of the day when I could grill the accountant, and get what I needed right away. But when I could finally do that, nothing changed. At that point, his help was no longer enough. I need his boss's input and couldn't grill him. It was the same no matter how much they promoted me. I am sure you know how it feels to get stuck in traffic on your way to the airport. You know you'll miss the plane, you yell and honk all you can, but nobody around you moves an inch. That's how I felt all the time. But now, working for myself, I feel like the highway is wide open. I still miss the plane once in a while, but it's always because I drive too slowly or don't leave on time.

The airplane analogy hits the nail on the head. If accounting gives you the numbers for your board presentation an hour late, you may have to wait for two weeks until the next meeting, just as missing the plane by five minutes can get you stranded for six hours until the next flight. These things will, of course, tremendously inflate your workload. Missing the budget cycle because you couldn't get the numbers approved by the board forces you to go through the entire budgeting process again during the next round of revisions.

Since you will always need the input of other people to do your job in a large organization, you must either learn how to lead them around obstacles to get what you need or resign and start a small business. Before you throw in the towel and go for the latter, consider the suggestions below, because there is hope, especially if you are willing to give up a bit of fame.

Do not frame anything as "your" project

Suppose that you are a supervisor for the small electrical appliance section of a department store. After careful analysis, you decide to switch the location of the toasters and juice extractors to allocate more space to hairdryers. You cannot simply move things around, of course. You must first get an approval from the person responsible for your floor and convince your staff that it is worth the effort. Now, what is the fastest and easiest way of doing this?

Classical management books will tell you to "champion" the idea by fully owning the process as well as the outcome. They claim that anything pushed forward by an enthusiastic devotee who is willing to be held accountable will move faster. But, if improperly applied, this approach creates far more problems than it solves and can slow things down to a halt. Problems start at the concept stage, while trying to get an approval. If you communicate the project as "your baby," the supervisor will have reason to be suspicious. Even if you make a perfect sales pitch, he will naturally hesitate to push the button because he cannot know if the floor personnel who will carry things around will buy into it. After all, this is just your baby and nobody else's.

Compare this with the alternative, where you first talk to your own people and convince them. After securing their support and collecting a diverse set of reasons why this will work, you approach your supervisor and put a completely different spin on it. Rather than portraying yourself as the owner and originator, you go to him only as an ambassador. You relay the message of a big crowd and explain why your people want it. This will provide greater reassurance that the idea is valid—people dealing with customers every day think so—and convince the boss that the process will run smoothly, since it already has a large following.

Next, you must go to the finance manager and obtain money for the new display shelves. Again, you may be tempted to demonstrate your commitment to the project, but this can easily create the wrong impression. If the finance manager feels that you are the only one crazy about this plan, he can safely reject the idea no matter how committed you are. If, however, you pitch this as the initiative of your team, the pressure on the finance manager will be much greater. Angering you is one thing, but making twenty enemies is another thing altogether.

The little you may lose in giving up the ownership of the idea is more than made up for by the gains in speed and efficiency. It is much better to be a contributor to a successful project than to be the originator and sole owner of a failure. Also, do not exaggerate the value of ideas. As a professor of mine in business school used to say, "Ideas are like butts and elbows, everyone's got them." What will benefit your career a lot more than ideas is the ability to gather people around a cause. If you must give up the ownership of some ideas for that, so be it.

When it comes to implementation, the same is true again. The more you make it look like your project, the more obstacles you will encounter. However, by emphasizing the contribution of other influential people, you will communicate that you are willing to give credit where it is due and give your people a reason to work harder. Besides, the slackers will have a tougher time. If it is only your idea, who will give them problems for taking it easy when you're not around? Yet if you show that numerous people suggested this change, they will know that a lot of eyes are watching them and put in a lot more effort.

Do not claim to have done the most work, even if you did

Assume that you rearranged the small appliance section and, as you expected, sales improved while theft went down sharply. Now it is time to sell the results to top executives who heard about your success and will visit your section. Focusing on your individual contributions during this process will only diminish the value of the accomplishment. If you constantly talk about how hard you worked and make it look like a one-man show, top management will conclude that it wasn't such a major project after all. If it was mostly you, how big a deal could it have been?

Yet if you talk about how helpful the finance department was, how the guys from the home entertainment section gave a hand, and how hard your own people worked you will create a totally different impression. Be specific when giving credit. By telling exactly what they did, you will make people look much better. "We couldn't have pulled it off if Joe hadn't stayed all night to get the budget approval" means a lot more than merely thanking Joe. In addition, this will emphasize the multitude of specialized tasks that had to be accomplished and communicate how large and complex the project was.

Keep in mind that top managers won't remember how your section looked before the remodeling. This is true in most projects. Due to their isolation from daily events, top management cannot assess the amount of work that goes into an assignment. Yet if they know how many people were involved and how hard each one worked, they will assume that you have made serious changes.

Superiors will see this skill of yours and put greater resources at your disposal. Your own people, the finance department, and everyone who witnessed the project will also be more willing to help the next time around. Why shouldn't they? It pays to work with you since you share the rewards. In the words of the legendary philosopher Lao Tzu: "To lead people, walk beside them... When the best leader's work is done the people say, 'We did it ourselves!' "

3 Key Points You Should Remember

- Do not portray yourself as the "champion" or "custodian" of a major project
- Give credit to others to emphasize the scope and significance of your projects
- Communicate the outcome of your efforts, as opposed to how much time you put in

CHAPTER 19

Gliding Through Obstacles with Action Plans

Perhaps the best definition of genius is "seeing the extraordinary potential in the ordinary." People who perceive the hidden potential in things and transform them into something special have always fascinated me. The 2000 Olympics in Sydney, Australia, was the site of just such a transformation. Until then, swimsuits were considered a necessary evil that slowed down the swimmer. The added layer created a micro-hill on the otherwise smooth surface of the skin and disturbed the water flow. Consequently, it had a very minor, yet still negative, effect on the swimmer's speed.

The traditional solution was to make the swimsuit as small as possible to minimize its impact. Adidas, however, saw the untapped potential and realized that the swimsuit could become a performance booster. By modeling a synthetic fabric after a shark's skin, the sporting goods company produced an extremely slippery surface and turned traditional wisdom on its head. Now it made more sense to cover as big an area as possible with this new fabric. The result was a giant suit that covered everything except a swimmer's head, hands, and feet. In the first high-profile use of this suit, Australia's Ian Thorpe broke the 400-meter freestyle world record. Thorpe went on to win two more gold medals in the 4 x 100 and 4 x 200 meter freestyle events.

This achievement was highly publicized, but equally creative feats often go unnoticed. I have seen numerous managers similarly transform action plans from a necessary evil to an office power tool. Most of us see action plans as bureaucratic necessities that slow us down by imposing an inflexible schedule. Just as swimmers do with swimsuits, the traditional response of managers is to shrink action plans as much as possible, while still covering their backsides. When asked what they'll do, how they'll do it, and when they'll do it by, they commit to as little as possible and don't want to put down any of those commitments on paper. Yet action plans can be transformed from drag producing add-ons into slippery body armor that will enable you to slice through the organizational jungle with far less effort. Let's see how.

Use action plans to demonstrate the difficulty of your job

A key premise of this book is that your coworkers will not understand the complexities of your job and therefore underappreciate your achievements. Thus, you must show them that your occupation is not as easy as it may look. As we saw in Chapter 13, an action plan can be a great way to communicate the multi-faceted nature of your job. Such a plan is also the most economical way to convey the constraints you must operate under. A particular type of action plan known as a "Gantt Chart" is especially useful for this purpose.

A Gantt chart is more of a picture, and thus worth a thousand words. This one, for example, not only shows how many tasks are involved in getting the new ice cream parlor up and running, but also demonstrates how many of them are interdependent. Armed with such a visual representation, it takes less than a minute to explain why you need 26 days to open the facility.

DAYS

| 1 | 2 | 3 | 4 | 5 | 6 | 7 | 8 | 9 | 10 | 11 | 12 | 13 | 14 | 15 | 16 | 17 | 18 | 19 | 20 | 21 | 22 | 23 | 24 | 25 | 26 |

```
Sign Lease            Refrigerators Delivered            Install Electrical System      Production Test
                           Neon Signs Delivered
                      Painting and Decoration       Certification Complete
Find Local Milk Supplier            Sign Supplier Agreement
Hire Full Time & Part Time Staff          Train Staff
Prepare Ads for Local Paper
Print Flyers
```

Refrigerators cannot be ordered until you sign a lease and know the dimensions of the shop. The electricians cannot work before both the refrigerators and neon signs are delivered. Neon signs are custom made and take longer to deliver than refrigerators. So electricians may have to wait for a while after the refrigerators have arrived. In contrast, the staff can be hired and trained right away, because the size of the refrigerators will not affect how they scoop the ice cream.

With the Gantt chart you can illustrate this immense amount of data far more quickly than by talking. Hence, it is especially useful when working with top managers. It also shows how many issues you must think of and how many constraints you are facing. This will reduce expectations, help you to get more credit for what you do, and obtain more help from coworkers. If purchasing is slow in approving the refrigerator order, for example, one e-mail with the above Gantt chart will show everyone the consequences of such a delay. This gives you tremendous leverage to increase the pressure on purchasing to speed things up. To maximize the power of Gantt charts, make them easy to grasp and ensure that the limitations and interdependencies come across at first sight. Use the same Gantt chart over and over to hammer the message into people's heads.

Use action plans to gain credibility and pull others into your projects

When we have to decide on a deadline, we almost always make an action plan like the one shown above. Whether we go through this process mentally or write it down does not make much difference. Whether we publicize and promote this plan, however, makes a huge difference. If, in order to not bore your colleagues with details, you simply say "The launch of our IT system is scheduled for July 12," you are not giving people a good reason to believe you. Managers in large organizations are so accustomed to phony deadlines that most will assume that this is your best-case scenario. You might have a very well thought-out plan in your head. But since others cannot read your mind, your words will sound empty.

Contrast this with putting an action plan on the table where you detail what needs to be done and explain why. Even if people don't understand the technicalities, they will be much more likely to believe in you and your venture. The fact that you thought about a strategy and have the courage to commit to a detailed plan is highly impressive. This makes it more likely that others will join or support your project, because it reassures them that their efforts won't go to waste.

Use action plans to show that things are moving ahead

Imagine these two scenarios. In the first case, you obtain detailed directions to drive from point A to point B and, by following the instructions, you arrive at your destination in two hours. In the second case, you have no directions and you go by your instincts, trying to guess which way to turn at every intersection. After two hours, point B suddenly appears in front of your tired eyes and the pain is finally over. Which of these do you think would feel shorter? Psychologists tell us that, although both journeys lasted two hours, the first one will feel significantly shorter.

In the first case, you know how much is left and feel a step closer to your target with each turn. It will almost be like watching a countdown. In the second case, however, you will feel lost and won't have this sense of edging closer to the finish line. When you arrive, you will say that you "finally" made it and think that the trip took an unnecessarily long time, even though this isn't true. Likewise, an action plan allows people to cross off items as you move along and creates a sensation of moving forward. This renews everyone's motivation.

Checking an item off your to-do list is one of the best feelings you can experience in an office. It is so liberating, especially after the item has been there for a while. People feel the same way when you announce that a key step in a project is completed and can now be crossed off everyone's mental to-do list. This lifts spirits up and creates momentum.

Furthermore, those who may jump ship midway through are less likely to do so when they see how well things are moving. The motivation to be part of a success and the peer pressure not to sabotage something that has already made a lot of progress will keep them on board.

Another advantage of an action plan is that it enables you to easily communicate your status to top managers. These executives rarely have time for details and often quiz you in an elevator or by the coffee machine. If you only published a deadline, but didn't bother to break it down into easily understandable pieces, all you can say when a director asks you about the project is "It's going great." With an action plan, however, you can say "It's going great. Our goal for July was to sign all agreements with distributors. We did that last week. Next, we'll do a test run in the factory, probably also a week ahead of schedule." Which one sounds better to you?

To take advantage of this phenomenon, break projects into enough steps so you can regularly pass small milestones. If a yearlong project only has three items, you will lose the audience between steps. If, on the other hand, you have so many items that you declare a victory every week, people will soon start to ignore you. Planning for the completion of one step every month is a good starting point.

To visually communicate how much progress you made, always present the entire Gantt chart even if most tasks on it are finished. Even a twelve-year-old who has never seen a Gantt chart can look at the following picture and see that you are almost there. A busy top executive, who can sometimes be harder to communicate with than a twelve-year-old, needs close to zero mental bandwidth and time to understand how much progress you have made after seeing this representation.

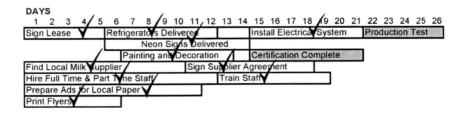

If most of the planned actions have been accomplished on or ahead of schedule, you can use a slightly different format to convey this information too. The list shown below can accompany the Gantt chart or, if you have only a few tasks left, it can replace the Gantt chart altogether. Whether people will read every date and realize how many of the tasks have been completed ahead of schedule does not matter. The transparency with which you operate and your courage to display your entire operation history will get the point across.

ACTION	TARGET DATE	COMPLETION DATE
Sign Lease	5-May	4-May
Refrigerator Delivery	12-May	12-May
Flyer Production	6-May	4-May
Advertising Approval	11-May	9-May
Neon Sign Delivery	14-May	13-May
Electrical System Installation	21-May	19-May
Milk Supplier Agreement	18-May	18-May
Training of Staff Complete	19-May	19-May
Facility Certification	**21-May**	
Production Test	**26-May**	
Days remaining to completion: 6		

Use action plans as an insurance policy

Very few major projects run as smoothly as planned. In fact, I have never seen one that did. While unforeseen problems cannot be avoided, you can overcome them much more easily by placing invisible insurance policies into your action plans.

i) If all tasks are equally difficult

If none of the steps looks more challenging than the rest, insert an extra step close to the beginning and another one near the end. These "insurance steps," which you can accomplish easily and independently of other tasks, will help you to keep the good news coming and preserve the momentum. A good example is legal filings, which lawyers can prepare ahead of time. Similarly, easy to obtain approvals from internal sources will serve you well. Although nobody will likely throw a party upon hearing that you accomplished a minor task, these will help you to communicate that you are still pushing forward and haven't stalled yet.

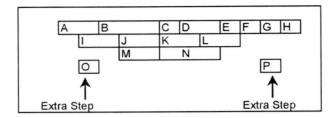

Step O in the above example is designed to do just that. If you encounter a problem after only accomplishing A and declare that B will be delayed, you will look really bad. As there is not yet sufficient investment, top management may even shelve the project. Besides, you will lose the audience's attention between A and B by not providing any news for too long. By having step O, however, you can cross one more item off the list while waiting for B, and show that things are still moving along. This way, the delay of B will attract less attention.

Step P is even more important. The last few tasks are the most likely to be delayed in most projects. Problems accumulated earlier often surface at this phase. For instance, production tests in the ice cream parlor can reveal a wide variety of problems, ranging from insufficient electrical power to temperature fluctuations in the refrigerators. Step P will prevent you from looking bad when you were so close to the finish line and help you to leave a good last impression.

ii) If one task will be particularly difficult

When you can spot the most difficult task in a project, insert an extra step right before it.

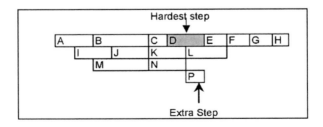

If D is the most challenging task, step P will act as the fallback item. It will enable you to deliver a piece of good news at exactly the right time even if D is delayed.

iii) If there is an unusually long gap between two consecutive tasks

Sometimes two consecutive tasks, neither of which is exceptionally difficult, are separated by a long break. You have no choice but to sit and wait during this period. For example, certain packaged foods must be stored under harsh conditions for several months to check the chemical integrity of the formula. Although practically nothing needs to be done during this process and results are rarely negative, the long wait can be disheartening. It is prudent to insert an extra step to be completed at around the midpoint of this long pause.

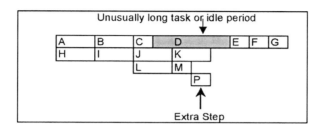

Scheduling the completion of packaging safety tests, a routine and easy procedure, around the midpoint of the storage period will keep the momentum up during the wait.

Use action plans to deal with inevitable failures

No matter how well you explain the constraints, top management will sometimes impose an unrealistic deadline—perhaps to present exciting, yet unattainable, forecasts to their own bosses. Another reason may be to force you to fail in order to demonstrate to the bigger guys that more personnel or a better infrastructure are needed. Although this sounds cruel, it may be better to get the point across with a forced failure in a medium-sized project before being pushed into a huge battle with insufficient resources. Or sometimes your superior will just not get it. You can explain all you want, but the boss will childishly insist that it can be done and ask for the impossible.

But no matter who pushed you in, all fingers will point at you when you fail, and you will have to defend yourself. A proper action plan is one of your best weapons in such a fight. Unless you had given a road map, nobody will know whether you were almost finished or have barely scratched the surface by the deadline. But if you can refer to your earlier plan and show that most of what was promised has been done, you will look much better—perhaps not even like a failure.

To create the proper effect, however, you must deliver a few strong results until the deadline. If you make the classical mistake of rushing everything, you will achieve a lot of mediocre results that will be of little use. In the end, you will fail to reach the ultimate objective, plus you will create the impression that the outcome would have been sub par even if you had plenty of time. When you know that you will fail no matter what, focus your energy on a single thing and achieve one spectacular result. In the ice cream parlor example, the early and highly visible task of painting and decoration must blow people away. Upon seeing a gorgeous yet unfinished store, people will think one of two things: that you will build the perfect shop if given more time or, at worst, that you are a competent but slow worker. Either one is much better than being thought of simply as a failure, which is unavoidable if people see both an average paint job and a missed deadline.

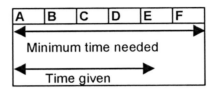

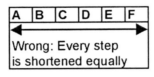

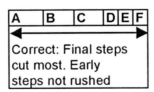

Use action plans to fight for more time or resources

Although some deadlines are carved in stone, most can be extended. Again, a carefully crafted action plan is your best bargaining chip. There is a world of difference between saying "Trust me, we're almost there" and putting a plan on the table to show that 85% of the tasks have been completed. If you have not produced such a formal plan in the beginning, however, it is now too late to do so. Pulling out a list that no one saw before, with most items already checked off, will just not be credible. If, on the other hand, everybody saw you progress as promised until you hit a roadblock, it is much easier to convince people that you can overcome the last hurdle with a bit more time or money.

Older managers, in particular, fail to understand this critical difference, because the economy has changed so much over the last two decades. Back in the old days, manufacturing made up a much larger proportion of the total output. Since we used to make things that we could touch, smell, and see, it was much easier to show where a project stood. If you are building a warehouse and get stuck at the last stage, you can take people to the construction site and show that when you put a roof on top, the damn thing will be ready. After seeing that you are almost there, few superiors would cut off your lifeline and let everything go to waste.

If, however, you are building an electronic database or wireless network—the kinds of things that we mostly do today—there will be nothing to show until you are 100% finished. Therefore, you must give people a sense of how much progress has been made, as this IT manager points out.

> The problem with practically every IT project is that most of the money will be spent up front but produce no visible results until the very end. And when the results start to come in, they'll usually be disappointing at first. A bug in the software or one missing file can mess it all up. These things can only be solved gradually. Tangible products—like a building—are best when they are new but deteriorate over time. The new economy produces things that get better over time, like software that you improve with use. People who are writing the checks must be made aware of this fact, or else they will think that they aren't getting their money's worth. You have to give them a road map of what to expect so they can check your status and know what will happen next. Otherwise, the IT guy always looks like a whiner, constantly saying that success is around the corner.

If you follow these directions, action plans will turn from a burden to a power tool. So use them as much as possible. Even relatively minor tasks, such as repainting eighteen delivery trucks, will run better and faster with an action plan. Announcing that you must first decide on the paint scheme and then proceed at a pace of two trucks a day will make it much easier to deal with potential problems. Should the task finish ahead of time or budget, this will be much easier to publicize and get credit for, if you produced a simple action plan in the beginning.

3 Key Points You Should Remember

- Use action plans to demonstrate the importance of the job at hand
- Use action plans for a visual representation of the progress you are making
- Use invisible "insurance policies" in action plans to deal with potential problems

CHAPTER 20

Turning Skeptics into Supporters

Although many years have passed since, I still remember the day so clearly. I had been working for a month as an assistant brand manager and had just finished one of the most brutal weeks of my life. Over the last few days, I had prepared every imaginable chart and graph (or so I thought) to justify the launch of a new pack size. Armed with that knowledge, my boss was finally talking to the marketing director behind closed doors. A decision was due any moment.

Since I was fairly confident that the worst was over, I had already made plans for the evening. This would be my first entertainment on a weeknight since I had started the job. It was also the last chance to smell the summer breeze. My hypothesis was simple: whether they approved the idea or not, the pain would end within minutes. If accepted, the plan was ready to implement because every detail had been addressed. We would push the button and launch the new size as quickly as it could be produced. A rejection would produce even less work, as it basically implied status quo. In any case, I would be free for the evening.

However, I was in for a big surprise. As the great biologist Thomas Huxley said, "The tragedy of science is the slaying of a beautiful hypothesis by an ugly fact." My beautiful hypothesis and plans for the evening were slaughtered at once, by an ugly fact I had never imagined. The marketing director could not make a decision either way and wanted to see even more analysis. Since we had already provided almost every bit of accessible information, his demands were extremely hard to meet. In fact, I had no idea where to get what he wanted. I knew, though, that I had to order a fairly large dinner soon, because it would be a very long night.

While it may sound dramatic, there is nothing unusual about this story. The inability to convince people always leads to exaggerated demands for information. The weaker your persuasive skills, the less people trust your conclusions. Consequently, they ask for every piece of relevant information to verify all of your opinions. These demands for progressively deeper analyses are among the biggest workload generators in large organizations. In the above situation, for example, superiors should take your word when you say that value-sized giant packs will not hurt the brand image. If you fail to inspire this confidence, you will be asked for a burdensome analysis, such as a list of prestigious brands that launched value-sized packs over the last year.

Furthermore, this skill will help cut your work hours by enabling you to enlist the help of others. While reward and punishment can help secure the co-operation of colleagues, someone who truly believes in your ideas will support you much more strongly than an ally cooperating only for short-term gain. In short, the ability to convince people can greatly reduce your workload.

Although the importance of persuasive skills is widely acknowledged, the relationship between personality traits and persuasiveness is often blown out of proportion. The focus in management media is mostly on abstract concepts such as charisma, personal magnetism, and manners. No wonder that most advice on how to convince people leaves the reader frustrated. Fortunately, persuasive skills can be distilled into more tangible elements. Since social interactions are fairly similar across large organizations, so are successful social strategies. More importantly, these strategies are independent of personality. If persuasive skills or other variables of success were determined by personality, the upper layers of large organizations would be full of a specific character type. But a quick glance proves that great managers come in all shapes, sizes, and personas. Therefore, skills such as persuasive ability must be learnable regardless of character.

To get to "yes," first block the public "no"

Dean Radin, a leading researcher on psychic phenomena, says, "When we are publicly committed to a belief, it is disturbing even to consider that any evidence contradicting our position may be true." He states that as a result, the scientific community won't even look at the ample proof confirming the super-natural. According to Radin, most scientists have publicly rejected paranormal concepts at some point and are afraid of losing face by taking a step back.

Whether psychic phenomena are supported by solid evidence is beyond the scope of this book. However, Mr. Radin correctly identifies the fact that be-ing committed to a public statement can paralyze our ability to reason. In fact, managers fall prey to this more often than scientists do. Deprived of time, they make snap judgments and quickly publicize their views. Once publicly commit-ted to a stance, they close their minds and turn into fanatical supporters of their ill-conceived ideas. If the matter is a new and unusual concept, the snap judgment is usually "no," because new ideas take time to digest. Defending this "no" can quickly become a matter of pride and seal the fate of the initiative.

Senior managers are particularly prone to this mistake. Suffering most from time-famine, they make countless premature judgments. In addition, they are usually surrounded by people, so their opinions instantly become public knowl-edge. And since top managers place so much value on their images, revising the opinion that they so confidently put forth can be close to impossible.

This scenario could play out as follows. In a meeting, you propose an un-usual product promotion, which, like all new ideas, sounds strange at first. After you explain the rationale, the denial on people's faces turns to indecision. Now you put the bug into their ears as planned and step back to revisit the topic after a few days. A top official, however, takes it upon himself to reach a quick verdict and kills the initiative on the spot. One cannot blame him, because the last thing he wants is another unresolved item in his gigantic to-do list. But now the top official will refuse to give a second chance to the idea he so readily dismissed in front of others. The concept is, for all practical purposes, dead.

To prevent this outcome, your first goal when introducing a new idea is not to get to "yes," but to prevent a public "no." Fortunately, you have many options.

i) Introduce the idea with an <u>incomplete</u> e-mail

Introducing people to new ideas when they are alone will prevent an immediate public comment. A brief personal e-mail is highly effective for this purpose. Although most people feel compelled to answer quickly to the spoken word, e-mails generate a slower response. Plus, even if the answer is immediate and negative, at least it will not be broadcast to the whole world. Additionally, the recipient will recall the matter every time he sees the message in his inbox, and like all unusual ideas, the concept will sound a bit more plausible every time it is reviewed.

To further discourage an instant response, make your message incomplete. State that you are continuing to look into the issue and will soon follow up with more details. This way, you can also keep the e-mail short and ensure that it will be read. A particularly effective method is to use a graph or chart, not as an attachment, but right in the body of the message. While some people don't launch attached files until much later, almost everybody looks at the message right away—often by single clicking on the message. A picture pasted into the body of the message is therefore almost impossible to miss and, like all pictures, it is worth a thousand words.

From	Date	Subject
Sales Support	19-May	April Sales Breakdown
Mary Brown	19-May	Monday's Meeting
Suzan Smith	20-May	Promotion Idea
Harry Morton	20-May	Request for information

Hi John,

As you know, the big concern with "half off" promotions was the high return rates after the last one. But upon close inspection, the numbers don't look bad at all in the Midwest, where we'll focus this time. I'll send you more data soon, but in the meantime I wanted to share this.

Susan

Returns After 2005 "Half off Promotion"

Florida	Midwest	California	East Coast
7.0%	6.2%	21.0%	11.4%

Even if the recipient only single-clicks on Susan's email to preview it, the chart with a strong visual message is displayed in the preview window below.

The graph in the above example is very hard to escape because, even if the recipient single clicks on the message, the picture will appear inside the display window at the bottom. In addition, stating that more data is coming soon will make it very hard for the person to react. Very few people would respond to such a message by saying "Don't bother sending more information, half-off promotions are out of question." If you send the entire data at once, however, the recipient can reasonably reach a verdict and kill your baby. When sending only a few data points, you can also pick the most compelling and impressive evidence, thus making it even harder for the person to reject the proposal.

ii) Hand them a page or two on the way out

Printouts handed at a strategic moment are another great way to introduce a project. Some top managers are so bad with e-mail that it can take them days to devote even a few seconds to your message. In other situations, printouts will have the upper hand over e-mail due to logistical reasons, such as the lack of time to power up a laptop in a cab ride. Clearly state that the few pages you are handing out do not include every single piece of relevant information, and catch the individual when he cannot stop to take a detailed look at the material. These precautions will practically eliminate the possibility of a hasty response.

It is even better to provide those pages right before a business trip or a brief vacation. The issue is more likely to get stuck in the recipient's mind and constantly bother him. This will force him to think about it and, as I said, the more people think about a controversial matter, the more they will warm to it. You probably have had this experience before. Someone makes an unacceptable proposal and walks away before you can say "no." Although you wish to get the matter off your mind by catching the person and declining the offer, you cannot reach him, and the issue keeps revolving in your head. By the time you talk to the individual again, you have spent so much time with the idea that it does not look that outlandish anymore and you are at least willing to discuss it. This is precisely what you want to accomplish with e-mails or printouts that contain incomplete information and/or are handed out when the person cannot reach a decision right away. A variation of this strategy is to hand out a few pages or send an e-mail right before you leave for a business trip where you will be hard to reach, and request that you have a meeting on the matter upon your return.

iii) Make it the last topic in a rushed meeting

Meetings are usually the worst places to bring up unusual ideas. There is rarely enough time to properly consider novel concepts. In addition, everybody witnesses the rejections, thus strengthening the skeptical manager's commitment to his public remarks. Sometimes, however, meetings can be your only gateway to specific top managers. These people may be very hard to reach, or they may be so senior that you cannot simply walk into their offices to pitch an idea.

If you must introduce a new idea in a meeting, one option is to bring it up at the end when there is no time to talk about it. Just as people are preparing to leave, kindly mention that you were hoping to discuss an issue, but do not want to hold everyone up. As a compromise solution, request that the topic be included in the agenda of the next meeting, then distribute a few pages that participants can read in the meantime. As usual, clearly state that the document is only an introduction and that more information will be revealed soon. You will eliminate the possibility of a premature public comment and keep the idea in their minds until the next meeting.

Pick arguments that require the least thought

Once you have stopped a premature "no," you are ready to launch an attack to get to "yes." To do so, you must replicate your argument in the other person's mind. If you can successfully convey the information as well as the logical connections that led you to a particular conclusion, chances are that the other person, too, will become a believer. This is the essence of genuine persuasion: to take someone through a thought process in order to help him see what you are seeing. Socrates, perhaps the highest master of this art, summed it up by saying, "I cannot teach anybody anything. I can only make them think."

Unfortunately, the chaos and complexity in a giant entity often eat up all the mental capacity of managers, leaving very little brainpower to listen to new ideas. People's heads are overflowing with analysis, and the last thing they want to do is to think even more. To make things worse, the senior managers whose opinions matter most have the least available bandwidth.

Most of the management literature tries to overcome this problem by resorting to charisma and personal magnetism. Here, instead of inviting the person to think with you, you implicitly ask him to suspend his intellectual capacity and accept *your* thoughts, since you are so intelligent. Even with all the charisma in the world, this produces short-term results. Fortunately, the problem can be overcome in another way.

When efficient managers must convince a busy executive, they make it as easy as possible for the other side to reconstruct the intellectual argument in his own mind. They identify all the reasons that can potentially lead to a conclusion, and then communicate the ones that conform most to the other party's existing beliefs. This way, the other person can understand you by doing the least mental work.

For example, suppose that you are bullish about stocks and wish to persuade a business partner to make an investment. First, ask yourself why you think that stocks will advance. Some of the bullish arguments you have constructed on your own or adopted may be the following:

a) Economic outlook in Europe is weak and the region presents few investment opportunities. So the U.S. stock market looks attractive to overseas investors and foreign money should flow in soon. Therefore, the stock market should recover.

b) Interest rates are very low and the Fed is determined to keep them low. Since businesses will borrow more to take advantage of the low rates, the economy should grow and, consequently, the stock market should go up.

c) This administration is more committed to economic recovery than the ones I saw in prior recessions. They also have a good plan in place and enough time before the end of their term. So they will succeed in reviving the economy. Therefore, the stock market should recover.

Your partner has never been to Europe and is largely disinterested in that region of the world. In addition, he constantly complains about declining prices for the product manufactured by your firm and resists borrowing money to increase capacity. Finally, he is a keen political observer and follows congressional discussions very closely.

Argument (a) will probably fail. Your views about Europe may be valid, but since your partner knows nothing about the region, you will have to educate him from scratch. You must give a long conference to show the weakness in Europe and prove a strong link between U.S. stocks and the European economy. Chances are you will lose him during this discussion. In the end you will have to ask him, implicitly or explicitly, to take your word for it because a busy manager can simply not give you enough time and attention to absorb this much information.

Argument (b) is even worse. Whereas he knew nothing about the matter in case (a), he has conflicting views about this subject. Since he does not want to borrow money despite the low rates, it will be very difficult to convince him that other firms will do so and prop up the economy. You must not only neutralize his existing views, but also replace them with something radically different. This will require a huge investment of time and mental energy by both parties and is unrealistic within the context of a large organization.

Argument (c) presents none of these problems. Since your partner is already familiar with politics, you do not have to educate him about that at all. All you need to prove is that the tax-cut proposal in the congress, which he already knows very well, will likely lead to a bull market. Putting up a historic chart showing past tax cuts and their impact on stock prices will do the trick, because this is the only piece of the puzzle missing in his mind. You only need a few minutes of your partner's time and a tiny bit of his attention to impart this much knowledge.

In addition, a logical argument will travel much better throughout a large organization than an idea force-fed solely through charisma. Your partner can promote your argument almost as successfully as you can and pull more people into your venture, as explained by this interviewee.

> I think that personal charisma can be enough when you are running a small operation or working independently, but in a big company it is not the best tool of persuasion. Since personal charm requires direct contact with your audience, your argument cannot travel beyond you. If you buy my point because of my charisma, you cannot sell that argument to someone else on my behalf. I must contact every person that I want to win over and charm them. But if I provide an easily digestible logical argument that everyone with average intelligence can understand, you can relay this to others. My thoughts can then travel beyond me, because every person I win over will turn into a walking billboard.

So remember, the less thinking and mental processing a given argument requires before it can be digested, the better you can convince a busy manager with it.

Support your arguments with the strongest authorities

To further reduce the mental work that the other party must perform, support your arguments with the strongest available authorities. The amount of thought one must put in before accepting a piece of information decreases in direct proportion to the reliability and objectivity of the data source. If, for example, I showed you an article where Harvard Medical School says champagne is healthier than beer, you would probably accept this assertion without much thought.

If, however, the same information came from a small, unknown research center, you would want to know where the study was published, what other research the same institution put out, and so on. In other words, you would utilize a lot of brain cells before accepting the thesis because the reliability of the source is suspect—not a desirable situation if you wish to convince a busy manager with little intellectual bandwidth. Similarly, if the same information was published by a champagne manufacturer, you would need to do a lot of probing. This time, the objectivity of the source would be in doubt. So which sources are perceived as most reliable and objective, and thus maximize your persuasive power? They rank as follows in descending order:

1—An independent institution with no vested interests in the outcome
Example: Food and Drug Administration

2—An independent institution with potential conflict of interests
Example: A medical school conducting a study funded by pharmaceutical companies

3—An independent institution paid by your organization
Example: A consulting firm hired by your company

4—A broad/diverse group or task force within your own organization
Example: A diverse team of managers investigating quality problems

5—A small/uniform group or task force within your own organization
Example: Five managers from the quality department investigating quality problems

6—You working alone with broad array of data
Example: You preparing a quality report with input from four departments

7—You working alone with your own data
Example: You preparing a quality report based on data you collected from the field

Not surprisingly, the most useful options are also the rarest and most expensive. A study by a trustworthy and independent institution that supports your point will really strengthen your hand. Consequently, reports prepared by an industry association or a federal body quickly become the industry standard. Unfortunately, these institutions are by definition independent, and you cannot influence when they will release something useful.

You can, however, diligently search the databases and keep your eyes open. New hires out of college and interns are especially useful for scanning long reports to pick out relevant facts, because they haven't lost their academic edge. When you have to tackle this task alone, check databases frequently and get on e-mail lists for regular updates, as opposed to reading a 100-page report once every two months. Remember that you can digest the information much better if you take it in small and regular portions.

Keep a particularly close eye on governmental bodies. There is a strong trend towards greater transparency in most governments around the world. Reports, forecasts, and sometimes even meeting minutes are available on the Web sites of institutions such as The Federal Reserve Board. While these documents can be wordy and hard to read, governmental agencies are still among the most trusted and objective sources, especially after the corporate scandals of late.

Sometimes an institution you wish to quote may be labeled as biased for no good reason. To efficiently convey the objectivity of the source, illustrate how its view has changed in response to new data. For example, show how the Food and Drug Administration started supporting the use of tea supplements only after the last study, tough it had been silent on the matter in the past despite efforts by tea makers. This will prove that the FDA is not afraid to take a stance and is probably objective. It also helps to mention the reservations and mild criticisms of the FDA about tea supplements to strengthen its image of objectivity. Another solution is to point out how the FDA slams many other similar supplements, often refuting the claims of giant supplement manufacturers. As a general rule, the fewer endorsements an authority gives, the more valuable each one of these will become.

Hire a consultant

If you cannot find a written or verbal statement by an independent authority to support your opinion, try to hire a consultant. As a general rule consultants are most useful when people either have too little or too much confidence in you. The first case is obvious; when your word alone is insufficient to sway the opinion of your superiors or coworkers, you can try to bring in a paid expert who will likely support your viewpoint. The important thing to remember during this process is not to give the impression of leading the consultant towards a certain conclusion. Most managers spend too much time with the expert in public, hurting the image of both parties. If you are seen taking the consultant to lunch every day and he delivers a report strongly supporting your ideas, how credible will he look? The more likely he is to support the ideas that you have been preaching all along, the more you should distance yourself from him. Limit your interactions to only providing the data that he needs to see the facts.

In the second case, an outsider might be helpful to reduce unrealistic expectations and alert the organization to the risks. Managers who are appointed to new divisions following a stellar success are often expected to repeat the prior miracle—now under even more difficult circumstances. Having seen the person walk on water during his prior assignment, few superiors will buy his claims that he needs a bit more slack this time around. If you find yourself under such excessive pressure, an outside expert may be able to open up the eyes of your superiors to the risks. Especially if your new assignment constitutes uncharted territory for your organization, expectations will likely be unrealistic and you should seriously consider hiring an expert for a reality check. A typical case that I witnessed several times was acquisitions. Since few management teams appreciate the pains of adding an entire business unit or company to an existing corporation overnight, the task almost always takes more time and money than initially planned. Should you be put in charge of such an integration, a feasibility analysis by an expert can be an invaluable tool for obtaining more resources for the task at hand.

Diversify your project/research teams

If a consultant is not an option either, you must prepare an internal report. While doing so, expand your team as much as possible, because the diversity of contributors is more important than the content. A mediocre joint report by quality assurance, production, and R&D about raw material problems has more credibility than a flawless study prepared by the quality assurance group alone.

Everybody will know that no matter how many people from quality assurance participated, the department head can manipulate the final report. Since their boss is involved and their goals are aligned, few people will object. The report will thus be viewed as "the quality assurance version of the story." On the other hand, it is much harder to manipulate several departments at once. The consensus of a broad group with varying interests makes their views much more credible.

Therefore, gather as varied a group as you can for your analysis. People may be reluctant to join such a task force, citing lack of time or other commitments. If you get such excuses, assure these individuals that not everybody will have to be involved to the same extent, and that they will need a negligible amount of time for the project. Depending on the scope of the task, even the inclusion of one assistant from finance in only one of your meetings may enable you to say "Finance was also involved." The role of such a person is not unlike the rabbi who supervises the kitchen of a kosher restaurant. The rabbi is not supposed to do the actual cooking and, therefore, won't need to spend a lot of time there. He only needs to see what is going on and approve the process. Similarly, people just want to know that someone from finance was around and saw how you came up with your profit estimates. This will significantly enhance your credibility, even if the finance representative doesn't ever touch a spreadsheet.

If such a task force would be too much for the matter at hand, include data from as many sources as possible in your analysis. Coming up with four bullet points that explain why the plant expansion will be profitable can be persuasive. But presenting four graphs from different departments, all reaching the same conclusion, is much better. Even just working with the data of other departments will boost your credibility. While the analysis may be yours, charts or tables can mention other departments as the source. This will not be as strong as an outright endorsement, but it will show that everybody's data is pointing in the same direction.

Finally, do not quote Web pages as a source. The Internet is still seen as an unreliable medium. The reaction may be that "you just got it off the Web," as if you had typed a keyword into Yahoo and copied the first page that came up. This will both diminish your credibility and understate the amount of time you put into the research. Instead of using the name of the Internet site, use the name of the organization that owns it. For example "CNN" is much better than "cnn.com."

Use a scientific style

As you have probably noticed, scientific works share common elements of style, regardless of the discipline. Certain cues give away the intellectual roots of a write-up or speech in just a few sentences. Although excessive reliance on these can bore the audience, careful insertion of a few hints will significantly improve your credibility.

First, list the assumptions you have made in your calculations and your data sources. This is much easier than it sounds and can be just a few sentences. When quoting a source, be specific. Instead of "Bureau of Labor Statistics," say "Bureau of Labor Statistics, Occupational Outlook Handbook, Transportation Section." This takes only a few more seconds but sounds more serious and shows that you read, or at least are familiar with, the entire report.

It is also reassuring to let people know how to obtain the data you have used. Knowing it is possible to replicate the calculations gives assurance to the audience, even if nobody attempts to do so. In a sense, like every scientist, you are saying "Here's how I got my results; rerun the numbers if you want." This openness shows a lot of confidence. For a brief study, a simple notice, such as the one below, is sufficient.

"Market share data has been provided by ABC Research Co. and is based on a retailer sampling in 32 major cities. Market size for cold cereals is assumed to be 3.8 billion boxes per year. For complete history of market share and advertising data contact Jsmith@xyzcereal.com."

Do not worry if a lot of your charts end with the same paragraph. As I said, this will actually make it easier to recognize who did them when they are distributed without the author's name.

Another trademark of scientific research is the author's willingness to explain the terms. Instead of assuming that readers will know what specific phrases mean, each key term is defined. Just like providing appendices and data sources, this projects an image of transparency. It shows that you are not using confusion as a method of persuasion. Remember, the more you expose something, the less people will probe it.

Finally, refrain from reaching absolute conclusions and always present the other side of the coin. A healthy dose of skepticism is an unmistakable attribute of science and rationality. Almost every scientific analysis concludes that "further research is necessary." We are so accustomed to this uncertainty that it rarely shakes our confidence. We don't expect the doctor to guarantee that the medicine will work. In fact, such a statement would alarm us, because it sounds more like a sales pitch than a medical diagnosis. We expect the doctor to mention risks and side effects, so we can make an informed decision.

Briefly mention the limitations and risks. Omitting them won't make you more credible; on the contrary, it will weaken your claims. Besides, top managers will probably bring up the risks anyway. By addressing them on your own, you can put the right spin on them and prove that you think like a top manager. It is worth remembering that, both at work and in life, mild self-criticism usually thwarts a much harsher condemnation.

3 Key Points You Should Remember

- Do everything you can to block a public rejection of your idea by top management
- Make your arguments easy-to-digest for busy minds
- Support your conclusions with information from various stakeholders

CHAPTER 21

Curbing the Customer's Insatiable Appetite

In Chapter 5, we saw why customers have an inherent power advantage and can be more dominant than even top management. As Sam Walton, the founder of Wal-Mart, said, "There is only one boss: the customer. He can fire everybody in the company from the chairman on down, simply by spending his money somewhere else." Because of this imbalance of power, managers find it very hard to say "no" to customers' never-ending requests. As a result, customers rank right up there with your immediate boss and meetings as the biggest workload generators in large organizations.

I am not implying that all customers are evil or will needlessly inflate your workload. But it is crucial to learn how to defend yourself against such people, because it takes only a very few abusive clients to make you miserable. It is equally important to spot a slowly emerging pattern of abuse and act before it turns into a chronic problem. Upon sensing that you must comply with virtually all of their requests, even reasonable clients can get spoiled over time, dumping more and more of their own work on you. As they say, power corrupts, and since clients are some of the most powerful people you will deal with, you must be prepared for that possibility.

The most common, and also the worst, strategy used to deal with abusive clients is to retreat into a shell to minimize client interactions. The appreciation of the customer is worth more than the Pope's blessing and, thus, is a tremendous efficiency booster. (Recall the salesperson in Chapter 5. He could do almost anything he pleased, because customers loved him.) A better response is to provide the best service you can, while neutralizing the power advantage of the customer. This will both satisfy him and put a cap on what he thinks he is entitled to ask for. You must also ensure that the client talks to your superiors when he is happy, communicating your superb performance. If you can accomplish all this, you will have a satisfied customer who praises you and refrains from making excessive requests. Sounds like the seller's nirvana, doesn't it?

Before I explain how you can get there, let me clarify two things. First, a customer is anyone who provides financial, logistical, or legislative support without which the organization cannot survive. Hence, you don't need to sell something to have customers. The fire department, for example, doesn't sell anything, but depends on the resources of the city and must treat elected officials as customers. Second, you do not need to have direct client contact to benefit from the following discussion. These strategies apply to all interactions in the office and can be especially helpful when dealing with other departments. Finally, the higher you climb in an organization, the more likely you are to deal with clients. So you will eventually need this knowledge anyway.

Now let's take a more detailed look at the intricate power struggle between buyers and sellers.

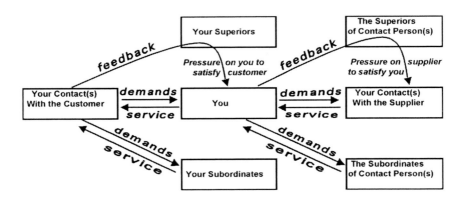

The figure on the previous page shows that there is a lot more going on between you and customers, as well as suppliers, than you may realize. Like it or not, there is a constant but subtle fight for dominance with external parties. Although you may see only a nasty Friday afternoon e-mail from a customer asking for a ton of donkeywork, the events leading up to this problem are multifaceted.

To start, the customer (or more precisely, your point of contact in the customer's organization) can attack you from all sides. Due to his power advantage, he can dictate the fronts where the battles are fought. Although you may not simply pick up the phone and call his assistants or superiors, he can request things directly from you, pressure you through your boss, and bug your subordinates. This generates significant workload. Your goal is to divert the communication to the channels that are most advantageous to you, minimize his demands, and maximize the positive feedback through those channels.

Make the customer ask for you in person
As demonstrated by the managerial value chain, a great result does not nec-

essarily do much good to the manager who is responsible for it. The implications of this principle are nowhere as profound as they are in customer relationships. Suppose that your firm makes a terrific patented product, delivers every shipment on time, and takes the client to Hawaii twice a year. Naturally, the customer will have every reason to be satisfied. Unfortunately, you, the salesperson, may not necessarily be one of these reasons. It is unlikely that this customer will insist on working with you and no other salesman. If your employer should decide to replace you with a cheaper manager who has no experience, the customer will probably not make a big fuss. He is just getting too good a deal to risk. In short, the customer is happy, but instead of making you stronger this only weakens your position.

Now imagine working for the competitor with an inferior product. Assume that your firm depends on superior client service to compete with the supplier in the prior example. This time, your position is very different. Now, your company cannot fall back on patents, flawless distribution, or promotional budgets to satisfy the customer and must rely on you. You must defend your firm against the giant rival by arranging custom lot sizes and shipment plans to maximize the client's productivity—something that you can do only if you know your client inside out. This may be a compromise solution, and the customer may be less happy than in the prior example. He will, however, value your input much more. To ensure the continuity of the satisfactory service, he will need to keep you. In other words, the customer's total happiness may be smaller, but a much greater percentage of that happiness will be attributed to you. Therefore, you will be much stronger, and can better resist the client's pressures for more work.

To ensure that the customer attributes most, if not all, of his happiness to you, as opposed to your employer, you must make him feel that he is receiving personalized service that only you can deliver. You have to provide him with a unique flavor every step along the way and slightly dissociate yourself from your employer. Instead of perceiving you as an extension of your organization, the customer must see you as a craftsman who molds the standard services of his employer into a unique shape to suit the client's needs. The suggestions in Chapter 17 about customizing your work provide a great starting point. Never send standard e-mails, files, or printed documents without at least some modification to make them more useful. Ideally, the customer should not even know what the company's standard files that you automatically download look like.

These modifications need not be time consuming. Saving a file under a more relevant and intuitive name, highlighting important columns in a spreadsheet, or underlining a few lines in a booklet all make a significant difference. While these may be minor changes, they save time for the end user. More importantly, they work as a quality control seal. If the client receives an unopened booklet from you in the mail, he cannot even tell if you actually read it, much less why you are sending it. It will look like you received a box of those reports, put them in front of the secretary, and asked him to send a copy to every account.

Anyone can do this. Why then should the client try to keep you? He would rather get a cheaper sales rep and a 0.5% price break. If, however, there is even a slight mark on the report, you must have looked at it and be convinced that it is worth the client's time. This is not to say that you must limit yourself to minor touchups. If you can modify your services even more, by all means do so. Custom shipment schedules, unique product specifications, targeted presentations, or anything that is substantially customized will strengthen your hand.

Another unique and valuable gift you can give your customers is to save them time. Know precisely when and when not to call them and make sure that they receive all electronic communications in a form they can use with minimal intervention. Keep track of what they do with every file you send them. If the end user will take weekly numbers and produce monthly figures, find an intern or secretary to do that. If he will summarize a long document in five bullet points, try to include proposed bullets.

Also, find out their preferred mode of communication and try to comply. No matter how much you prefer e-mail, use the phone if this is what they like. Know if they prefer long and infrequent meetings or short but frequent ones. Find out if they wish to completely switch over to teleconferences instead of regular meetings. (Multitaskers who can do other things while on the phone, save a lot of time with teleconferences.) If they are coming to your office for a meeting, ask if they would like an empty room before or after the meeting to work in peace and arrange convenient transportation. These may not be rocket science, but they can only be performed by someone who knows the client. Therefore, they give you a unique edge.

Make sure that the good news reaches your superiors

To ensure that your effort pays off, you need a channel of selective communication between the client and your superiors. The key word is "selective." You do not want potentially abusive clients to talk to everyone in your organization all the time. In that case, you would lose control over your image and give him too many contacts to pressure you for more work. Ideally, you should control the information flow and put the client in touch with superiors only when he expresses satisfaction.

One way to connect the client and the boss at the right time is by offering to make permanent changes in your services. If, for example, you arranged a Sunday morning express shipment of raw materials and made the client really happy, you can propose to do this on a regular basis. It is accepted practice for you to ask the client to talk to your boss about such a major change. When he does, he will almost certainly mention how pleased he was with your performance. Since he will be asking for something extra, he must give a bit in return, which usually will be praise for you. The conversation will probably start like this, "Listen, the Sunday shipment arranged by your guy was outstanding. We think it would be great to do that more often."

Even something as small as providing the customer with easy-to-process receipts, which may require a bit of hassle with the accounting department, can do the trick. Kindly tell the customer that your boss has more authority over other departments, and ask him to help you convince your supervisor. Again, the customer will be asking for a favor and will have to bring up your recent satisfactory performance to get what he wants. Such innovations also attract the attention of top management and are often used as case studies throughout the organization. This will further advertise your customer focus and creativity.

Another effective strategy to get your boss involved at the right moment is to call on his expertise. If the customer is having problems at his warehouse, for instance, you can bring up the fact that your boss worked as a warehouse manager in his prior job, and offer to visit their facility together with your boss to see if you can be of help. If you can time this well and do it when the client is in a good mood, he will probably sing your praises. When the client has something great to say about you, mention a relevant experience or skill of your boss and create an opportunity to bring those two sides together as soon as possible.

A more direct approach is to simply tell the customer that you can give him a better deal if he can help you convince your boss that doing so will increase the volume of business. Whenever your client asks to take the relationship further, he will have to imply (or openly state) that the foundation is solid enough to build something bigger—in other words, that he is happy enough with you that he would like to work with you even more closely. An interviewee explains below.

> Show the client that he can get a better deal by praising you. I am not talking about bribery here, but a mutually beneficial deal. I'll tell him, "Look, I know we can do more volume and make more money for both companies. I'd love to hire an assistant dedicated to you, give you bigger promotions—or whatever it is that I can offer—but I need the backing of my boss. If you think the same way, share your thoughts with him so we can take this to the next level." If you selected the right person, he will do that and also tell your boss how happy he is with your services. He has no choice but to say that he's happy with you. Otherwise, it makes no sense for him to ask to take the relationship further.

A final possibility is to use the satisfied customer as a test subject to implement a new tool or system. If, for example, your employer is working on a new industrial lubricant and wants to test it under realistic conditions, nominate your most satisfied customer. Regardless of the success of the test, the customer will end up talking to important people within your organization, and inevitably mention how satisfied he is with your services. Similarly, joint press conferences, co-branding a product, or even a golf outing can work wonders. The idea is to bring together the people who have good things to say about you with those who need to hear those things.

Clarify the scope of the interaction

As we saw, it can be very difficult to say "no" to a customer. Therefore, if you do not clearly agree on what you will and, more importantly, will not do for him ahead of time, you may end up doing everything. The worst example I saw was a client who used a market research company practically as a back office. Due to the failure to clarify the scope of their service, the researchers were forced to present and summarize any research as many times as the client wanted.

They would be asked for a "one-page summary" to be added to the advertising brief, a "quick two-paragraph summary" to be printed in the monthly highlights report, and then a "crisp, presentable summary for the CEO." Since the boundaries were not defined up front, the research firm had no defense against these demands. Over time, they had lost all control and had no way to stop the exploitation short of terminating the relationship, which they couldn't afford to do.

To avoid such disasters, define the scope of the relationship as early as possible. Get something in writing, at least via e-mail, before the first piece of work is started. Although you probably won't pull up an e-mail in case of an unjust demand, these informal agreements will discourage the other side from going too far. Such agreements are much easier to obtain at the start of the relationship. Asking the client to clarify what services you will perform so you can give a price quote, or "only to make sure that you are on the same page going forward" is all you need.

Trying to formalize the relationship at a later stage, however, will signify erosion of trust and is rarely acceptable. If you are going to sign a prenuptial agreement, for instance, you are supposed to do so before the marriage or, at the latest, within the first few months. Bringing this subject up several years after the wedding will send a terrible message to your spouse. By that time, you are supposed to have forgotten about formalities, let alone trying to further structure things.

Proposing such a contract, especially after a dispute over money, will bury the marriage alive. Similarly, you cannot ask to clarify the scope of your relationship with the customer after a nasty Friday afternoon e-mail that asks for a ton of donkeywork. This is just as bad, and therefore just as difficult as saying "no." So, at the start of the relationship, and each time things are taken to a new level, first agree on details.

Fix price and volume with long-term contracts

Another easy way for the buyer to manipulate suppliers is to constantly switch back and forth between them. If the client can shift the volume at a moment's notice, especially if only one person makes this decision, suppliers will be at a huge disadvantage. One awful example I witnessed was the relationship between a major snack manufacturer and a few firms specializing in distributing samples. The client was working with several such firms, but had only one liaison person coordinating the whole operation. This individual had the sole authority to decide whom to give the business to because, due to her background in distributing samples, she was the only one seen fit to make that decision.

To make things worse, brand managers rarely had a preference for a particular distributor. Even if they wanted a certain company, none of them had the knowledge to push for their specific choice. A remark by the liaison person such as, "I have doubts about that firm. They always station their people at the wrong intersections in that city" would silence anyone who lacked the expertise to challenge the liaison person. Unfortunately, this included everyone in the company.

As a result, the liaison person had tremendous power over distributors and obtained amazing concessions. She made them drive for hours to pick up samples instead of making a few calls to arrange a shipment, and forced them to write every report that she was asked for. Knowing that the liaison person could cut their lifeline at any time, suppliers had to comply. While the contracts signed with the distributors fixed the price, details such as pickup location of samples weren't regulated. Most importantly, a minimum volume wasn't specified.

To prevent such exploitation, fix not only the price but also a minimum volume with long-term contracts. Any agreement that leaves the volume decision to one person, or a group that can be manipulated by one boss, will put you in a highly vulnerable position. The time span of the contract is just as critical. A detailed agreement is of little use if it must be renewed every three months. In that case, the supplier can blackmail you with the threat of not renewing the contract a few months down the road.

The buyer may resist a minimum volume. If so, try to include a clause in the agreement to penalize ridiculously low purchases over the duration of the contract. One solution can be a declining price structure. For example, instead of a price of $4 per unit for an expected one million units, propose a price of $4.4 that declines by ten cents for every 100,000 units purchased during the year. If the volume happens to be one million units as expected, the average price will be around $4, but absurdly low amounts will increase the average price.

If the liaison manager in the prior example had been bound by such a contract, it would have been nowhere as easy to push the suppliers around. Her power came from the fact that nobody saw what she was doing. Despite the pain she inflicted on suppliers, the samples were getting distributed and the firm was paying a fixed price. So nobody in her organization had a reason to inquire. But if costs had swelled when volume was unevenly spread out between distributors, at least the purchasing department would see the abnormal prices and ask a few questions.

Protect your subordinates from abusive customers

To further avoid the exploitation of abusive customers, protect your subordinates; they are your Achilles heel. While it may be difficult for you to say "no" to clients, it is often outright impossible for your subordinates. A seemingly innocent question by the customer such as "Could you maybe get us those numbers going back to 1987?" can lead to disaster. Forced to give an answer on the phone, the subordinate may have to say "yes." And since backtracking after such a commitment will look terrible, he may get unfairly stuck for hours. Even worse, this will set a precedent. Every time you reject a similar request, the comment will be "But you did it before. Actually, let me forward the old file to you so you can fill in the missing cells. That'll clarify it."

To defend against these attacks below the belt, isolate your subordinates from abusive clients. Personally send all files and e-mails to such customers, even if your subordinates prepare them. Although I advised that you do not give out your cell phone number, problematic clients constitute an exception. To prevent them from speaking with your subordinates when you are not around, provide your cell phone number to those people and always answer their calls.

Furthermore, encourage such clients to use e-mail as opposed to the phone. The phone favors the caller and you or your people may say "yes" when caught by surprise, even if the right answer should be "Hell, no." Subordinates can also show you client e-mails before they commit to anything, but they will be forced to give some answer on the phone right away. Encourage the use of e-mail by responding to e-mails ASAP and cutting phone conversations as short as you can. When you receive a call from one of these clients, ask to call him back, and do so later rather than sooner.

Finally, instruct your subordinates not to commit to unreasonable customer requests. It is better for them to sound naïve and say, "I don't know if we have that, can I get back to you right away?" and get you involved, instead of being stuck for hours doing something silly for a customer. Keep in mind that you can transfer close to a minute of your own work to your subordinates for every minute you save them. So do not let anyone abuse them.

Diversify your contacts

While you should try to be the only direct contact person for dangerous customers (except for good news, where you will open up a selective channel of communication, as we saw) talk to several people within their organization. This prevents the dreadful situation where a single person's word about you is taken as gospel. Such arrangements leave you extremely vulnerable to exploitation. If you get stuck with one person, shift as much of your communication to e-mail as possible. This way, you will at least have some proof that you are doing a reasonable job.

By diversifying contacts, you can also pick the easiest people to satisfy. Instead of bending over backward to get the weekly numbers to A, who is always out, you could find a B, who is easier to reach. If so, you can gradually turn to B and eliminate your dependence on A. The operative word is gradual. Start by CC'ing messages to B and after a while move him to "TO," while also keeping A there. Monitor A's reactions before you start to call B directly. In the beginning, call B only when you cannot reach A. Keep A in the loop and let him know that you had to call B and watch his response. As a result of your unequal enthusiasm when dealing with these people, the interest of A in the subject matter should slowly decline, while that of B should grow.

Do not try to become friends with the customer

In Chapter 7, we saw why, contrary to popular belief, it is a bad idea to get too close to top managers. A similar myth is that spending long hours with customers or becoming friends with them can help you. This is, at best, a waste of time. As I explained before, the closer you get, the greater the risk of a dispute. In addition, the client may worry about losing his authority when you become friends and even feel that you are trying to manipulate him. To make matters worse, meeting clients requires much more time than hanging out with your boss. While it takes only minutes to go to the cafeteria with the supervisor for lunch, a client visit takes much longer, especially in a city with heavy traffic. On top of it all, the friendship will only dilute your image.

You want the customer to see you as a professional who helps him to do more in less time. Since most people draw strict lines between their personal and professional lives, it is very hard to be both a business ally and a friend. If you force friendship into the equation, you may be quickly removed from the professional category and pushed into the friend segment. Excessive closeness may also lead the client's superiors to accuse him of giving the business to friends.

Spend as little personal time with the customer as possible. Show that you are busy, but will juggle tasks to talk to him. Do not be unconditionally available at all times. Just as work expands to fill the available time, clients will use up your time until you say "enough." When he calls at a bad moment, do not feel obliged to talk. Just promise to get back to him promptly and do so.

If you strive too hard to accommodate his schedule, he may conclude that you have nothing else to do. This will make you look insignificant and diminish the perceived value of your work. When you must entertain the client, do so irregularly but make it really special. If you take him out to lunch every week, it will soon turn into a duty and fail to impress. Instead, save your budget and take him to the most expensive place you can afford once a month. This will be remembered for much longer, save you time, and give him something to look forward to.

Preserve your power advantage when working with suppliers

Before I conclude this chapter, I would like to add a few remarks about what to do when you find yourself as the customer—in other words how to handle supplier relationships. Whenever you are the customer, you will have an inherent power advantage, and must maintain your superiority.

Even if you are the biggest client and the other side cannot survive without you, do not become too complacent. A skilled supplier might not only neutralize your dominance, but turn the balance in his favor.

To maintain superiority, avoid trapping yourself with very long-term agreements. If you are obliged to buy a certain amount at a fixed price for the next two years, why should your contact person try to satisfy you today? Especially if he plans to change jobs before the end of the contract, you may end up asking him for favors, instead of the other way around. Fixing every detail of the work with a contract, especially if the supplier has much more experience in the field than you do, will have similar results. While it isn't wise to abuse the market research company by forcing them to write a dozen summaries of the same report, the opposite end of the spectrum is just as unfair. You do not want to end up with 400 pages of statistics and realize that the research firm will charge an arm and a leg to produce an executive summary. If you have never commissioned that type of work before, you simply cannot plan for every contingency. Therefore, you must give yourself some contractual freedom to make added demands.

Do not sever your ties with old suppliers when you switch to a new one. Purchasing everything from one supplier may be economical, but at least keep your options open. If the seller realizes that you have no clue about other suppliers, his incentive to satisfy you will greatly diminish. One purchasing manager I talked to asks multiple sellers to fax him their rock-bottom price proposals and scatters those faxes on his desk before meeting with suppliers. That shows that he is fully aware of all alternatives and actively shopping around. Small

Christmas gifts with the suppliers' logos displayed around his office serve the same purpose.

Finally, do not forget to reward good deeds. Be aware of the significance of your comments for your contact person at the supplier and provide positive feedback to his superiors when he deserves it. When he makes you really happy, tell him how pleased you are with his service and ask whom to call to express your satisfaction. You will almost certainly be given the name of an influential manager and be able to open up a line of communication with that individual. This will provide a big incentive for your contact to do a proper job, as his good deeds will not go unnoticed. Should things turn sour, you can use the same top manager to gently pressure your contact person. Since by then you will have a longstanding relationship, the complaints will have greater impact. The top manager will know that you give credit where it is due, and take your criticism much more seriously.

5 Key Points You Should Remember

- Do not let the customer view you as a replaceable extension of your employer
- Ensure that the positive customer feedback reaches your superiors
- Make the customer understand the boundaries of your responsibilities in advance
- Sign long-term, binding agreements with customers whenever possible
- Be in touch with multiple individuals in the organizations that you serve

CHAPTER 22

Three Classic Mistakes That Drain Your Power

In the preceding four chapters, we have seen how managers can accumulate power and use it to reduce their workloads. Now, let's see how they can lose it. The following mistakes are extremely common in large organizations, but fairly easy to avoid if you know what *not* to do.

Beware of the static promotion

Before I started working for a large organization, I used to associate promotions with a lot of change. I was probably influenced by the movies, where the manager's life would be turned upside down whenever he rose in the firm. The Hollywood version of a managerial promotion starts with a happy celebration dinner, followed by an emotional farewell to the old department. Then the manager moves into a bigger office, takes over a troubled division, slowly gains the confidence of his new subordinates, and finally turns things around. Bingo!

In reality, few advancements involve so much fanfare. Some of them can be so silent that most colleagues don't notice the change until they see your new business card. You may be given an assistant, a bigger budget, and more responsibilities, but essentially do the same job as before. This is what I call a "static promotion"—your location in the organization, the people around you, and your duties remain mostly static. Although you need to invest very little time to learn new skills in such a promotion, the potential workload reduction is also minimal.

First of all, a static promotion hampers your ability to make structural changes in the job. As we saw in Chapter 14, you are usually granted a learning period after substantial career moves. Investing in long-term projects during that period makes it easier to shine later. Unfortunately, this learning period is much shorter in a static promotion. Since you will do basically the same job as before, you will be expected to deliver right away. Therefore, you must start to chase short-term results immediately, as opposed to focusing on substantial changes that will pay big dividends later.

More importantly, you will lack the justification for structural changes.

When you are assigned to a new place, it is relatively easy to argue that the system of the old manager is inadequate and needs to be overhauled. But criticizing the previous person becomes much harder in a static promotion—you were the previous person. Personnel changes are also immensely difficult. When relocating, you can often take a few trusted associates with you and lay off a few problematic workers in the new place. But being promoted within your area and immediately firing long-time coworkers can result in a public relations disaster. Remaining workers, as well as external observers, will take this as an obvious sign of corruption and feel extremely insecure.

Leaving the structure intact, on the other hand, can lead to other problems, as people may fail to give you the respect that your new position deserves. Since perceptions change only gradually, your old image will stick for much longer than you would like. Former peers who may now be below you will have a difficult time mentally upgrading you. Any effort to accelerate this process will get you labeled as a jerk. But in a relocation, you will walk in without this baggage. Your new subordinates will not remember your history in a lower position and treat you just like their new boss.

Imagine that, on a scale from 0 to 100, district managers (DM) have an image/power rating between 51-60 and senior district managers (SDM) are rated 61-70. In a static promotion from DM to SDM, you will start at 61 in the eyes of most coworkers. On the one hand, they will want to treat you as an equal as they always did, but on the other hand, they must acknowledge your new position. To minimize this conflict, they will rate you at 61. This will change your status as little as possible, while still giving you the minimum respect due to a SDM. If, however, you become the SDM of another division with different employees, you will start at 65—the average score for that position. This relative lack of power and prestige in a static promotion will make it harder to direct the efforts of the people around you, inflating your workload.

> I was recently promoted within my department, but didn't get new subordinates. So now I must ask my old peers to do things for me. I am not their direct boss, but I am ranked higher and, in theory, I have the right to give them some work. In practice, though, it is not happening and I end up doing more than my fair share. Since these are my old buddies, it's an uncomfortable situation for everyone. Sometimes I feel bad about asking them to do the boring work and sometimes they resent me for doing so. The executive secretary who is now supposed to take my calls too supposedly said that I have changed since I got promoted. I don't think I changed as a person. If anything, I am more sensitive to people's feelings. But am I more demanding? Absolutely, because I am now asked to do a lot more.

When an opportunity for a promotion appears, ask yourself this: Do you value stability or do you prefer long-term workload reduction in exchange for some short-term investment? If the former sounds better, go for a static promotion. But if you prefer the latter, try to get relocated. This doesn't have to involve moving to another city or asking for a more prestigious assignment. You just need to need to handle slightly different tasks, and work with different people who do not have a longstanding image of you as someone in a lower position.

Do not surround yourself with too much passion

To survive in a large organization, you need a support network. Typically, such networks start to expand horizontally, then move upward, and finally reach downward. Regardless of the level at which you join the organization, your first friendships will probably be formed with peers, most likely with people hired at around the same time. As you get settled, a few superiors will notice you and take you under their wings. While they can act as mentors and take a genuine interest in your personal growth, some of them may only be trying to nurture a long-term strategic partnership. As you grow further and accumulate more power, you, too, will start to reach downward, taking some people under your own wings.

If you are an ambitious and passionate individual with lofty goals, you must avoid the mistake of filling your support network entirely with like-minded people. If practically every person you can ask for advice is a go-getter, you will likely make biased decisions, take excessive risks, and burn out too soon. Especially if you must manage a team of such individuals, a great deal of your energy will be spent containing internal clashes, which are inevitable if too many tigers are locked inside one cage. To maintain a more balanced outlook, keep close ties with a few individuals who are more settled—the kinds of people who will ask you whether you have considered all the risks, as opposed to pumping you up to bet the house on the next big thing.

When building a team or a taskforce, keep the same principle in mind and include a few of these "cool heads" who can slow things down a bit when the group gets too bold. These people are also ideal for some of the easier and less inspiring tasks that the team must perform. The last thing you want is a team where every member wants to save the world even if it involves 90-hour weeks. More than likely, you won't be able to find anyone in such a group willing to do the easier and less glamorous things, such as updating presentations, in exchange for shorter work hours and a smaller salary. Remember, the worst army is one composed entirely of generals.

Never apologize via e-mail

This final point is about how not to undermine your own position at work through inappropriate use of e-mail. Unfortunately, e-mails can be kept on record indefinitely and forwarded at will. A message with a generous apology can be later taken out of context and treated as an admission of fault. To make matters worse, recipients save those messages where you express regret with particular care, often seeing them as a way to cover their backs.

When you must apologize, do so on the phone and agree on the next step. Then send a kind, but unapologetic, message where you make it clear that there has been a mutual understanding about the action you will take or are taking with the e-mail. A comment such as "The attached file contains the figures we agreed upon in our earlier conversation" makes it extremely difficult to use the e-mail against you in the future.

And a word of caution...
Do not leave a bad taste in anyone's mouth
The strategies we saw in this part are potent tools that will significantly boost your power. With power comes responsibility. At some point, you will be in an extremely strong negotiating position and be tempted to take more than what is fair. You are most prone to this mistake after a major success, such as the completion of a big project or a promotion. As Napoleon Bonaparte said, "With victory comes your weakest moment."

For your own good, do not leave a bad taste in people's mouths by pushing them too far. Just like workload, power is a dynamic quality that can fluctuate wildly. You can never know when the tables will turn and you will become dependent on the other person. You may remember the example in Chapter 6 when my partner and I were left with a broken computer in the advertising agency and there was only a single IT person in the building. We avoided a major disaster that night only because my partner had not abused his power when he had a chance to do so. Later on, when the IT person had all the power, she was willing to save us.

CONCLUSION

A Day in the Life of an Efficient Manager

Before we close, let us review the principles of managerial efficiency in action once again. Let us follow our heroine, Athena, through a typical day and see how, just like her namesake, she solves the toughest problems with wisdom and strategy as opposed to brute force or sheer hard work...

6:45 AM Sweet dreams

Athena is still asleep but her dreams are approaching their happy endings because she is about to face a demanding day. This mother of two works as a relationship manager in ENIGMA Corporation, a large industrial conglomerate that produces a wide assortment of equipment used in the assembly of microchips, LCD screens, and imaging devices. Athena has been with the company's microchip department for five years. Her division manufactures, sells, and services robotic arms that cram millions of circuits into a tiny piece of silicone. Due to the high cost and complex nature of the products, her company relies on relationship managers to act as a buffer between customers and the R&D, sales, and technical service departments.

During the purchase of new equipment and upgrades of existing ones, Athena works with her sales department to offer different leasing and payment plans to clients. After the sale, she constantly communicates with R&D to develop customized upgrades and involves the technical service for the repair and maintenance of the equipment. She must juggle a lot of responsibilities and work with a wide variety of individuals within her company, often with conflicting interests. No wonder they call it ENIGMA Corporation. Luckily, she has two bright associates to help her out. Nelson has been with the company for three years and could almost do Athena's job, if he needed to. In fact, Athena is lobbying to get him in line for the next available relationship management position. Judy, on the other hand, is relatively new. She has only nine months of work experience, but is learning fast.

For the last two days, Athena was out of the office visiting a prospective client that she has been pursuing for over a year. This mobile phone maker has very different needs than any of ENIGMA's existing clients. Specializing in low-cost, disposable mobile phones, it will need large numbers of inexpensive assembly robots, which will have to be serviced frequently. When the opportunity arose to work with sales and bid for this contract, Athena immediately volunteered. She always tries to differentiate her client portfolio, as well as her responsibilities, from those of her peers. This relieves the pressure of peer comparisons, since there is no one else in the company who performs a comparable function. So, instead of having to beat the year-end sales figures and satisfaction scores of eight other relationship managers, she only competes against her own past results. In addition, she is also the sole expert in numerous fields. While most relationship managers are interchangeable, very few people have the expertise to handle the unique needs of Athena's clients. This improves her bargaining power (within her company as well as with clients) while also giving her more freedom in how she works. Like most of her clients, the mobile phone maker will involve a steep learning curve at first, but the later payoffs are well worth it.

7:00 AM A fresh start

Athena wakes up with a kiss from her husband and proceeds to prepare the kids for school. After dressing up Jeremy (9) and Linda (7), she asks her husband, Stuart, to prepare breakfast and quickly checks her e-mail while the omelet is cooking. Having checked her messages yesterday before leaving the prospective client's office, she doesn't find an overwhelming number of new e-mails. She quickly scans them and sends responses to colleagues who will arrive in the office before her. This gives her some visibility, which she needs since she was out for the last two days. Since she often sends such "remote" messages, her coworkers know that she doesn't have to be in the office to be productive. As a result, people are much more understanding when she leaves at six while everyone is still at work. Checking messages from home also enables her to clean up her inbox and get right into the more serious matters when she arrives at the office. After finishing breakfast and sending the children off to school, Athena leaves for work. She has a difficult day ahead, but wisdom and confidence are on her side.

8:30 AM Let the games begin

Athena arrives in the office and runs into David, the head of West Coast sales, in the elevator. When David asks how her trip was, Athena provides a brief but informative summary in 15 seconds. She doesn't have to think at all because she already knew which aspects of the trip she wanted to communicate to her coworkers before she even left the client's office. The four bullet points in her mind will also be featured in the e-mails she will send out shortly. She tells David that the cell phone maker is planning to set up 14 assembly lines for the upcoming disposable handsets. She also adds that the project team is running ahead of schedule and will make an official bid before the August 1 deadline.

None of these comments are accidental. Knowing that sales is primarily concerned with volume, she starts by mentioning the large number of assembly lines that the customer will need to fill with new equipment (this will also be the opening of the e-mail she will send to the sales team.) This immediately captures David's attention. She then communicates how she is performing better than expected by stating that the project is running ahead of schedule. Since she had published a step-by-step plan before starting the project, she can now communicate her progress easily and quickly. In the absence of such plans, however, no one will know how fast is fast and all she can say is "the project is going really well," which is not nearly as impressive.

Unfortunately, Jack from international sales overhears the conversation. After David gets off the elevator, Jack asks Athena to send him "whatever material she has about the prospective client." He made similar demands before Athena's trip, claiming that the international subsidiary of the cell phone maker is a potential target for his division. In reality, the client's international operations are fairly small and not worth Athena's or even Jack's time at this stage. Athena is well aware that Jack actually wants to squeeze himself into the ongoing project and claim some of the credit if the effort bears fruit.

Although the thought of having to deal with Jack upsets Athena, she erases the negative expression from her face and enters her floor with a smile. There is no need to demoralize the people she depends on. Athena knows that the more quality work her subordinates can fit into their days, the less work she will have to do. Before going into business matters, she asks her subordinates how they are and genuinely listens. Although neither of them reports anything unusual, Judy looks stressed. She also sounded a bit frustrated over the phone yesterday. Athena has no idea what the problem is, but she makes it her highest priority to find out and asks Judy to come into her office in 15 minutes. This should be enough for Athena to clean up her desk.

Since she had read all urgent e-mails and checked voicemail regularly during her trip, Athena does not find Post-Its stuck on her screen by desperate coworkers or printouts on her chair. All she has to take care of are a few phone messages left late last night and early this morning. After checking her voicemail, she quickly scans a major news site on the Internet and logs on to a Web site that specializes in the microchip industry. The last thing she wants is for her boss to storm into her office and start talking about the breaking news that Athena is unaware of. That would only create the impression that things are slipping out of her control and give her boss a reason to get more involved in Athena's work. Very few things are worse for one's efficiency or image.

Soon after Athena is done checking the headlines, Judy comes in. Although

Judy is an introvert by nature and doesn't share her feelings easily, she trusts Athena. She knows that Athena never shoots the messenger and keeps her cool no matter how bad the news. Over the last nine months, Judy has learned that sharing problems with her boss earlier rather than later saves time, effort, and frustration. The problem, it turns out, is that Jack has called Judy four times over the last two days, asking for documentation regarding the cell phone maker. When Judy kindly declined (Athena had instructed her not to send any files to the international sales department in her absence), Jack got progressively nastier and pressured Judy. Athena comforts her, reiterating that she did the right thing, and asks Judy to forward all of Jack's calls to her no matter where she is.

With the urgent issues out of the way, Athena sends three e-mails about her trip. Unlike other relationship managers who send a long and boring e-mail to practically everyone in sales, R&D, and technical service departments after such trips, Athena sends short but customized messages. Her e-mail to R&D explains that the prospective client's factory is hot and humid, which can cause problems for the assembly robots. The e-mail she sends to sales gives a brief overview of the target client's potential order size and includes a cost estimate that the sales rep can use to shape up her bargaining strategy. Since these e-mails contain only the relevant bits of information, they are short, so recipients actually read them. As a result, people realize how active Athena was during her trip and how much she accomplished. All in all, Athena spends no more than 20 to 25 minutes for three e-mails, but gets a lot more out of them than other relationship managers who spend half an hour to compose one gigantic message that no one really reads.

9:30 AM Homework time

After sending the messages, Athena notices that she only has an hour left before the weekly status meeting at 10:30, where she will present her project to top managers from numerous departments including several board members, and immediately starts to prepare. Over the next half-hour, she will look at caller IDs and take only the most important calls. Athena prioritizes brutally; instead of doing two things improperly, she chooses to do one thing perfectly. Next, she prints out the minutes of the prior meeting and takes notes in the margins. These will ensure that she brings up all pertinent issues during the fast-moving meeting and visibly demonstrate that she has taken the time to prepare beforehand. Additionally, Athena makes extra copies of the meeting minutes, since some people will certainly forget to bring their own copies. The VPs of sales and relationship management are among those who often depend on Athena for this type of logistical support. These little gestures take mere minutes but really help her stand out. Next, Athena opens up the handouts that she had asked her staff to prepare about the prospective client while she was away, and makes a couple of editorial changes. She then sends the file to Judy, and asks her to produce 12 copies.

Finally, she reviews the preliminary profit and loss projection prepared by Nelson, makes a few edits, and e-mails the file to Karen, the sales representative who covers Athena's clients. Customarily, the P&L projection is prepared by sales with the support of relationship management. However, Karen is overwhelmed and there was no way for her to finish the projection on time for this meeting. Sensing that from earlier phone conversations, Athena had asked Nelson to prepare a projection with the help of Karen's assistant. In her e-mail, Athena gives most of the credit to Karen and her subordinate, although Nelson did most of the work. This is crucial for two reasons. First, it ensures that Karen will champion the idea and present it with enthusiasm in the meeting. The message is: "Go ahead and take credit for this in front of the board. I won't try to steal the show by hinting that I did the number crunching." Second, it shows to Karen how profitable it can be to cooperate with Athena, strengthening the alliance between the two parties. The support of sales will be extremely important as the project progresses.

10:30 AM Show time

Athena promptly arrives at the meeting, where among other things, the acquisition plan for the cell phone maker will be discussed. She kicks off the discussion by distributing her handouts and briefly explaining where the process stands. She displays her ten-step plan, where seven of the goals have already been accomplished and checked off. This "opening ceremony" has two purposes. It shows how much progress has already been made and how much the company has invested into this venture. The message is: "You can't pull the plug on this thing now." Additionally, it helps to kick off the conversation without revealing critical information. The departments involved in the project have conflicting goals and, despite a significant profit forecast, R&D is opposed to going after the cell phone maker. The task of designing a completely new assembly robot for this customer appears unattractive to R&D, so they are dragging their feet. Before revealing her cards, Athena wants to hear the objections. This light opening is a perfect way to hit the ball into the opposition's court.

After finishing her brief speech and creating a sense of optimism, Athena turns to Melvin, the VP for R&D, and says, "So Melvin, do you guys have a budget estimate for developing the new robots for this client?" Melvin is not quite sure how to respond. He was planning to say that developing a completely new set of robotic assembly devices for a single client would be infeasible. In her speech, however, Athena constantly stressed how the disposable cell phone market is poised for tremendous growth, and explained that many other manufacturers may soon jump on the bandwagon. Therefore the "it's just a single client" argument may not work. Furthermore, the VPs of sales and relationship management appear highly motivated after Athena's speech. Melvin runs the risk of getting isolated by sounding too negative. So, he only throws in a mild criticism, pointing out that the development cost of $280,000 may not be recoverable in the near term.

This is where Karen comes in. Armed with the profit and loss estimates provided by Athena, she easily invalidates this argument and explains that the investment is recoverable in less than six months. Had Athena not taken the time to help Karen prepare the P&L estimates, this golden opportunity would have been lost. Another key point was that Athena made it very clear in her earlier e-mail that she had no intention of taking credit for the P&L projections. If that had been the case, Karen would not have been nearly as enthusiastic during her presentation. The risk of an annoying comment by Athena to show the participants that her subordinate had prepared the P&L numbers would have forced Karen to talk about another issue in order to advertise her own work. But by spending half an hour doing someone else's job without asking to be compensated for it directly, Athena gained an ally and vastly improved her position.

Finally, it is Athena's turn to speak again. She decides that she has built sufficient support and does not need to force Melvin to change his position at this stage. She only needs to prevent a public rejection by Melvin, which would force him to stick to his position later in order not to lose face by flip-flopping. She respectfully acknowledges Melvin's concerns and points out that they will soon find out more about the precise specifications of the assembly robots that need to be built. She requests that R&D look at more cost-effective alternatives when the new data arrives. This gives Melvin a chance to withhold his final verdict about the issue. In the end, the board decides to move ahead with the project and finalize the official bid that will be submitted to the prospective client in the next status meeting. By then, it will be too late for R&D to derail the project. The meeting proceeds with other issues and goes on until 12:30.

12:30 PM Killing two birds with one stone

At the end of the meeting, Karen thanks Athena for her help and requests that they meet with the technical service to get a sense for the service and warranty costs. Karen is notorious for her marathon meetings. Since spending another two hours locked up in a conference room just to talk to the tech guys sounds like a waste of time, Athena proposes that they walk over to Jose's office right away to briefly discuss the issue. As always, Jose, the director of the service department, is quick on his feet and gathers all the data he needs for a preliminary cost estimate in ten minutes. The trio decides to talk again on Friday and splits up. Athena makes sure to use the phrase "talk" as opposed to "meeting" and is confident that they can get the cost estimate with a similar ten-minute visit.

These short, stand-up meetings serve two purposes. First, they save a lot of time. By talking as soon as an issue arises instead of waiting until the next formal meeting, things are resolved easily and painlessly. People are also more efficient when they are standing up and talking to only the relevant parties. Athena prefers to hold such meetings in the offices of colleagues. While she can always excuse herself from someone else's desk, it is much harder to kick people out of one's own room. Second, stand-up meetings are much more visible. A large number of people see that you are working and interacting with other parts of the organization. When locked in a conference room for half a day, however, people may even suspect that you took the day off.

1:00 PM Just a little getaway

Upon returning to her desk and quickly checking her voice and e-mail messages, Athena thanks her subordinates for their help and invites them out to lunch. Instead of going down to the cafeteria, she takes her staff to a restaurant and pays for the meal. She often makes such gestures to help her people relax following difficult assignments. Besides, the change of air is good for her, too. While most of her coworkers eat a sandwich at their desks, Athena can afford to take an extended break to recharge her batteries. As a result of her significantly higher efficiency during the rest of the day, she still accomplishes more and manages to leave the office earlier than her colleagues who work 12 straight hours.

2:00 PM It's not over yet

After lunch, Athena has a brief discussion with Nelson to tell him what the meeting minutes should include. Whenever possible, Athena volunteers to write and distribute the minutes of a meeting. Although it takes no more than half an hour, this gives her control over a tremendously important tool of communication. Since top officials who could not attend the meeting will only see the minutes, the precise wording is critical to get the right message across. Just one wrong bullet point such as "The R&D department pointed out that the cost of developing a custom solution for the prospective client would be prohibitively expensive" could easily kill this project. Also, certain action items may never be attended to unless they are put down on paper. Unfortunately, not everyone has the same motivation to put down detailed commitments in meeting minutes.

While going over her notes from the meeting, Athena realizes that the VP of sales noted how most of the consumer driven clients, such as the cell phone maker, had healthy balance sheets and made prompt payments. She recalls that one of her own recent reports included an analysis about client balance sheets. So, she asks Judy to send an e-mail to the VP with the relevant graphs as well as a list of all similar studies. This whole operation will take Judy no more than 15 minutes, because Athena's team keeps a list of all major presentations and reports. When such an opportunity arises to advertise their work, they copy and paste a few lines into an e-mail to inform the other party that they have a substantial amount of relevant analysis and would be happy to forward any of it if the recipient is interested.

When Judy later sends the e-mail to Athena so she can forward it to the VP, Athena asks Judy to send it herself. This will give valuable exposure to Judy and lift up her image; very few assistants send such valuable e-mails to VPs. She also needs a morale boost. Again, this gesture comes at no cost to Athena. The VP will certainly know that there were no assistants in the meeting and realize that it was Athena who listened carefully even to his casual comments and went the extra mile to help. All in all, the team gets a wonderful return from a total of 15 minutes of investment.

3:00 PM *Taking care of problems and problem people*

Athena spends the next hour on the phone with clients whom she could not contact over the last two days. In one of these conversations, she finds out that a new assembly robot recently sold to a digital camera manufacturer has over-heated for the third time since its installation. Although the technician assigned to the facility flew to the site each time and fixed the problem, Athena decides to investigate the issue with the help of the technical service department. This investigation may take a lot of time over the coming weeks and lead to delays in some of her ongoing projects. She must therefore find a way to inform her boss about this matter. Otherwise, she may look too slow and get little credit for all the work she will be doing to solve the client's problem. She tells the client that the issue can be resolved faster if the VP of customer relationships—her boss—gets involved and asks whether she can conference him in. This is a natural and noninvasive method of informing her boss about what she is spending her time on. Involving him also puts more horsepower behind the initiative, which means that the project will move along faster.

Afterward, she calls Jose from technical service and explains the problem. However, in the middle of this conversation, Judy knocks on the door and tells Athena that Jack is on the line, yet again asking for files regarding the cell phone maker. Athena asks Jose if she can call back later and picks up Judy's line. Jack is surprised that Athena picked up and tries to convince her that Judy can handle this minor request. He knows very well that the young and inexperienced Judy is afraid to anger him and is more likely than Athena to provide the files he wants. Athena explains that she would be glad to talk about the issue and asks several questions, such as why Jack needs the documents and to whom he will send them. Jack gives vague and evasive answers, claiming that it is mostly for his own infor-mation. He says that he wants to be prepared if the same client should decide to build a similar factory overseas.

While it may seem easier to ask Judy to prepare what Jack wants instead of hassling with him, this would only be a short-term solution. The behavior would set a precedent, and Jack would come back with more demands, monopolizing Judy's time and stealing the credit that should go to Athena's team. In the end, Jack becomes uncomfortable because he does not have a single good answer, and decides not to push further. He settles for the P&L analysis that Athena offers to forward to him. This is a fairly safe solution. Since the file was presented by Karen earlier, it will be difficult for Jack to claim it as his work.

Athena goes one step further and e-mails the file to several people in international sales. She explains that Jack pointed out that the international sales team may find the analysis helpful and encourages them to contact her for further information. This message establishes Athena as the legitimate contact for the project. It will not only be difficult for Jack to claim credit for the file within his department, but he will also not be credible if he comes to Athena in the future saying that his boss wanted him to obtain certain information. After this e-mail, the boss should know that he can get the data directly from Athena. In addition, this sends a strong message to Jack: "Don't distribute my work as your own, or I will expose you."

4:30 PM Timing is everything

When Athena checks her notes again, she realizes that Melvin, the VP in charge of R&D, will soon leave for a two-day business trip. (To free up her mind, Athena constantly takes notes throughout the day and checks them often.) This is a wonderful opportunity to gain the support of the only skeptical VP. She calls her assistant Nelson and they immediately prepare a three-page handout for Melvin. When she receives a phone call from her biggest client while preparing the handout, she asks the client if she can call him back and concentrates on the work at hand. She quickly visits Melvin in his office and hands him the material. She states that she was unable to convey some critical issues during the earlier meeting due to time constraints and wanted to pass along additional information. She stresses that her team continues to talk to the prospective client and will soon circulate further analysis. Melvin says that he cannot look at the information right now, but that he will read it during his trip—precisely what Athena wanted.

This is an absolutely brilliant maneuver for several reasons. First of all, by catching Melvin when he cannot stop to review the information, Athena eliminates the possibility of a hasty rejection. Even if his immediate reaction is negative when he later reads the handout, Melvin will not be able to announce his feelings to the entire company since he will probably be in an airplane or hotel room. He will have two full days to think and rethink the issue, and may therefore see that it is not such a bad idea after all.

The second reason this timing works well is that the project is still in the development phase, which gives Athena justification for providing incomplete information. If she had waited for the project to mature, Melvin could ask for a complete feasibility analysis. Now, however, he will accept just a few bullet points, which gives Athena the option to select only the most compelling pieces of data that support her theory. This way, she can also keep the handout short and ensure that it will be read. Finally, it is not by accident that Athena prints out the material as opposed to e-mailing it as an attachment. Over the next few hours, Melvin will probably find himself in a tight cab or a cramped seat in an airport, where he may not have the time or space to power up a laptop. Being a busy top manager who cannot afford to spend much idle time, he will likely reach for the first printout and read it. Therefore, Athena's handout will not compete against all the unread e-mails in Melvin's inbox and has a very high chance of getting reviewed soon.

While walking back from Melvin's office, Athena is stopped by the district manager of the technical service department. He asks when the customer satisfaction survey for June will be published and requests that Athena prepare a historical analysis for the clients that he serves. Upon returning to her desk, Athena opens up the file that she will use to update the satisfaction report on Monday and inserts a huge purple textbox to remind herself about the request. This way, she can remember to send the information without cluttering her to-do list or having to work her brain. Knowing the district manager, she figures that he will push until he gets what he wants. She will look much better if she takes the initiative and sends him the information before he calls again. This involves no extra work, yet greatly helps to solidify Athena's image as an attentive and hardworking manager. It also motivates the district manager to return the favor by helping Athena in her upcoming project where she will investigate her client's quality problems.

Next, Athena calls back the client whom she was unable to talk to earlier. Barring a crises situation, Athena refuses to be unconditionally available to even her most important colleagues or clients. This would make it impossible to concentrate for more than a few minutes and, more importantly, give the impression that Athena is not very busy. Besides, she cannot make a good impression when caught off guard, whereas now she can open the client's last e-mail and gather her thoughts before making the call—advantage, caller.

5:45 PM Wrapping it up

After a short break and a cup of tea, Athena is ready to wrap things up for the day. Looking at her notes, she sees that she needs to send an e-mail about the upcoming investigation of the overheating machine. She starts to compose a message that explains the rationale for the project and lists five goals that need to be accomplished, together with deadlines. This list once again shows the wide variety of critical issues that Athena needs to worry about in her job and subtly emphasizes her contributions to the firm. A solid game plan also gives her credibility, making it easier to obtain a bigger budget and more time for the project.

Before Athena can finish the message, Judy walks in with a few questions. Athena decides to save the incomplete e-mail as a draft and send it from home tomorrow in the morning. After helping Judy, Athena calls her husband to ask if he can show up an hour late at work tomorrow, so they can have a leisurely breakfast with the kids. Athena does that at least once every other week. By coming in an hour late, she can drive the kids to school, enabling them to leave the house later and giving the family a chance to spend a little more time together. Since she comes in at a reasonable time on most days, such luxuries rarely attract unwanted attention. By forwarding her office line to her cell phone when she will be out and checking e-mail from home, she keeps in touch with work and demonstrates that she is working despite the fact that she is away from her desk. Even in the absence of e-mails from colleagues that she can respond to, she always has draft messages to work on when she is out. At 6:30, while most of her colleagues are still working frantically, Athena leaves the office to pick up some of the waffles that the kids love for breakfast.

EPILOGUE

This has been a long book. Considering that the typical reader is a busy manager, I really must thank you for your time. Whether this book was worth the time and money you invested in it does not depend on the number of specific recommendations, interviews, or quotations you can recall at this stage. That is of secondary importance. What truly matters is whether this book has helped you look at your career in a significantly different way.

If you are like most managers employed by large organizations, you probably had the unspoken assumption that you were required to perform a set of unalterable tasks every day in order for someone to give you a paycheck. In other words, you perhaps thought that to earn your salary, you just had to make a certain number of phone calls, attend a given number of meetings, and type a fixed set of emails. You could maybe skip a call here and there and make up an excuse to miss a meeting or two per week, but for the most part, you had little control over the nature and quantity of the work that was awaiting you upon walking into the office everyday. When you begin with such an assumption, the only thing you can do to leave the office earlier is to squeeze those tasks into less time. Essentially all that you have at your disposal are the traditional time management tools. While those tools may help to some extent, they almost always fail to solve the real problem.

What I have tried to show you in this book is that there are much more powerful tools. The number of phone calls, presentations, and meetings that need to be taken care of before you can earn your paycheck and a decent promotion are not fixed. You can actually get the compensation, promotion, and appreciation you are looking for with less work. By understanding the dynamics in large organizations, you can create more value for your employer, help people better appreciate the significance of your accomplishments, and get more credit for what you do. And while doing all of this, it is still possible to reduce your workload. If I was able to get this fundamental fact across, the book has fulfilled its purpose, regardless of how many of the specifics you can recall at this moment. Armed with this awareness, you can return to the book and pick up the specifics with great ease. I am also confident that you will discover countless new ways to reduce your workload by examining the world around you with this attitude. If this allows you to smell a few more flowers on your way home or spend a few more minutes with your loved ones each day, I will surely be a happier man. Thank you and good luck...

ABOUT THE AUTHOR

The son of a Turkish diplomat, Hunkar Ozyasar grew up in Turkey, Germany, and the UK. He began his career as an assistant brand manager at Unilever, where he developed a strong interest in understanding managerial efficiency. He continued to interview managers for When Time Management Fails in his subsequent jobs as an entrepreneur and then as a copywriter at J. Walter Thompson. To pursue his passion from an academic angle, he completed an MBA degree at one of the world's top business schools, Kellogg Graduate School of Management at Northwestern University. Taking advantage of the school's exchange program, he completed part of his studies in Thailand, gaining valuable insights into the work habits and challenges of Southeast Asian managers.

Upon graduation, Ozyasar joined Deutsche Bank. Following his first assignment in London, he settled in New York, where he was subsequently promoted to Global High Yield Bond Strategist. During his tenure with Deutsche Bank, Ozyasar was quoted in numerous financial publications including *Financial Times* and *The Wall Street Journal.* In order to focus on his book, the author left Deutsche Bank in February 2005.

As a passionate athlete, Ozyasar enjoys studying natural means of enhancing sports performance. When his schedule allows, he writes in *Master Trainer*, a bimonthly magazine dedicated to the subject.

653904

Made in the USA